THE CHOOSING PEOPLE

VOTING BEHAVIOR IN ISRAEL

ALAN ARIAN

THE PRESS OF
CASE WESTERN RESERVE UNIVERSITY
CLEVELAND & LONDON
1973

Library of Congress Cataloging in Publication Data

Arian, Alan.
  The choosing people; voting behavior in Israel.

  Bibliography: p.
  1. Elections--Israel. 2. Voting--Israel.
I. Title.
JQ1825.P365A748   324'.2   72-7828
ISBN 0-8295-0249-1

cC

*In memory
of my brother, Phil*

CONTENTS

LIST OF TABLES

LIST OF FIGURES

PREFACE

WHILE WORKING ON THIS PROJECT, I have had the good fortune of receiving stimulation, encouragement, advice, cooperation, and aid from a number of sources. The many hours spent in conversation with Prof. Yonathan Shapiro of Tel Aviv University's Sociology Department on matters relating to the study were very helpful to me. His insights and his friendship were important to me as the work on this book progressed. Among my colleagues in the Political Science Department of Tel Aviv University I owe a debt of thanks to Dr. Gabi Arieli, Dr. Zvi Gitelman, Dr. Ehud Harari, Dr. Michael Kahan, Professor Gerald Pomper, Dr. Efraim Torgovnik, and David Sommer, who commented on various chapters of the manuscript. At the Political Studies Center of the Institute of Social Research at the University of Michigan at Ann Arbor, Professor Samuel Barnes and I discussed many of the ideas contained in this study; during the same period, Klaus Liepelt of DATUM in Bad Gotesberg in West Germany was also at the Center in Ann Arbor, and I benefited from conversations with him as well. Professor Samuel Krislov of the University of Minnesota, as always, provided sagacious advice and a helping hand.

But these expressions of gratitude relate only to the last link in a long and involved process which forms the backbone of the study presented here. The interviewing upon which most of the book is based was conducted in three waves in the summer and fall of 1969. That project was jointly directed by Professor Louis Guttman, Dr. Emanuel Gutmann, Dr. Michael Gurevitch, and me and was funded by the Hebrew University of Jerusalem, Tel Aviv University, and the Israel Institute for Applied Social Research. The interviewing was conducted by the Institute, and the third phase of this project was part of the Continuing Surveys sponsored jointly by the Institute and the Institute of Communications of the Hebrew University. Uzi and Ziona Peled of the

Institute were very helpful in both administrative and substantive matters.

Professor Haim Ben Shachar, who was then Dean of the Faculty of Social Sciences at Tel Aviv University, took special interest in the project and furthered it in many ways. His help at the top was matched at various other levels by numerous assistants, interviewers, coders, programmers, secretaries, and typists at Tel Aviv University, The Institute for Applied Social Research in Jerusalem, and the Center for Political Studies of the University of Michigan. My thanks to them all.

I am particularly grateful to Mr. Arye Pincus, Chairman of the Jewish Agency Executive, whose support at a critical stage of the analysis was very important. Thanks are also due to the Memorial Foundation for Jewish Culture and to its Executive Director, Mr. Mark Uveeler. Throughout the work on planning and executing the study, the Research Committee of the Social Sciences Faculty of Tel Aviv University was very supportive.

One chapter of the book (Chapter 9) is the result of collaboration with Dr. Shevah Weiss of Haifa University on our long-standing interest in split-ticket voting. Our first published work on the topic was in *Megamot* in October 1968, and an English version of the same article, "Split-ticket Voting in Israel," appeared in the *Western Political Quarterly* in June 1969; the latter is reprinted by permission of the University of Utah, copyright holder. While these articles discussed split-ticket voting through the 1965 election, another pair of articles brought the topic through the 1969 elections. The Hebrew version appeared in the *Social Research Review,* January 1972, and the English version appeared in the volume I edited entitled *The Elections in Israel—1969,* published by the Jerusalem Academic Press in 1972. Chapter 9 represents a compilation of these articles, and I thank Dr. Weiss for agreeing to let me publish this material here.

Portions of Chapter 3 also appeared in *The Elections in Israel—1969* volume, as did Chapter 7. A Hebrew version of Chapter 3 appeared in *Megamot,* February 1973; Chapter 7 is reprinted with the permission of the *Public Opinion Quarterly,* where it appeared in June 1971.

The focus of Chapter 8 was greatly influenced by Professor Roger Benjamin of the University of Minnesota. A grant from that University's Office of International Programs and the considerable assistance of Uzi Arad made these analyses possible. Chapter 8 has also been used in a comparative perspective in *Patterns of Political Development: Japan–India–Israel,* by Roger W. Benjamin, Alan Arian, Richard N. Blue, and Stephen Coleman, copyright 1972 by David McKay and reprinted by permission of the publisher.

This formidable list of individuals and institutions can only be praised for what they did; what came of all their help is my responsibility alone.

THE CHOOSING PEOPLE

CHAPTER 1

INTRODUCTION

IT HAS LONG BEEN accepted that democratic government in a modern industrial state cannot possibly mean rule by all of the people. Problems of assembly and communications, of disseminating information and expertise, of critical war-or-peace decisions with a lead time of minutes have convinced even the most utopian of democrats that other forms must be developed. The idea of authority and legitimacy deriving from the people has remained valid in the West, but the forms of democratic decision making have tended toward a hierarchical structure, with final power at the pinnacle of the pyramid.[1]

Israel is no exception to this pattern. On the contrary, the characteristics of centralization of political power, hierarchy, and oligarchy are a major part of modern Israel's historical experience. The leadership and ideology of one party—Mapai, now called Labor—have dominated the political system and through it the economic structure as well. Democratic forms are very important for the leadership, and deference to these forms is broadly accepted by the mass public in Israel. But this does not alter the fact that major political decisions must have the support—or at least the acquiescence—of the party.

The public is heard from only rarely. One way of explaining this is to point out that since the parties reflect the opinions of the public, additional efforts at communication become superfluous. A more plausible explanation is the centralized nature of the system itself. There are so few points of effective access to the system that politicians tend to mobilize the public only after they have exhausted the various parliamentary, bureaucratic, and political-bargaining alternatives. Because the country is very small and the leadership believes that it maintains close touch with the people and its problems, few appeals to the public are made.

Two other factors contribute to the relative unimportance of the

3

mass public in Israeli politics. One is its deference to the dominant leadership, which is reflected in the stability of the election results over the seven elections and a quarter of a century of Israeli independence. The public can be "counted on," both at the polls and when presented with the political arguments of the leadership. This encourages the habit of taking the public for granted. The second factor is that very few issues in Israeli public life are not already being processed. It is very hard to find an issue that might raise public attention which is not already being discussed, debated, studied, or researched by a government, public, or semipublic agency. The absence of free-floating issues makes the public less potent and gives a tremendous advantage to any group (in Israel's case, the dominant party) that can regulate the introduction of issues being processed into the political system. The timing of the infusion of issues into the system, as much as anything else, allows the power holders to nip in the bud movements that might otherwise gain public momentum and to divert attention to the areas they favor.

These points can be more fully understood by referring to Figure 1.1.[2] Any political system can be considered to consist of three main actors: the decision maker, the public, and the broker. The major actor is the decision maker, since politics is "the authoritative allocation of social values" and the decision maker is the allocator.[3] The decision maker may be the public, as in a referendum, but more often than not it is an elected or appointed official. The political contest focuses on him, for the ultimate test of power is success.

The public is a "phantom," to use Lippmann's term.[4] In any democratic society, it is probably misleading to consider the public a continuous, ongoing actor in the public sphere. Such an amorphous mass is structured and activated on specific occasions in response to certain stimuli. It is more helpful to think of many publics rather than one. On any given issue, a new and previously unactivated public may be formed. It is possible that the public that has the interest, information, and capacity to express its opinion on foreign policy does not speak out on matters of pollution. Obviously certain sections of the public are more susceptible to stimulation and activation. Usually those groups that are better educated and have better incomes and more leisure as well as interest, whether altruistic or otherwise, in the subject are likely

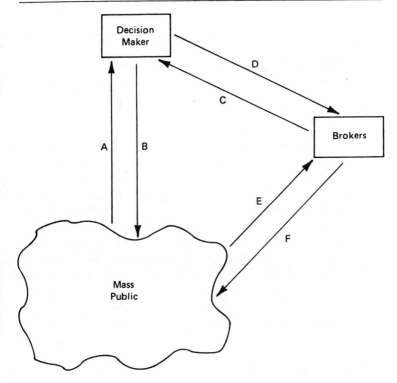

Figure 1.1 A Representation of the Political System

to be responsive to a specific stimulus. Such groups have been referred to as the active public.[5]

The brokers process, augment, aggregate, and articulate public inputs to the decision maker.[6] In addition, they are often called upon to relay the decision to the public and to recruit support for it. The brokers, which include political parties, pressure groups, labor unions, and the mass media, play a major role in democratic politics as the linkages between the public and the decision maker.[7] They are not simply passive relayers of messages, however, but activators of a public. As such, they often develop ideological and organizational interests of their own.[8] The brokers include a disproportionate number of individuals who have the prerequisites usually associated with membership in an active public. Editors, television announcers, and party officials act as brokers, but their choice of positions and issues is not indiscriminate. They are likely to represent and activate members of a public similar to them in background and social class; they are also likely to provide representation for their class which other classes are not fortunate enough to have.

The workings of the system vary from issue to issue. Building a power plant will activate different publics, brokers, and decision makers than will altering a nation's boundaries. In Israel, however, almost all issues have in common the potential of being processed by the dominant Labor party.[9] It is in the councils of the Labor Secretariat, or the Labor Ministers in the Cabinet, or the Labor Delegation in the Knesset (parliament), or the Labor members of the Central Committee of the Histadrut (General Federation of Trade Unions) that tough political decisions are made. Of course not all issues arrive at the pinnacle and receive the attention of the top leadership. But the facts that Labor is the country's largest party, consistently winning a plurality of the votes in the national elections and a majority in the Histadrut elections, that it is more than twice as big a vote-getter as its nearest competitor, and that this base of power is some fifty years old, beginning before the establishment of the state in 1948, makes it unlikely that any crucial issue will be settled without the blessing of the party.

The amorphous quality of the public, the lack of free-floating issues, the stability of the electoral results, and the centralized nature of the political system all increase the importance of the brokers in the system. Of the six channels of communication depicted in Figure 1.1, my guess would be that channels C and D are most heavily used. It is through those channels that the myriad memos, reports, letters, editorials, studies, position papers, surveys, informal meetings, background interviews, and consultation flow. This characteristic pattern results from and perpetuates the centralized nature of the political system. The concentration of the flow in two channels is also facilitated by the relative homogeneity of the decision makers and brokers. The schooling, life styles, values, stereotypes, and prejudices of each group probably have more in common than those of either to such characteristics among the mass public. The brokers are the makers and gatekeepers of the consensus that characterizes the entire Israeli system.

The brokers use channels E and F in an imbalanced way. The mass media obviously rely on channel F, and parties and pressure groups use it for informational purposes as well. But the parallel use of both channels E and F is rare. Though letters to the editor are frequent and even petitions are widely used, these add up to a mere trickle in the potential flow of communication in channel A. The decision maker uses channel B for educational and informational purposes, just as the brokers use channel F.

A possible activation of channel E occurred on the eve of the Six Day War, when a public clamor arose to appoint Moshe Dayan Minister of Defense, a job which had been held by Prime Minister Levi Eshkol. The case illustrates well the difficulty of pinpointing the factors related to the mobilization of public opinion and the difficulty of establishing boundaries between the brokers and the public. Dayan was a member of Rafi, a party which had split from Mapai before the 1965 elections (and which merged with Mapai and Ahdut Haavoda to form Labor in 1968). His mentor, Ben Gurion, and Eshkol had had a serious falling-out, mostly relating to the Lavon Affair and the subsequent investigations of it. The tension between Rafi and Mapai was based on personality clashes and organizational competition. The Labor party headquarters in Tel Aviv were picketed immediately before the war by individuals calling for Dayan's appointment as Defense Minister, and there seemed to be a feeling of relief when the decision to appoint him was finally made. (This may have reflected the satisfaction with getting news of some decisive action—even if it wasn't directly about the approaching war—after many days of frustration and waiting.) But, in addition, it must be remembered that many newspapers campaigned on Dayan's behalf and that Gahal conditioned its joining the National Unity government on his appointment. Considerable pressure was also brought to bear on Eshkol from within Mapai and from its longtime coalition partner, the National Religious party. It is not at all clear that Dayan's appointment in 1967—often cited as evidence of public opinion effectiveness in Israel—resulted from popular pressure. A good case could be made that the play of forces among the brokers determined the outcome. More likely, it was a little of the former and a good deal of the latter.[10]

The major use of channel A occurs once every four years on election day. But even when the mass public democratically elects its government, the brokers are extremely active. For the Israeli election system is one of proportional representation in which each political party presents a list of candidates to the citizenry. The voter selects a party, not a candidate, and each party is then represented in the Knesset in proportion to its strength at the polls. The head of the largest party is asked to form a government. Thus the election is in reality a combined use of channels A, E, and C.[11]

Of the four phases of the election process—the composing of the lists, the campaign, the vote, and the formation of the government coalition —the mass public is directly involved in only the second and third. And only in the third is the citizen active. In the campaign he is passive, since the active role is played by the brokers. In the phase of composing the lists, the political party and its affiliated pressure groups are the major participants. The groups strive for maximum representation in those places on the 120-man list that seven elections have indicated are likely to be the winnings of the party. A representative of the kibbutz movement of the National Religious party knows that putting one of his men in the fifteenth spot is not good politics, since the party has consistently won eleven or twelve seats over the years. The fifteenth candidate of the party would be—optimistically—third in line in the case of vacancies in the party's Knesset delegation or—pessimistically— out of a job.[12]

The phase of forming the government coalition takes place after the voter has had his say. Here back-room politics is king. The trading that takes place in order to form the government is not actively affected by the mass public, although it would be if dramatic changes were to occur in the election results. This phase is characterized by bargaining among the party brokers.

The conception of representation prevalent in Israel and the electoral laws that reflect it give the broker, with his organizational power, an advantage over the individual citizen. The notion that the political movement should represent the interests of the citizens and that the party should be active in many aspects of the individual's existence has deep roots in Israel, especially on the left. The party is the political arm of the movement, whose goal it is to advance the ideology and interests of the class. The structure of the party is hierarchical, with the ultimate authority for decisions resting at the top of the pyramid.

Not all Israeli parties follow this pattern, but those that have been more powerful on the political scene have tended to do so. The parties of the left in Israel have been able to attract a plurality of the electors and have developed a broad network of supporters.[13] The advantages that have accrued to Mapai because of its dominant position have indicated that the party could count on widespread support without tightly organizing its electors. Some smaller parties in the Israeli political system, such as Mapam and the National Religious party, have made strenuous efforts at organizing their electors. The extreme left-wing socialist party and the religious party have in common the ideological passion that necessitates organizing in the face of the political rival.

The center and right parties have been less conscientious in their organizational efforts; this partially explains why they have been rather ineffective in their competition with Mapai. Dominant since before the establishment of the state and identified with its struggle for independence, the left—and especially Mapai—has advantages that allow it to foster its favored position at the expense of the other parties.

One of these advantages has been the establishment of a series of social services in the Histadrut, the labor union federation in which Mapai has always had a majority. These services were of special importance to the newly arrived immigrant, and often Mapai rather than the Histadrut or the state was identified as the patron. The Histadrut's wide range of services can easily serve as a social network into which the citizen can fit. No other party can be as clearly identified with a competing social network; the right has always been loosely organized and demurred at the type of socialist organization that ultimately worked effectively for Mapai.

Religious observance is the basis of a social network that might perhaps have competed with the Histadrut network. But the relationship between religious parties and individuals who observe religious tradition is loose at best. Although Israel is first and foremost a Jewish state, this dogma is shared by almost every one of the political parties and is not unique to the religious parties.

The dominance of Mapai, then, coincides with the dominance in the society of the Histadrut network, which Mapai (Labor) heads. It is useful to discard the usual taxonomies of political party systems and consider Israel as a prominent case of the dominant party model, a model unfortunately neglected by political scientists. In place of the stable two-party model or the unstable multi-party model, it is best to picture a system in which one party has dominated for more than a generation and has been the pivot of every coalition formed. Even if government turnovers take place frequently (as in Italy), the political system remains competitive and relatively stable.[14] As Etzioni has pointed out, one of the major adjustments that the dominant party in Israel makes after the election is to construct the new coalition in light of shifts in public opinion.[15]

This book is primarily a voting study. Building on the impressive tradition of these studies in many countries (especially the United States and western Europe), I have attempted to analyze problems it raises in describing and explaining the political system of Israel. In doing so, I have expanded on many of the themes outlined above. The socioeconomic bases of dominance of the Labor-Mapam Alignment in the 1969 elections are discussed in Chapter 3. The other social network of some importance—the religious—is analyzed in Chapter 4. Chapter 5 presents the intersection of these two networks, and considers the impact of the resulting four major blocs. The effect of the dominant party on the structure of competition in Israeli politics is explored in Chapter 9.

Since this is the first empirical study of the vote in Israel, many traditional topics are developed: in Chapter 2, for example, participation, interest, communications consumption, and political efficacy are studied, and Chapter 6 presents a detailed analysis of the determining factor of the vote. In addition, the nature and role of public opinion are explored in Chapters 2 and 7. Chapter 8 attempts to associate voting behavior with level of modernization. This, it will be shown, is more successfully done for the non-Jewish population of Israel than for the Jews.

Elections in Israel are periodic occurrences that have given a vote of confidence to the previous division of power within the society. It is clear that the results have yet to change dramatically the personnel or policies of the government. Nevertheless, the elections are valuable in providing the citizen with a means by which he can symbolically identify with the state and in keeping open for him the options of bringing about political change. Given this channel of communications, the brokers and the decision makers must keep him in mind, if only by ensuring that no rift develops in the consensus they all share. The very stability of the vote is a monument to the effectiveness of the dominant party and the system to accommodate change while perpetuating political power.

NOTES

1. See, for example, Joseph A. Schumpeter, *Capitalism, Socialism and Democracy* 2nd ed., (New York: Harper and Bros., 1947), and Robert A. Dahl, *A Preface to Democratic Theory* (Chicago: University of Chicago Press, 1956).

2. For a somewhat similar treatment, see Bernard C. Hennessey, *Public Opinion* (Belmont, Calif.: Wadsworth, 1965), esp. ch. 6.

3. See David Easton, *The Political System* (New York: Knopf, 1953).

4. See the work of Walter Lippmann, including his *Public Opinion* (New York: Macmillan, 1922) and *The Phantom Public* (New York: Harcourt, 1925).

5. For the American case, see V. O. Key, Jr., *Public Opinion and American Democracy* (New York: Knopf, 1961).

6. See David Easton, *A Systems Analysis of Political Life* (New York: Wiley, 1965).

7. For a discussion of linkages, see Norman Luttbeg (ed.), *Public Opinion and Public Policy* (Homewood, Ill.: Dorsey, 1968).

8. A good example of this is found in Robert Michels, *Political Parties* (New York: Collier Books, 1962).

9. See Peter Y. Medding, *Mapai in Israel* (Cambridge: Cambridge University Press, 1972).

10. The events of this period are chronicled in Shlomo Nakdimon, *Likrat Sheat Haefes* (Tel Aviv: Ramdor, 1968).

11. For an introduction to Israeli government and politics see Leonard J. Fein, *Politics in Israel* (Boston: Little, Brown, 1967).

12. Many of these issues are discussed in Alan Arian (ed.), *The Elections in Israel—1969* (Jerusalem: Jerusalem Academic Press, 1972).

13. For a theoretical discussion relevant to Israeli parties, see Maurice Duverger, *Political Parties* (New York: Wiley, 1963).

14. See Alan Arian and Samuel H. Barnes, "The Dominant Party System: A Neglected Model of Democratic Stability," *Journal of Politics,* forthcoming.

15. Amitai Etzioni, "Alternative Ways to Democracy: The Example of Israel," *Political Science Quarterly* 74 (1959): 196–214.

CHAPTER 2

ELECTIONS IN ISRAEL

I

ELECTIONS IN ISRAEL, like so many other features of the nation's political and social life, can best be understood in terms of the institutions and arrangements that existed before the state was declared. The proportional representation system and the associated multiplicity of parties can be traced back to the First Zionist Congress in Basle in 1897.[1] Democratic reforms were gaining ground in Europe, and suffrage was being expanded throughout the continent. Many of the delegates were lawyers, and they stressed the importance of the democratic nature of elections. Herzl, himself a parliamentary correspondent of a Viennese paper in Paris, was conscious of the need to establish a solid democratic foundation to the organization he wished to build.

The delegates preferred a system that would permit the broadest and most exact representation of the constituent groups and therefore opted for a proportional list system. They saw the major goal of the Congress as uniting Jews of various countries under an umbrella organization that could represent them before the various governments. Matters of execution and efficiency were less important than accuracy in representation. In those countries with a sizeable Jewish population, parties developed to compete for places on the delegation. The Congress in effect recognized the parties by dividing the delegations among the parties according to electoral strength. As a result, many of the procedures and parties established at the first Congress at Basle were to reappear later in the politics of Israel. Some of the parties active in Israel today can be traced back to that first Congress. Herzl's saying that in Basle he established the Jewish state can be expanded: in Basle the parliamentary and electoral groundwork of Israel was also laid.

13

In Palestine itself the desire to establish a parliament was expressed very early in the history of the Jewish resettlement on the land. But it was not until the period of the British Mandate after the first World War that the idea of an elected assembly was realized. Although there was some organization under the Turks before the war, it was only at the beginning of the British Mandate and with the democratic renaissance in the world that the movement toward parliamentarism gained strength among the Jews in Palestine.

In May 1920 the first elections for the Meeting of Electors (Asefat Nivcharim) was held.[2] This was to be the supreme representative organization of the Jewish community in Palestine. The Assembly chose its own executive—the National Committee (Havaad Haleumi)—which accepted its subordination to the World Zionist Federation in all matters pertaining to the establishment of a national home. This assured the eclipse of the Meeting of Electors and the National Committee while facilitating the prominence of the Zionist Federation and its executive arm, the Jewish Agency, since the crucial issues of foreign policy, immigration, and money-raising among Jews in the world would be in the hands of the latter.[3]

Democratic procedures were established in the elections for the specifically Jews-in-Palestine body, but two additional problems developed. One involved lingering doubts about the legitimacy of setting up a Jewish parliament while most of the Jews of the world were outside Palestine and the legitimacy of doing so while the country was entrusted to a foreign power in the form of the mandate. The second problem had to do with the extension of the vote to women. The debate over the right of woman's suffrage split the community along religious-secular lines. The religious camp opposed; the left advocated the policy in terms of the democratic principle of one man-one vote, and in order to stress the equality granted women in the pioneering society they were building. Patterns that would become familiar after the founding of the state were evident: the religious threatened and sometimes withdrew their support of the dominant left. The left, realizing the importance of the religious groups in providing the additional support needed to form a working coalition, walked the line between acquiescence and obstinacy by concocting elaborate compromises.

Knesset Israel was in effect a voluntary state. Its citizens were Jews who lived in Palestine, although one could have his name removed from the rolls (and hence from "citizenship") upon request. The activities of this stateless state centered on health, education, and welfare. Elections were to be held every four years but were actually held less often: in 1920, 1925, 1931, and 1944. During this entire period the leftist parties dominated. Besides the lack of authority, the widespread non-cooperation by extremist religious factions undermined Knesset Israel's legitimacy. The parties of the right, on the other hand, provided strong opposition to the left by virtue of their strength in the urban centers and their control of many city halls.

On the eve of the establishment of the state, the National Committee decided that members of the Executive of the Jewish Agency and the Executive of the National Committee would serve as a temporary government. The legacy of the pre-state period was immense. Most of the leaders of this period continued in their leadership positions after the founding of the state. There was also organizational continuity as the parties, well trained in parliamentary and electoral matters, and their ideologies moved into statehood. The dominance of the leftist parties was a continuation of a familiar pattern. The parliamentary tradition was also established upon statehood. The practice of proportional-list elections continued as a matter of course, and political arrangements that were set before the state was founded transferred into statehood naturally. Even the pattern of a weak parliament and a strong executive was well known from the pre-state period. For these reasons, the 1949 elections—even though they were the first of independent Israel—were thoroughly in keeping with established traditions.

The first parliamentary elections in 1949 were largely overshadowed by other problems. The problems of foreign policy, security, immigration, and economics were massive for the 650,000 Jews of Israel. To add to these problems, the technical arrangements necessary to conduct elections seemed inappropriate to many in a time of war. Decisions had to be made about the size of the Knesset, the right to vote for Jews in transit camps in Cyprus, and so on; lists of eligible voters had to be assembled—all of this while a shooting war was being waged and while talks at Rhodes were being held with delegates of Arab states through the mediation of Ralph Bunche.

The campaign was highlighted by public rallies and meetings in theaters and coffee houses. A large part of the political campaigning was conducted through the various immigrant associations. Radio time was provided for, with each party receiving fifteen minutes air time and each list ten minutes.[4] But public interest in the campaign was low. Tens of thousands were still on active army service, and the public was preoccupied with international developments. Also, there was no real issue that divided public opinion.[5] This was in sharp contrast to the previous elections for the Meeting of Electors and the Zionist Congress, where bitter arguments over military "activism" and the Jewish or binational nature of the state had split the public and the parties. By 1949 the issue had become less clear-cut. Almost all the parties promised "an uncompromising fight for our rights" and the addition of Jerusalem to the new state. Only the Progressives raised domestic issues, and most discussions concerned foreign and defense policies.

In 1949 Mapai was clearly the party of leadership. Ministers from its ranks included the Prime Minister and the Ministers of Defense, Foreign Affairs, Treasury, Education, and Transportation. It was generally conceded that Mapai, with its power bases in the kibbutz and moshav movements, the Histadrut, and the pre-state national institutions, would be the strongest winner. Its leadership, which included Ben Gurion, Shertok (later Sharret), and Meirson (later Meir), was already prominent.

The results of the elections to the First Knesset in 1949 (see Table 2.1) reflected a pattern familiar to observers of Israeli politics before the establishment of the state—and one that continues to thrive years after these first elections. Mapai was the biggest winner, although its 36 percent of the vote fell short of an absolute majority. The second biggest winner, in this case Mapam, was less than half as successful as Mapai. The rate of participation was very high (86.8 percent). In retrospect, it is fascinating to note that ethnic parties did well in this election even though the large waves of oriental immigration had not yet begun. In 1949, the oriental community comprised 15 percent of the total Jewish population, and the two oriental lists (the Sephardic list and the Yeminite Union) won five mandates between them. In 1969, with over half of the population oriental, not one ethnic list was successful in placing a candidate in the Knesset.

The first wave of massive post-state immigration coincided with the

TABLE 2.1   KNESSET ELECTION RESULTS (120 SEATS)

YEAR OF ELECTION KNESSET	1949 I	1951 II	1955 III	1959 IV	1961 V	1965 VI	1969 VII
Left-of-Center							
Communist[a]	4	5	6	3	5	4	4
Mapam	19	15	9	9	9	8 ⎱	
Ahdut Haavoda[b]	–	–	10	7	8 ⎱	45 ⎰	56
Mapai	46	45	40	47	42 ⎰		
Rafi	–	–	–	–	–	10 ⎰	
State List	–	–	–	–	–	–	4
Center and Right							
Free Center	–	–	–	--	–	–	2
Herut	14	8	15	17	17 ⎱	26 ⎱	26
Liberal[c]	7	20	13	8 ⎱	17 ⎰		26
Independent Liberal[d]	5	4	5	6 ⎰		5	4
Religious							
Mafdal	16 ⎱	10	11	12	12	11	12
Aguda and Poalei Aguda	16 ⎰	5	6	6	6	6	6
Arab and other	9	8	5	5	4	5	6

a. In the 1965 and 1969 elections, the New Communist list won three seats of the four.

b. Ahdut Haavoda included in Mapam for the first two elections.

c. "General Zionists" through 1959 election.

d. "Progressives" through 1959 election.

e. In the 1965 and 1969 elections, Aguda won four seats of the six.

January 1949 elections. By the middle of 1949 the new state had absorbed some 200,000 new immigrants since independence. Most of them were settled in abandoned Arab sections; when these were filled, tent encampments sprouted. In the wake of the difficult crowded conditions in these camps came the resignation of the government and the second elections, which were held in 1951. The crisis centered on the education policies of the government, and especially on religious education in the camps of new immigrants from religious backgrounds. The fact that the crisis was between the two major elements of the ruling coalition—Mapai and the religious parties—explains why the election was earlier than required by law and why the campaign was so bitter.[6]

The campaign introduced into the voting public new waves of immigrants who knew little of the social and political problems facing the country. This rapidly expanding electorate was courted by the various political parties, often with material rewards. The number of voters jumped to 869,500 between the 1949 and the 1951 elections—an increase of 70 percent. Even so, the range of parties which presented itself to the voters in 1951 was almost identical to the one which appeared in 1949. Some interpreted this to mean that the new immigrants had been successfully absorbed into the existing political structures. A more likely explanation has to do with the large-scale division of immigrants among parties and their functionaries immediately upon arrival in the country. Since this division closely resembled the strength of the various parties in the previous elections, it is less surprising that the balance between the parties remained stable even when dramatic changes in the demography of the country were taking place.[7]

While the international and security situations were relatively stable during the 1949–1951 period, internal problems were very trying. The large-scale immigration from eastern Europe and later from Arab lands brought many impoverished immigrants. Social problems—religious education in the immigrant camps being only one of them—troubled the population, rationing was decreed, and even the weather was burdensome, with floods damaging many of the immigrant camps. The General Zionists, who came out most strongly against the economic policies of Mapai, touched a respondent chord in a population wearied by rationing, long lines, inefficiency, inflation, high taxes, and the black market. Mapai, in arguing against the General Zionists' call for free enterprise and a more liberal economy, presented itself as the people's party, the gathering point of the exiles, and the champion of independence. Ben Gurion was perceived as a messianic figure by some new immigrants. The campaign was very intense, with bitter denunciations common and vote buying widespread, especially among the new immigrants. The religious parties, which in a sense caused the early elections, were torn by internal arguments and were unable to form a united front. The results of the election show that the General Zionists became the second biggest party after Mapai, with Mapam losing four mandates.

The period of the Second Knesset witnessed the gravest crisis of Israeli parliamentarism—the question of reparations from Germany. Herut was prominent in its opposition, and bitter debates in the Knesset coincided with violent demonstrations outside on the street. The issue was finally settled by accepting the government's policy, and a new era in Israeli economics was introduced as a result of the infusion of money that the reparations brought to the country.

Mapai, especially Ben Gurion, bemoaned the difficulty of leading the country under a coalition and called for a majority of the vote in order to promote governmental stability. Before the 1955 elections, this line of reasoning led to a suggestion that the electoral system be changed to district representation. The General Zionists by 1955 had lost much of their appeal, since the economic situation had improved and since the party had joined in the Mapai-led coalition for two and a half years of the Second Knesset. Herut instead became the standard bearer of the opposition. The salient issues of 1955 were foreign and defense policy, and it was Herut that provided alternatives to the voters. In addition, it adopted a liberal-bourgeois platform in the hope of coopting many of the General Zionists' former supporters. In the field of foreign affairs, Herut called for militant and activist policies against the neighboring Arab states and an explicit pro-West policy. The labor camp underwent change before the 1955 elections: Mapam had split, and the more moderate socialists, who called for activism in defense policy (Ahdut Haavoda), separated from the more Marxist, pro-East group, which retained the name Mapam.

The campaign was intense. Although the parties claimed they intended to avoid a repetition of the 1951 campaign, accusations of vote buying and personal attacks on prominent leaders were rife. The highlight of the tension and bitterness came when a bomb was exploded at a public meeting of the General Zionists.

Eighteen lists competed in the 1955 election, and eleven of them received more than the 1 percent necessary for representation in the Knesset. Mapai was the biggest loser, winning five seats less than in the previous elections. Herut emerged as the second biggest party, but with well under half the strength of Mapai. The General Zionists lost seven mandates. Ahdut Haavoda did very well, winning ten seats; together with Mapam they won nineteen seats, an increase of four over their performance in 1951, when they had run together. The activist parties, Herut and Ahdut Haavoda, did best on the whole.

The years before the 1959 election brought relative quiet on the borders and impressive economic achievements. Mapai rode the wave of success, and leaders of the security effort, including Dayan, Peres, and especially Ben Gurion, were the heroes of the day as a result of the successful Sinai campaign. But other, less spectacular issues brewed close to the surface. Labor unrest, the question of Who is a Jew? and the ethnic riots in Wadi Salib all indicated that internal problems were widespread. Mapai played the role of the dominant party to the full: it encouraged identification of the state's achievements, including the military victory in 1956 that achieved a relatively peaceful situation on the frontiers, as its own. Even issues of corruption Mapai turned to its own advantage by claiming that it was the party which uncovered these antisocial acts. The "you've never had it so good" theme was used widely; the voter was asked to compare his station in life with that of a short eleven years ago. The charismatic appeal of Ben Gurion was also developed as a theme in Mapai's campaign with the theme, "Say yes to the old man." The only specific issue that was raised was electoral reform, but that stirred mainly the politicians, not the man in the street.

Herut's campaign was emotional, calling for Mapai's dethronement. Herut was at best perceived as the second biggest vote getter, but not as an alternative to Mapai or as a potential coalition partner in the government. It is understandable that Herut won much of the protest vote; the chances of being influential in government were greater for the General Zionists, whose economic platform was similar to Herut's. After the 1956 war, Herut's call for activism also sounded hollow, since Mapai had clearly dealt a harsh blow to the neighboring Arab states. Ahdut Haavoda had the same problem in differentiating itself from Mapai by trying to stress its activism. But, unlike Herut, it campaigned actively for a role in the coalition to be formed after the elections.

The 1959 elections strengthened Mapai's dominant position. The three non-Communist leftist parties won an absolute majority, with Mapai performing better than ever. The General Zionists continued to lose votes and even relinquished the mayoralty of Tel Aviv after thirty-two years of control. Herut emerged as the largest opposition force and the second largest party.

In the fall of 1960 the Lavon Affair became a heated topic of political debate. The failure of a secret mission in 1954 became controversial in later investigations through the discovery of forged documents. There was also the question of the level in the chain of command at which the order to carry out the mission had been given.[8] The ensuing investigations wrought great bitterness in the ranks of the establishment and Mapai, and eventually new elections were called for. The campaign raised the question of the security-first mentality, in which some saw an erosion of democracy; more indirectly, the long-time dominance of Mapai was also made an issue.

In the campaign for the 1961 elections Mapai was split internally. Meanwhile, the Progressives and General Zionists had merged to form the Liberal party. Mapai streamlined its campaign organization and introduced the small home meeting to discuss political issues and to reach the electorate more effectively. This was Mapai's last solo appearance, but its loss of five seats was less than many had foreseen.

In the period after the Fifth Knesset elections in 1961, Ben Gurion left the premiership permanently, after having taken leaves of absence previously, and was followed by Eshkol. On the eve of the elections to the Sixth Knesset in 1965, it appeared as if voters would be confronted with a drastically changed political map: Dayan, Almogi, and Peres, all stalwarts of Ben Gurion, left Mapai and formed Rafi; the Communists split into two parties; the Liberal party resplit, with the former Progressives emerging as the Independent Liberals and the former General Zionists, now retaining the name Liberal, forming a bloc with the Herut Movement to become Gahal.

Rafi appeared to be Mapai's biggest challenge. Formed by Ben Gurion to challenge the Mapai he had so long headed, it attacked the entrenched bureaucracy of the party and spoke of modernization, science, young leadership, and fair representation. Mapai reacted by forming an alignment with Ahdut Haavoda, hoping thereby to strengthen the left from the attack by the right and center. Rafi appeared unique in that it was a party that developed in Israel, without roots in the pre-state era, and its leadership had been part of the establishment.

The 1965 campaign was the longest, bitterest, and most expensive in Israeli electoral history. The Alignment (Mapai and Ahdut Haavoda) again managed to put up a good show, and, although it lost seats, Mapai remained the country's dominant party. Rafi's ten mandates were not all won at Mapai's expense: Gahal and the Independent Liberals combined lost three seats compared with 1961, and the religious parties, the communist parties, and Mapam all lost one each. Despite the expectations of political change, the 1965 elections were more similar to previous ones than different from them.

The 1969 elections were held in the wake of the Six Day War of 1967 and the war of attrition that followed it. In 1968 Rafi returned to the mother party and, along with Ahdut Haavoda and Mapai, merged into the Labor party. A portion of the Rafi group refused to return to Mapai and formed the State List. The newly formed Labor party and Mapam aligned and put up one list. Again the newly united left hoped for a majority of the vote, but their hopes were in vain once more.

Gahal, which had joined the national unity government on the eve of the June 1967 war, had won a measure of respectability. It remained in the government through the 1969 elections until August 1970, when a cease-fire went into effect and the Rogers initiative brought about the reactivation of the Jarring mission. But in the government the respectability Gahal had won was neutralized by its association with the government's policies. The results of the 1969 elections demonstrate continuity with previous elections. The 1969 Alignment won fifty-six seats, less than a majority but a strong plurality.[9]

The seven elections indicate remarkable stability. The left-of-center parties have never won fewer than sixty-four mandates of the 120-seat Knesset and never more than sixty-nine. The center and right parties range from twenty-seven to thirty-four seats, and the religious parties have won no fewer than fifteen nor more than eighteen mandates. While the institutional arrangements among and within parties have varied, electoral change in Israel over the long run seems minimal, with various factions and leaders dominating, regardless of the formal names used to refer to them.

Much greater change is obvious in Mapai's coalition formation. Mapai has always been the pivot of the government coalition and from the beginning it has had as a constant partner the National Religious party. This has been the basic characteristic of all governments formed, and it has influenced the special role of religion in the state.[10] In contrast to the stability of the election results and the permanence of the National Religious party in the coalition calculations of Mapai, there have been three major turning points in Mapai's strategy since independence through the 1969 elections. It is useful to see these changes in light of the election results immediately preceding the coalition negotiations.[11]

It was in 1952, after the impressive showing of the General Zionists in the 1951 elections, that they were brought into the government coalition. After the 1955 elections and the rise in electoral strength of the leftist parties, Mapam and Ahdut Haavoda were included in the coalition. Herut for the first time and the General Zionists (Liberals) were added on the eve of the Six Day War. These three turning points seem to have been in response to shifts in public opinion that were perceived by the Mapai leadership and were recorded in the election results without depriving Mapai of its dominant status. This adaptive behavior is one of the most potent weapons of a dominant party, for it tends to coopt the opposition party and the public support behind it and eventually identifies the dominant party with the demands expressed in the election results. By the next elections it is then natural to again identify the dominant party with the achievements of the state.[12]

II

Elections in Israel take place within a political culture that emphasizes the importance of democratic norms. Although one party has been dominant for so many years and has provided the pivot of the coalition of every government since the establishment of the state, competition for political power is a procedure that undergirds the Israeli political system. While no fundamental changes have occurred in seven elections, the majority of Israelis in 1969 felt strongly that elections are significant. The most impressive proof of their attitude is that more than 80 percent of the population voted in elections. In addition, 60 percent of the sample[13] disagreed with the statement that elections cannot change policy.

It has been argued, however, that the very essence of Israeli democracy is threatened by the continuing dominance of one party (once Mapai, now Labor). Rejecting the line of reasoning that asserts that the forms of democratic decision making can be maintained within the context of the give and take between groups within the dominant party and among parties in the coalition, this argument asserts that an actual changeover of the ruling party is a necessary condition of democratic government. Two-thirds of the population do not accept this argument.[14] They are quite willing to see the dominant party stay in power so long as it is doing a good job. This is especially interesting, since only 46 percent of the voters supported the dominant party. At least an additional 20 percent of the population who did not vote for the Alignment were willing to concede that parties should be judged on performance and not on length of time in office.

The Israeli electorate demonstrates a very high level of interest and participation in politics.[15] Interest in and discussion of public matters is extremely widespread (see Table 2.2). Even if we take into account

TABLE 2.2 INTEREST IN AND DISCUSSION OF PUBLIC MATTERS[a]

AREA OF INTEREST	FOREIGN & DEFENSE POLICY	ECONOMIC POLICY	SOCIAL POLICY	LOCAL POLITICS
Interested	86%	66%	67%	46%
Think average citizen should be interested	94	89	84	81
Discuss often or sometimes	84	63	63	b

a. From phase 1; see Appendix II.
b. Not asked.

the fact that the survey reported here was conducted during the war of attrition that followed the Six Day War, the rate is strikingly high. In this period of tension and intermittent shooting, interest in news and discussion of foreign and defense matters may have been higher than for a "quieter" period. But the high rates of response for economic and social policies, which serve as a check of sorts, indicate that the rate is generally high. Only for local matters does the rate fall off, but even there the norm is high.

These formidable rates of interest and discussion also reflect the very smallness of the country. A family feeling is pervasive, especially during a time of crisis or tragedy. Few public issues do not directly relate to the individual or to someone he knows. Foreign and defense matters are often at the center of public interest. All newspapers give these issues extensive coverage, both as news stories and in separate sections devoted to opinion and commentary. Discrete diplomatic moves as well as political or bureaucratic debates usually find their way into the press. The alertness and sensitivity of the public and the small size and integrated character of the society facilitate the rapid circulation of news, political gossip, and rumors.

Communications networks are widespread and relatively homogeneous. The radio and television are under the government's broadcast authority and have a monopoly on transmission. Newspapers are widely read and cover many aspects of public life and political gossip. Some 41 percent of the sample[16] reported that they listen to the radio for more than three hours a day. A high 84 percent of the total sample indicated that they listen primarily for news and information; two-thirds said that they watch television primarily for the same reason. Israelis not only consume news avidly; they also tend to believe what they read and hear. Yet here there is an interesting difference: whereas only 48 percent reported that they find the newspapers generally reliable, 70 percent said that they generally trust what they see and hear on radio and television.

To complete the portrait of the interested, discussing, and mass-media-consuming Israeli citizen, we must also note that he tends to be quite clear about what the government's policies should be. A total of 58 percent of those sampled said they know what policies the government should pursue, with 17 percent being absolutely certain and 41 percent quite certain. This high level of self-confidence in opinions and attitudes (some call it dogmatic) is familiar to many who know Israel or Israelis. Whatever the psychological or historical underpinnings of this self-assertion, the data document the generally held impression of Israelis as articulate and often dogmatic in their opinions. One might expect this confidence to be moderated with education, as the complexities and subtleties of the real world are realized more fully, but in fact the opposite is true. The higher the educational level attained, the more self-confidence about how things should be done. Those with low education are the least self-confident, and Asian-African-born are much less certain of knowing what policy the government should pursue than either European-American- or Israeli-born.

An election campaign generally intensifies patterns of political interest and discussions. Three out of every four respondents claim to be interested in the election results, and this is very closely associated with level of education (see Table 2.3). The European-American-born are the

TABLE 2.3 INTEREST IN THE ELECTION RESULTS BY
PLACE OF BIRTH AND EDUCATION[a]

BIRTH AND EDUCATION	N	VERY INTERESTED	INTERESTED	NOT TOO INTERESTED	NOT AT ALL INTERESTED
Place of Birth					
Asia-Africa	436	26%	39%	20%	15%
Europe-America	957	36	44	14	7
Israel (father Asia-Africa)	85	20	55	14	11
Israel (father Europe-America)	231	44	44	8	4
Israel (father Israel)	94	35	35	20	10
Total	1803				
Education					
Elementary or less	603	24	39	20	16
Through high school	856	33	47	14	6
More than high school	353	51	39	7	3
Total/Averages	1812	33%	43%	15%	9%

a. From phase 3; see Appendix II.

most interested, and this interest is even stronger among their Israeli-born children. The Israeli-born cohorts of Asian-African-born fathers are also more interested in the election results than are their fathers. This would seem to indicate that patterns of interest in politics are likely to continue and even grow in the future.

There are other indications of widespread interest in politics. Five percent report that they attend party meetings often, and 29 percent do so occasionally. For the period before elections the corresponding figures are 8 and 17 percent, respectively. This type of participation before elections is weakly related to both place of birth and education. The Asian-African-born are slightly more likely to be active in this than are European-American-born or Israeli-born, in that order. Those with less education tend to attend political meetings slightly more than those with higher levels of education.

Party membership is claimed by 18 percent of the respondents, with an additional 37 percent stating that they are "sympathetic" to a party. There is a slight trend away from party membership when the Israeli-born sons are compared with the foreign-born fathers.

The use of television in the 1969 campaign for the first time introduced a new form of potential political communication and participation. While only 40 percent of the respondents reported that they had television sets at the time, 57 percent watched the parties' campaign broadcasting.[17] Each party was allotted a given amount of time by a prearranged formula. On the whole, the campaign's novelty was the television broadcasting, and many parties counted heavily on the medium.[18] But while the television campaign had some effect on political opinion, it had very little effect on the vote. Forty percent of the sample[19] reported that the television campaigning led them to change previously held opinions, while 55 percent said that the campaign strengthened their previous ones. The campaign had little effect on the vote, however; 84 percent reported that the campaign did not affect their vote decision and 12 percent that it reinforced their decision to vote for the party of their choice. Only 4 percent maintained that the campaign affected their decision.[20]

Although Israelis are interested in politics, discuss it quite a bit, vote in great numbers, and believe that elections can change policy, they do not have much faith in their own ability to influence policy (see Table 2.4).[21]

The data indicate that the *lower* on the social scale the Israeli citizen is, the more likely he is to feel efficacious. Asian- and African-born are more efficacious than are any other groups. Israelis born of European and American fathers are the least non-efficacious. More can be learned about the phenomenon by examining the rates of the place-of-birth and education groups in claiming no efficacy at all. There the Asian- and African-born and especially their Israeli-born children stand out as having the highest percentage. The lowest rate is shown for the European-

TABLE 2.4 EFFICACY BY PLACE OF BIRTH AND EDUCATION[a]

"To what extent can you and people like you influence policy?"

BIRTH AND EDUCATION	N	A VERY GREAT DEAL	A GREAT DEAL	SOMEWHAT	A LITTLE	NOT AT ALL
Place of Birth						
Asia-Africa	296	5%	14%	26%	23%	32%
Europe-America	629	4	11	34	27	24
Israel (father Asia-Africa)	89	7	8	23	26	37
Israel (father Europe-America)	213	3	11	43	29	14
Israel (father Israel)	68	3	2	39	29	26
Total	1295					
Education						
Elementary or less	372	4	11	23	22	39
Through high school	640	5	11	36	27	20
More than high school	280	2	11	38	30	18
Total/averages	1292	4%	11%	33%	26%	25%

a. From phase 2; see Appendix II.

American-born, and especially for their children, with the Israeli born of Israeli fathers between the Asian-African and the European-American. But when the two low-efficacy categories are combined, much of this effect disappears. Those of lowest education still have low efficacy, but the two higher education groups show similar patterns.

We have seen that there is a slight tendency for place of birth to maximize the efficacy of groups such as the Asian-African-born. When efficacy is related to income, this slight inverse relationship still holds. Only for the lowest level of education is the lack of efficacy apparent. There is no direct relationship between education and efficacy in Israel, although the *lack* of efficacy grows as education decreases. These findings are rather surprising, considering that in other countries a direct relation is usually found. The direct relationship between efficacy and education, for example, is usually explained by the fact that as one moves up the social ladder in one area—say, education—one progresses in other parallel areas at the same time—status, income, political influence. But, as Table 2.4 indicates, no such pattern holds in Israel. If the slight inverse relationship warrants explanation, it is possible that as the

Israeli moves up the social class ladder, he becomes more realistic and realizes that his chances of penetrating the relatively closed political system are very slight. On the other hand, it may be that the notion that social class is parallel to political influence simply doesn't hold for Israel. Other correlates of political influence—family ties, youth movement membership, place of employment, and the like—are more important than social class.

The tension between the high rate of voting turnout and the low level of efficacy is apparent in the response to the question of whether politicians pay attention to the opinions of the ordinary citizen. A quarter of the population is certain that they do, a third of the population thinks that perhaps they do, 38 percent believe that politicians do not. The data seem to indicate that the Israeli citizen is fundamentally passive, identifying with democratic forms, confident that the politician is concerned with his opinion, yet basically unconvinced about his own ability to influence policy.

Within the democratic context this civil passivity seems to have given rise to a desire for assertive political leadership. In spite of—or perhaps because of—the brilliant military victories and impressive achievements in other areas, many Israelis seem to be waiting for a leader to fill the gap left by the retirement of Ben Gurion. The cumbersome parliamentary process is at times criticized for its inefficiency, and politicians are often taken to task for their lack of imagination and resourcefulness. Indeed, many have wondered how so much progress has been achieved, considering the lackluster political leadership and the ever-present bureaucracy. When offered strong leadership as an alternative to "all the debates and laws" (see Table 2.5), two-thirds of the sample agreed with the leadership alternative as being potentially more helpful to the country. Those born in Asia and Africa were more extreme in their support than were other groups. Israeli-born children of Israeli-born fathers were the most supportive, Israeli-born children of European- and American-born fathers least. There was a slight inverse relationship between agreement and education, but the differences were not very large; on the whole, the statement was supported by all groups.

We might seek an explanation for these findings by noting that Israel is a nervous, energetic nation. The doer—pilot, manager, builder—is rewarded heavily both materially and symbolically. Much of this ner-

TABLE 2.5 IMPORTANCE OF LEADERSHIP BY
PLACE OF BIRTH AND EDUCATION[a]

"There are those who say that a number of strong leaders would help
the country more than all the debates and laws. Do you agree?"

BIRTH AND EDUCATION	N	DEFINITELY	SOMEWHAT	NOT TOO MUCH	NOT AT ALL	DON'T KNOW OR NO ANSWER
Place of Birth						
Asia-Africa	297	43%	22%	13%	19%	3%
Europe-America	642	38	23	19	17	3
Israel (father Asia-Africa)	89	38	29	16	13	3
Israel (father Europe-America)	214	32	30	21	16	0
Israel (father Israel)	69	41	33	12	14	0
Total	1311					
Education						
Elementary or less	379	42	23	16	15	5
Through high school	646	40	25	16	16	2
More than high school	283	30	26	23	21	1
Total/Averages	1308	29%	25%	17%	17%	3%

a. From phase 2; see Appendix II.

vous energy is expended in the army, but its expression can also be witnessed in moments of anonymity—for example, on the highways and on the buses. There Mediterranean friendliness merges with this nervousness to produce a fundamental Israeli characteristic. Hemmed in on many sides by bureaucratic regulation, this condition expresses itself in less formal, less structured situations. And yet the need for guidance, for structuring, for leadership remains strong. Hence the high rate of agreement evident in Table 2.5.

This thirst for leadership is evidently shared by all classes and political trends.[22] There is a slight decline in agreement as monthly income increases, and the moderate left is less supportive than the center and right. But even these low groups score about 60 percent in support of the statement. Asian- and African-born may agree more because they lack experience with democratic forms, but most of them have now been exposed to Israel for many years. A better explanation is the tone of the country, which emphasizes doing and leadership, although the political arena gives the impression of being devoid of both. Israelis will deliberate, go to the polls, and obey the law, but many of them would be agreeable to stronger leadership "to put things in order."[23]

The resulting syndrome appears paradoxical, but its elements actually mesh nicely. On the surface there is a cockiness and assurance about running the country—and many less important issues, for that matter. At a more fundamental level there is also a desire for order, for security, for leadership. The former provides the semblance of the latter: in place of the desired authority comes an assertive dogmatism. Whether this fundamental insecurity has its roots in the individual psyche or the educational system (or in one of any number of other sources), it is an appropriate subject for future research. At the public level, however, it provides a very fertile soil for cultivating widespread support for positions associated with leaders invested with legitimacy. Public opinion in Israel is unstable and can be brought to support the dominant position with speeches and appeals by the appropriate leaders.

A good case in point is the fate of the national unity government. Its formation introduced Herut (a partner in Gahal) into the government for the first time in the history of the state. Herut was the organizational continuation of the rightist groups that actively and violently opposed the Establishment in the period before statehood. During that period a deep split occurred between the moderate Hagana and the more extremist elements over the proper policy toward the British mandatory power. A situation verging on civil war developed. Twenty years later, just before the June war in 1967, these former antagonists joined together to form what amounted to a war cabinet.

The dissolving of the national unity government in August 1970 was no less traumatic than its formation. The government had to weigh the advantages of the broad-based government and the political quiet it insured against its assessment of its position vis à vis its American allies. The public was treated to an intense display of rhetoric and soul-searching on the part of the politicians. After overwhelmingly supporting the national unity government through the 1967 and 1970 crises, public opinion seemed to be neutralized by the end of 1970 (see Table 2.6). Even this position is entirely in keeping with the Labor party leadership's position that it was Gahal that left the government and thus

TABLE 2.6   QUESTIONS RELATING TO THE NATIONAL UNITY GOVERNMENT[a]

TIME PERIOD	N	QUESTION	RESPONSES	
June 11–13, 1967	708	Did you think it advisable to add new ministers to the government before the war?	Definitely	39%
			Yes	28
			Perhaps	14
			No	17
			Definitely not	2
June 11–13, 1967	708	How long should the enlarged government remain in existence?	Should be disbanded immediately	1%
			There should be a deadline (end of the war, arrival at a settlement, etc.)	33
			It should always exist	50
			Don't know, no answer	15
August 2–7, 1970	509	If Gahal should leave the government, how would that be?	Definitely desirable	6%
			Desirable	13
			Not desirable	51
			Definitely not desirable	30
Nov. 11–Dec. 28, 1970	1829	Do you think Gahal's leaving the government hurts or helps in having an appropriate foreign policy?	Definitely hurts	5%
			It hurts	21
			It doesn't hurt and it doesn't help	52
			It helps	17
			Definitely helps	6

a. The results are from surveys conducted by the Israel Institute of Applied Social Research.

broke national unity; the implication was that the remaining government leaders would be pleased if Gahal would reconsider and return. Despite its concessions in foreign policy, the government (and especially the leaders of the Labor party) was successful in convincing public opinion that Gahal's participation in the coalition was not essential for an appropriate foreign policy three months after the overwhelming majority of the population (and the government) thought it was.

As this demonstrates, Israeli public opinion is most malleable when leaders of stature attempt to alter its course. The results of the opinion polls tend to change in accordance with the arguments of the dominant leadership. In the Israeli situation, this ability to appeal to and win the support of the population is a characteristic of the leadership that the dominant-party democracy has fostered. But since politics is played by the party elite, the populace is rarely considered. Public opinion enters the political arena, on the whole, only when it is mobilized by one of the political actors. More generally, pressure groups fight it out among themselves and with the government and administrative agencies, with infrequent appeals and activation of public opinion. Power is sharply focused at the center, as is the pressure of interest groups. Since there are very few points of access into the decision-making process and since both sides think they know the measure of support a position enjoys among the relevant groups, few appeals are made to the public.

The one outstanding exception is the election process itself. Although the public is called upon to vote, the election results have not shown dramatic shifts. Changes in public opinion do tend to be taken into account by the dominant party in its coalition formation policies, but they have never brought about a serious discontinuity in the distribution of power. Elections are nonetheless of paramount importance in Israel: they provide the voter with a symbolic means of expressing his identification with the state and the political system.[24]

NOTES

1. The best general source in English is Ben Halpern, *The Idea of the Jewish State* (Cambridge, Mass.: Harvard University Press, 1961). In Hebrew, see for example Israel Cohen and N. M. Gelber, *History of Zionism* (Jerusalem: Rubin Mass, 1962).
2. See Moshe Attias, *Knesset Israel* (Jerusalem: National Committee, 1944), in Hebrew.
3. See Halpern, ch. 6.
4. *Haaretz,* January 9, 1949. The elections synopses are taken mainly from the daily press of the period.
5. For an enlightening discussion of election issues and political change, see David Butler and Donald Stokes, *Political Change in Britain* (London: Macmillan, 1969), ch. 15.
6. Discussion of the crises in which the religious parties were involved is found in Ervin Birnbaum, *The Politics of Compromise: State and Religion in Israel* (Rutherford, N.J.: Fairleigh Dickinson University Press, 1970).
7. See Chapter 8.
8. See Amos Perlmutter, *Military and Politics in Israel: Nation-Building and Role-Expansion* (New York: Praeger, 1969).
9. Many aspects of the 1969 elections are discussed in Alan Arian (ed.), *The Elections in Israel—1969* (Jerusalem: Jerusalem Academic Press, 1972).
10. See Chapter 4.
11. This notion was first suggested by Amitai Etzioni, "Alternative Ways to Democracy: The Example of Israel," *Political Science Quarterly* 74 (1959): 196–214.
12. For an example, see Chapter 7. Details on the Israeli governments is found in Asher Zidon, *Knesset* (New York: Herzl Press, 1967) and Birnbaum, *The Politics of Compromise.*
13. From phase 2; see Appendix II.
14. The question reads, "There are those who say that it is desirable to switch the party in power even if it is doing a good job. What is your opinion?"
15. For comparisons with other systems see Lester M. Milbrath, *Political Participation* (Chicago: Rand McNally, 1965); Seymour Martin Lipset, *Political Man* (Garden City, N.Y.: Doubleday, 1963); Robert E. Lane, *Political Life* (New York: Free Press, 1959); Angus Campbell, Philip E. Converse, Warren E. Miller, and Donald

E. Stokes, *The American Voter* (New York: Wiley, 1964); Gabriel
A. Almond and Sidney Verba, *The Civic Culture* (Princeton:
Princeton University Press, 1963); and the symposium on citizen
participation in *International Social Science Journal,* Vol. 12,
No. 1, 1960. For Israel, see Leonard J. Fein, *Politics in Israel* (Boston: Little, Brown, 1967), pp. 141-45, and Emanuel Gutmann, pp.
53-62 of the 1960 *International Social Science Journal* Symposium.
16. From phase 1; see Appendix II.
17. See Michael Gurevitch, "Television in the Election Campaign: Its
Audience and Functions," in Arian, *The Elections in Israel.*
18. See Leon Boim, "Financing of the 1969 Elections," in Arian, *The
Elections in Israel.*
19. From phase 2; see Appendix II.
20. From phase 3; see Appendix II.
21. Comparison with other countries can be found in the sources mentioned in footnote 15.
22. See Alan Arian, *Consensus in Israel* (New York: General Learning,
1971), Table 3.
23. I should caution against reading a tendency toward dictatorship
into these data. They certainly cannot support such an interpretation. The type of appeal that Dayan had—but failed to bring to
fruition before the election of 1969—was never based on the nega-
tion of democratic principles.
24. See Richard Rose and Harve Mossawir, "Voting and Elections: A
Functional Analysis," *Political Studies* 15 (1967): 173-201.

CHAPTER 3

ELECTORAL CHOICE

I

ISRAELI ELECTORAL STRENGTH is lopsided: the dominant Labor party and Mapam, which together in 1969 formed the Alignment, received more than twice as many votes as the second strongest list, Gahal. When party vote is considered by socioeconomic indicators, the Alignment receives more than half of the responses in virtually every category. To be sure, there are variations and patterns generated by these indicators, but the primary fact is that in almost every category reports of party vote for the Alignment exceed half of the sample.

We must always keep in mind that almost every other voter supported the Alignment in 1969 (or the parties that comprised the Alignment in earlier elections). In fact, in each of the seven elections since 1949 the parties of the Alignment of 1969 received roughly one out of every two votes cast; Gahal, and its constituent parties, rather consistently received about one in every five votes, and the religious parties about one in every eight votes.[1] All this while enormous demographic, economic, and social changes were occuring in Israel.

The Alignment has achieved this remarkable record of success in part because it has been Israel's dominant party. It has harnessed itself to the nation's needs and identified itself with Israel's successes. This party embodies most closely the value patterns of the general society. The circular effect here is important: since the Alignment is the dominant party, national success tends to accrue to it. Its goals, its methods, its ideology easily spill over into other areas and onto other institutions. The boundary between nation and party is often blurred; the party has caught the spirit of the nation at a crucial historical moment and has provided leadership to serve the nation's—and its own—interests.[2] Having achieved the position of leadership, it enhances its stature and power by accepting the position of dominance "thrust" upon it. Harkening to the trumpet's call and sacrificing for the good of the nation are

37

"luxuries" which a dominant party can afford, for from its position of power it can only benefit from heeding the "public will."

Duverger, writing in 1951 about political parties in general, gives an amazingly accurate description of Labor, Israel's dominant party before independence and to the present day: "A party is dominant when it is identified with an epoch; when its doctrines, ideas, methods, its style, as to speak, coincide with those of the epoch. . . . Domination is a question of influence rather than of strength: it is also linked with belief. A dominant party is that which public opinion *believes* to be dominant. . . . Even the enemies of the dominant party, even citizens who refuse to give it their vote, acknowledge its superior status and its influence; they deplore it but admit it."[3]

Evidence for the applicability of this generalization to Israel is provided by survey research on Israeli voting behavior. The very difficulties that attend such research lend support to his observation. One of these is that the survey results about party vote differ considerably from the actual outcome of the elections. This coincides with the fact that about 30 percent of the sample[4] avoided indicating vote behavior. This group divided into two, with 17 percent refusing to answer to the direct question about vote intention, while an additional 13 percent avoided naming a specific party in response to the question. Because the interviews were conducted both before and after the election, a wide variety of reasons was obtained. Before the election, many claimed that they had not yet decided how to vote or if they would vote at all; afterwards, some claimed that they had not voted, others that they did not recall how they had voted. Both before and after the election, many respondents refused to discuss the question, citing the democratic right of the secret ballot.

The likelihood that those interviewed actually voted is higher than in the general society. The people interviewed knew Hebrew and were found at their registered home address. Many others who could not be located or did not know the language and were therefore not interviewed, although they were included in the sample, were better candidates to refrain from voting on election day. The overall rate of participation in the election in 1969 was 81.7 percent. A refusal rate of 30 percent of those interviewed is high, even if one grants the sensitivity of the question and the secrecy of the ballot. It is high by comparative standards as well. Butler and Stokes report in their study of British electoral behavior that 12 percent in 1964 and 17 percent in 1966 did not vote, refused to answer, or did not recall their own voting behavior.[5] In Italy, where the party array that confronts the voter is certainly as complex as the Israeli system, 21 percent refuse to disclose party vote.[6]

Despite the high rate of refusal, the Alignment received a disproportionate share of the party vote in the survey. Duverger's suggestion that the dominant party is the one people believe to be dominant is in evidence here. Even if they did not intend to actually vote for the Alignment, or had not voted for it, a substantial proportion of the voters seemed to perceive the Alignment as the "right" answer to be given to the interviewer.[7] The Alignment received an inflated proportion of the reported party vote (see Table 3.1), which, for the total sample, is below the actual vote won by the four party groupings. But the discrepancy rate between the percentage actually won in the election and the party vote as a percentage of the actual vote shows that the differences between parties are not random. The tendency among respondents to avoid answering the party vote question increases as we move from the Alignment through Gahal and the religious parties to the minor parties.[8] For the Alignment, the discrepancy rate is about 10 percent (46.2 - 41/46.2); for Gahal and the religious parties it is about a third; and for the other parties it is almost 60 percent.

TABLE 3.1   PARTY VOTE FOR THE ELECTORATE AND A
NATIONAL SAMPLE, 1969

PARTY	ELECTION RESULTS	AS % OF TOTAL SAMPLE	AS % OF PARTY IDENTIFIERS		
			BEFORE ELECTION	AFTER ELECTION	TOTAL
Alignment	46.2%	41%	57%	59%	59%
Gahal	21.7	14	20	20	20
Religious[a]	14.7	9	13	12	12
Others	17.2	7	9	10	9
N	1.4 mil.[b]	1825[c]	434	858	1292

a. Including Mafdal, Agudat Israel, and Poalei Agudat Israel
b. 81.7 percent of the 1.75 million eligible voters participated in the election.
c. Some 30 percent did not identify a party.

Forty-one percent of the sample gave the "correct" answer, Alignment, while another 30 percent refrained from mentioning the name of a party. If the refusers had actually voted for the Alignment at the same rate (41 percent of the 30 percent), the total Alignment vote would have been 54 percent rather than the 46 percent they actually won. The "rightness" of the Alignment response is of course maddening to the survey analyst, but it indicates the way in which people perceive the political power and position of the dominant party. Respondents are less anxious to proffer the Gahal or religious alternatives regardless of their voting behavior. The eleven other, small parties, none of which won more than 4 percent of the vote, are barely visible in a sample of this size. (The absence of the Arab parties and the Arab Communist party must be discounted in the calculation, since the Arab sector was not included in the sample.)

If the reasons for avoiding answering the question about party vote operated equally on all types of respondents regardless of party vote, each party's vote would be reduced by the same proportion in the final survey results. Evidently additional processes are at work. Some respondents, using less than democratic assumptions, might wish to give the "right" response since the interviewer might really be working for the tax authorities, the party, the municipality, or the police. This is the type of sensitive question best not to answer; but if you must answer, answer "correctly." This apprehensive mood leads to a strong tendency among some to inflate the position of the dominant Alignment.

Whether the question about party vote is asked before or after the election evidently does not make any difference.[9] In both time periods, the strength of the Alignment is heavily exaggerated compared to the actual results when only the party identifiers are considered (see Table 3.1). Looking at the responses of those who identified their party vote, the Alignment is exaggerated out of proportion to its actual success. The Alignment's discrepancy rate for this group is more than 25 percent *above* its actual poll (59 – 46.2/46.2), the report on vote intention of all the other lists is *below* the actual poll, but the ordering of the parties remains as it was before. Gahal is less than 8 percentage points below its actual vote, the religious parties are almost 20 percent below, and the other lists combined are nearly 50 percentage points down.

These striking differences cannot be argued away by pointing out that the sample was drawn only from the urban Jewish population and thus tended to inflate discrepancies when compared with the national vote. In fact, the deflation of Gahal is even more severe when the discrepancy rate is calculated on the basis of the vote in veteran Jewish cities.[10] The discrepancy rate for Gahal actually rises from less than 8 percent to 25 percent below its actual poll on election day. That is, Gahal received 20 percent of the reported party vote of a national sample of urban Jewish adults, but it received 26.5 percent of the vote in veteran Jewish cities and 21.7 percent in the country at large. Using the veteran Jewish cities vote as the base of the calculation of the discrepancy rate, the religious parties stay about the same (14.6 percent in the veteran Jewish cities, compared with 14.7 in the whole country), and the Alignment goes down slightly (45.4 percent in the cities, 46.2 percent in the whole country). The greatest shift occurs in the other parties: they won 13.5 percent of the vote in the Jewish cities and 17.2 percent in the country as a whole. The discrepancy rate between reported party vote and actual vote is about 30 percent, as opposed to some 60 percent using the nationwide base.

The hint that these data supply about the dominant position of the Alignment in the political perceptions of Israelis is of utmost social and political significance. But it must not be forgotten that the information provided about their vote by the great majority of respondents was evidently accurate. Most people vote Alignment and report it as their party vote. The distortion in the report of party vote inflates the proportion of the Alignment and deflates all other parties. But the contours that emerge are basically correct.

II

Analysis of socioeconomic correlates of voting in Israel must be estimates, influenced by the high refusal rate and the tendency noted to identify with the Alignment at the expense of other parties when reporting party vote. Among the most powerful indicators of party vote are sex and age (see Table 3.2). In each age group women support the Alignment more than men by 5 to 11 percentage points. And for each sex group support for the Alignment increases with age. The reverse

TABLE 3.2   PARTY VOTE BY SEX AND AGE

SEX AND AGE	N	ALIGNMENT	GAHAL	RELIGIOUS	OTHER
Men					
18–24	97	38%	33%	14%	14%
25–29	55	47	27	11	15
30–39	111	56	27	11	6
40–49	153	61	18	12	10
50+	252	61	15	17	8
Women					
18–24	96	49	25	18	8
25–29	67	54	27	9	10
30–39	157	62	17	9	12
40–49	113	66	22	7	5
50+	189	68	12	12	8
Total/Averages	1290	59%	20%	12%	9%

tendency generally holds true for Gahal. Men, in each age group, support Gahal more than women, and the young tend to support Gahal
more strongly than the old, regardless of sex. Support for the religious
parties is strongest among the very young and the very old. For each
age group except for the very young, men provide more support for the
religious parties than do women.

The data in Table 3.2 give some idea of the basis of support enjoyed
by the Alignment. The Labor party appeals to and is supported by
moderate or even conservative Israel. The highest vote getter, it has the
image of being the nation's builder, defender and provider.[11] It concen-
trates within it and radiates from itself a large share of the political
power of the country. Its voting support is widely diversified but tends
to come disproportionately from the secure, moderate, middle strata of
Israelis. They represent the "extreme center" of Israeli politics; they are
the conservative elements in the society, in the etymological sense of
that term. They are relatively pleased with their position and anxious to
preserve it. Ideological statements aside, they are hardly the stereotype
of the militant working class. For socialists who have become plump
(few get fat in Israel), proletarians who are enjoying the fruits of their
revolution and who want to keep on enjoying, change is not the foremost consideration in the voting decision; on the contrary, preventing

change seems much more important. It is not surprising that this type of approach to politics is more prevalent among women than men, among the old than the young.

Israel's dominant party finds support among all groups, but especially among those who identify with the epoch in which the party rose to its peak and to that period's dominant values. The highlight of Mapai's (Labor's) epoch probably was the achievement of independence. All the projects undertaken by the Jews in Palestine—immigration, building the land, security—were highlighted by this event. After the founding of the state, these undertakings were continued, sometimes within different organizational settings and institutional arrangements, but with much of the same symbolism and ideological justification. Anyone who lived through the independence epoch in Israel is more likely to identify with the dominant party (see Table 3.3). Jews who immigrated to Israel before independence and immediately thereafter support the Alignment heavily. The rate falls off for those who arrived after 1955, and for Israeli-born the rate is fully 10 percent below the sample average, although it is still almost 50 percent.

The year of arrival in Israel and the way a respondent relates to the epoch of independence are mediated by age. An adult and a child who immigrated at the same time may well react differently because of the differences in their previous and subsequent experiences. Cross tabulations of the age and year of immigration for party vote reveals that while both variables retain some explanatory power, age is more powerful. For each immigration cohort, age remains closely associated with the Alignment choice and inversely related to the Gahal choice. In each age grouping, the influence of the year of immigration diminishes. The pattern seen in Table 3.3 is dispersed; especially, those who immigrated before the founding of the state are shown to be somewhat less supportive of the Alignment by age cohort, in comparison with the overall group not broken down by age. Identification with the epoch and with the party of the epoch retains its importance, but the social fact of aging in Israel, with all that entails regarding social welfare and expectations of stability, seems to be even more powerful in attracting votes for the Alignment.

Much of the program and appeal of the dominant Labor party in the epoch of independence must be seen in the light of the social and

TABLE 3.3 PARTY VOTE BY YEAR OF IMMIGRATION,
PLACE OF BIRTH, EDUCATION, AND INCOME

BACKGROUND	N	ALIGNMENT	GAHAL	RELIGIOUS	OTHER
Year of Immigration					
Before 1947	398	63%	18%	11%	8%
1948–54	472	63	17	13	7
1955 and after	119	57	19	18	7
Born in Israel	275	49	26	14	11
Total/Averages	1264	59%	20%	13%	8%
Place of Birth					
Asia-Africa	312	55	26	13	6
Europe-America	694	64	15	12	9
Israel	279	49	26	12	14
Total/Averages	1285	59%	20%	12%	9%
Education					
Elementary or less	424	61	20	16	4
Through high school	621	59	21	11	10
More than high school	240	55	16	11	18
Total/Averages	1285	59%	20%	12%	9%
Income					
Under I£. 600	335	56	17	19	9
I£. 600–I£. 1000	539	61	21	10	8
Above I£. 1000	384	57	20	10	12
Total/Averages	1258	58%	20%	12%	10%

political realities that the Labor leadership knew in Eastern Europe during the first decades of the twentieth century. The further one is away from this reality, the hazier the values of the epoch become. The precarious position of the Jew, the restrictions on his economic and political activity, the unbalanced nature of the occupations followed, the spread of nationalist feeling, the undermining of traditional religious belief and behavior—all these led to the creation of the socialist-Zionist experiment. The Labor leaders, almost exclusively of East European origin, developed a party and an ideology that answered the needs of the nation as they saw and experienced them. Gahal, on the other hand, using a different emphasis and a different ideological idiom, finds its support (relatively) among different groups. The Alignment is notably successful among the earlier immigrants and among those born in Europe and America (see Table 3.3). Gahal appeals more to the native-born than to any of the immigrant groups, and more to the Asian-African-born than to the European-American-born. The symbols the Alignment uses in order to evoke the epoch of independence and nation building are more effective among the old than the young, among those who came before independence than those who came after independence or were born in Israel, and among those born in Europe than those born in Asia or Africa.

It is no coincidence that Duverger's description is so adequate for Israel. The Labor party, its organization and its leadership, is in the tradition of European political parties that he knows so intimately. The Israeli political system, and the Labor party above all, is historically, if not geographically, an extension of European political experience. And, indeed, those born in Europe and America provide the highest level of support for the party. The Israeli-born who sometimes question the relevance of Labor answers to Israel's problems have the lowest rate of support for the Alignment. Both the Asian-African-born and the Israeli-born support Gahal at a high rate. But, unlike the Asian-African-born, the Israeli-born tend to turn to other parties for the political answer.

The Israeli-born in the sample have higher rates of high education and high income than do the other place-of-birth groups. Evidently those introduced into the system from outside are more likely to identify with the dominant party than those brought up within the system. The success of the political socialization process that leads to support of Mapai is greater for immigrants, probably because more of the agents of socialization of immigrants are under party control than are the similar agents that affect sabras. [12]

The social and economic structures of Israel have been greatly influenced by the ideas and policies of the dominant party. While the fidelity of the party's program to original socialist ideas may be debated, on the whole Israel is an egalitarian state. This is expressed in the general informality of relations, the universal service in the army, the tax structure, and the relatively low income differentials. More than two-thirds of the sample identify with the middle class, with another 15 percent categorizing themselves as working class. It is the average respondent, then, that we would expect to support Labor—not too rich, not too poor; not too much education, but some; in short, comfortable. And this is in fact the case (see Table 3.3). As education increases, support for the Alignment falls off. But, interestingly, support for Gahal does not increase with education, though support for *other* parties does grow dramatically. Increased education is probably related to greater independence of decision. While many Israelis enjoy job security and relative financial security, the ability to consider party alternatives—or indeed, to consider the possibility of weighing alternatives to the traditional vote—is probably greater among groups with higher education.

Additional support for the notion that the Alignment dominance is based on the electorate's middle is found in the income data. The middle-income group is the most supportive of the Alignment. Moreover, Gahal's greatest support (by only 1 percentage point of difference) comes from the middle-income group. The low-income group gives disproportionate support to the religious parties, and the upper-income groups is highest in its support for other parties. All sections of Table 3.3 show that the most liberated (or distant) group from the dominant Labor party—the educated, the Israeli-born, the upper-income group—report other parties more often than groups closer to the "extreme center."

A breakdown by education and place of birth (Table 3.4) provides additional support for the analysis of the Alignment as the party of the middle strata. For the elementary school and partial high school cate-

TABLE 3.4 PARTY VOTE BY EDUCATION AND PLACE OF BIRTH

EDUCATION AND PLACE OF BIRTH		N	ALIGNMENT	GAHAL	RELIGIOUS	OTHER
Elementary	As-Afr	179	55%	27%	16%	2%
or less	Eur-Am	182	69	10	18	3
	Israel	63	53	32	5	11
Through	As-Afr	121	56	27	7	10
high	Eur-Am	364	65	16	11	8
school	Israel	136	46	28	14	13
More	As-Afr	12	58	0	25	17
than	Eur-Am	148	58	17	8	18
high school	Israel	80	49	18	15	19
Total/Averages		1285	59%	20%	12%	9%

gories, the pattern by place of birth is the same as reported in Table 3.3: those born in Europe and America provide the highest support for the Alignment, followed by the Asian-African-born and then the Israeli-born. For the group of respondents who have completed more than high school, the difference between the two foreign-born groups is erased, but the small size of the Asian-African group that had more than high school education can support only some hesitant conclusions. When place of birth is held constant, the following relationships hold: for Asian-African-born, almost no differences are found when party vote is considered by level of education. For European- and American-born, however, support for the Alignment decreases as education increases. The Alignment is especially successful among those born in Europe and America, but it is also the party of the little man—the clerk, the factory worker, the farmer. The Alignment loses some of its hold in terms of the place of birth most receptive to it as educational level increases. It does best among Israeli-born—more than 50 percent—who have not gone beyond elementary school.

Gahal also does best among Israeli-born who have not studied beyond the elementary level. As education increases, support for Gahal decreases steadily among Israeli-born. Among those born in Europe and America, support for Gahal increases with education; among the Asian-African born, it is very high for the lowest and middle categories of educational achievement, but then it falls off. (The number of cases is very small, however, and might be misleading).

In Table 3.3 the religious parties were shown to be relatively more successful among lower educational achievers, while there appeared to be no real difference by place of birth. Table 3.4 presents a very different picture. The European-American-born are true to the original description: support for the religious parties decreases with educational attainment. Among the Israeli-born, however, religious parties support increases with additional education. The pattern for the Asian-African-born is harder to ascertain, since so few of the respondents in this category have more than a high school education. What is clear, though, is that between the first two categories of educational achievement, there is an extreme decrease of support for religious parties among Asian-African-born as education increases.

As noted earlier, support for other parties increases within each place-of-birth group as educational level increases. Within each educational grouping, the Israeli-born are most likely to support other parties. If these patterns hold and, as time passes, more of the voting population is Israeli-born and educated longer (if not better), relative party strengths might well be altered. The potential pool of Alignment supporters will grow as socioeconomic conditions improve, and, in addition, more votes will go to the small parties on the fringes of Israeli politics and power. These changes are unlikely to lead to a two- or three-party system. More probably, many of the other parties will benefit, not only the Alignment's nearest competitors.

Table 3.5 provides further confirmation of some of these observations. The density of living conditions (persons per room in the house) is more than an economic indicator. Behind it lies the life style of the voter, and this index is related to some of the variables already considered. Crowded living conditions affect educational attainment, large families and low incomes are more prevalent among the Asian-African born, and so on. The picture is clear: support for the Alignment and other parties decreases as the index increases; support for Gahal and the religious parties increases as the index increases. Support for Gahal and the religious parties combined is highest (43 percent) among people living in the crowded conditions. For people living under the least crowded conditions, Gahal and religious parties' support combined amounts to only 22 percent.

The Alignment gains more of its support among the moderately well-to-do than among other groups. The moderately well-to-do have been found more likely to support other, smaller parties as well. The religious parties, more than others, gain the support of the "underdog"— those with low education and low income, those living under crowded

TABLE 3.5 PARTY VOTE BY DENSITY OF LIVING CONDITIONS

PERSONS PER ROOM	N	ALIGNMENT	GAHAL	RELIGIOUS	OTHER
Less than 1	176	65%	15%	7%	13%
1.0–1.9	716	58	19	13	10
2.0–2.9	304	59	22	13	6
More than 3	100	51	26	17	6
Total/Averages	1296	59%	20%	12%	9%

conditions, and those (although the tendency is slight) born in Asia-Africa. Since having been in Israel "at the creation" carries with it some intangible symbolic value and snob appeal, we might also note that these "underdogs" who immigrated after 1955 also support the religious parties relatively heavily. Gahal, composed of the lower-middle-class Herut and the bourgeois Liberal party, presents a more variegated picture.

The Alignment, especially successful among the middle strata of Israeli society, the moderately secure and satisfied, has become less than militant in its program and policy. It has turned from what Duverger calls the real left to the apparent left, and this shift coincides with the support it receives from the electorate. Duverger points out that "domination has an obvious stabilizing influence. It slows the rhythmic swing of the pendulum; it diminishes the violence of any trend to the Left. For the dominant party takes up an attitude analogous to that of parties with a majority bent; the continued exercise of responsibility for government diminishes demagogy and the need for innovation. When a left-wing party becomes dominant its appetite for revolution is dulled; apparent leftism is strengthened, but real leftism is weakened."[13]

The Labor party and Mapam, both of which define themselves as socialist, are supported heavily by individuals who report their own political tendency as to the right of the left.[14] The domination of labor has coincided with the ideological moderation of the electorate—and of the Labor party itself, albeit at a slower pace. The factors that facilitated the domination of Labor have also led to a weakening of ideological positions in the population as a whole. This pattern is documented in Table 3.6. Less than half of those who vote for the Alignment report their political trend as left or moderate left. A high 20 percent of the Alignment voters report that they have no interest in politics. The Alignment appeal is spread over all the political trends. In the eyes of many voters, it is evidently not so much a party as the symbol of self-rule and independence. Hence it is supported without regard to platform or program.

The Alignment receives its votes from all sectors of the political trend continuum. It is true that most of the respondents who identified their trend as left or moderate left voted for the Alignment, but more than

TABLE 3.6
POLITICAL TREND BY PARTY VOTE

	N	LEFT	MODERATE LEFT	CENTER	RIGHT	RELIGIOUS	NO INTEREST IN POLITICS
Alignment	728	7%	37%	23%	13%	1%	20%
Gahal	241	2	3	31	46	1	17
Religious	154	1	2	11	9	74	3
Other	114	8	20	36	18	2	16
No decision	114	2	11	23	20	3	41
Total/Averages	1351	5%	23%	24%	19%	9%	19%

PARTY VOTE BY POLITICAL TREND

	N	ALIGNMENT	GAHAL	RELIGIOUS	OTHER
Left	66	77%	6%	3%	14%
Moderate Left	300	89	3	1	8
Center	304	56	25	6	13
Right	237	38	47	6	9
Religious	123	4	2	92	2
No Interest in Politics	207	70	19	2	9
Total/Averages	1237	59%	19%	12%	9%

half of the center trend respondents and 38 percent of the *right* political trend respondents voted Alignment. Even 70 percent of those who had no interest in politics did so. These figures document well the attraction of the Alignment. Gahal's support comes mainly from the right political trend, although less than half of the right votes Gahal. The most faithful of all are those who vote for religious parties; this is all the more noteworthy as "religious" political trend was not suggested to the respondents. Nonetheless, 74 percent of those who voted for the religious parties volunteered "religious" for their political trend; and of those who did so, 92 percent voted for one of the religious parties.

In Table 3.6 the responses of those who avoided naming a political party in answer to the party vote question are provided. Many of them claim that they have no interest in politics, suggesting that for at least some of the respondents the two consistent answers should be accepted at face value. Others—43 percent—identify with the center and right. If their vote was also center and right (Gahal, for instance), they may have chosen to refrain from answering the party vote question rather than name a party other than the dominant one.

A party system characterized by domination lacks an effective parliamentary opposition by definition. While some parties may go through the motions, the operative condition for opposition is missing: the ability and possibility of providing an alternative to the party in office. "Domination takes the zest from political life, simultaneously bringing stability. The dominant party wears itself out in office, it loses its rigour, its arteries harden. It would thus be possible to show . . . that every domination bears within itself the seeds of its own destruction. By and large, however, domination produces some fortunate consequences, especially in multiparty systems. It allows of the formation of a relatively solid majority round the dominant party, whether, in exceptional cases, it obtains the majority alone, or forms the centre of a coalition, or constitutes a homogeneous minority government with the support of allies." [15]

This state of affairs is, of course, very heartening for the supporters of the dominant party, and discouraging for others. The political leadership of other parties has become accustomed to the impossibility of dethroning the Alignment and seems to be content to hold on to the small successes of past elections. By some weird mutation of the usual rules of political striving, Israeli politicians whose party has gone from 3 percent in the first election to 3.2 percent in the second have claimed victory, while the leaders of a party which might have fallen from 40 percent to 38 percent have behaved as if the defeat were total. The electorate seems to take a more realistic, "usual" view of the electoral results than do politicians. Their assessment of their parties' chances of being influential in the Knesset are quite accurate, even before the election (see Table 3.7). More than 90 percent of those who voted for the Alignment saw its chances as very good or good, while 85 percent of Gahal supporters voted the party's chances as good or fair. More than three-quarters of religious parties supporters saw their parties' chances as fair or poor, and more than half of the supporters of other parties saw the chances as poor. The electorate evidently is aware of the position of domination enjoyed by the Alignment and realizes that a vote for a party other than the Alignment is a vote "wasted." But this knowledge does not prevent some 53 percent of the electorate—and

TABLE 3.7 LIKELIHOOD OF PARTY BEING
INFLUENTIAL IN THE NEXT KNESSET

BY PARTY VOTE	N	VERY GOOD	GOOD	FAIR	POOR
Alignment	730	55%	38%	7%	0%
Gahal	250	10	47	38	5
Religious	151	4	19	49	27
Other	120	4	10	32	53
Total/Averages	1251	35%	35%	21%	10%

BY PERCEIVED PARTY STRENGTH	N	ALIGNMENT	GAHAL	RELIGIOUS	OTHER
Very Good	438	92%	6%	1%	1%
Good	435	63	27	7	3
Fair	258	19	37	29	15
Poor	121	2	10	34	53
Total/Averages	1252	58%	20%	12%	10%

some 42 percent of the sample—from voting non-Alignment. It is not unreasonable to speculate that many of these are protest votes.

A dominant party such as Labor perpetuates its strength by means more subtle and effective than is indicated by the term "mobilization." It creates support in unobtrusive ways by blurring the distinction between itself and the state. Hence it is most effective among those who are most susceptible to massive societal influences. The dominant party does not and need not organize tightly because of the other advantages of power that accrue to it. This is demonstrated by the fact that only a quarter of the Alignment voters are party members, while over a third of the religious parties' voters are. (The comparable figure for Gahal is 14 percent.) By the same token, the dominant party is likely to be most successful among respondents whose politicization has been weakest. When primary groups provide cues regarding appropriate political behavior, the individual tends to respond in accordance with these cues. Among those individuals who are not provided such cues, however, the success of the dominant party is likely to be greatest. Because it sets the mood of the political scene, the dominant party is in the best strategic position to attract those who are undecided. In a sense, it has the facilities to provide the cues not provided by the primary group.

TABLE 3.8 POLITICIZATION AND PARTY VOTE[a]

"Do you vote as your family votes?"

BY ANSWER	ALIGNMENT	GAHAL	RELIGIOUS	TOTAL/AVERAGES
Yes	32%	39%	55%	35%
No	61	56	37	58
Doesn't know how family votes	7	5	8	7
N	750	139	98	987

BY PARTY VOTE	YES	NO	DOESN'T KNOW HOW FAMILY VOTES	TOTAL/AVERAGES
Alignment	69%	80%	79%	76%
Gahal	16	13	10	14
Religious	16	6	11	10
N	345	572	-70	987

a. Phases 1 and 2; see Appendix II.

Table 3.8 confirms this point. The supporters of the religious parties, followed by Gahal supporters and only then by Alignment supporters, vote like their families. Evidently primary group pressures are most perceived and pervasive among religious voters. Alignment supporters have the highest rate of out-family voting, which indicates that forces have been exerted that can overcome the pull of the primary group.

Another indication of this pattern is evident when we study party choice by politicization (see Table 3.8). Among those who vote as their families do, more than two-thirds vote for the Alignment. But for those individuals who report they behave in a manner contrary to the primary group, four-fifths vote for the Alignment. The dominant party is a powerful magnet that draws individuals to it, especially if their roots are tenuous. The dominant party is not a tightly organized mobilization structure, but a party that oozes throughout the society and engulfs many diverse types of individuals.

How different is the picture for the religious parties of Israel. We shall see in Chapter 6 that they are likely to be the most influenced by the party in determining their vote; their members also show the highest rate of membership compared with the other groups. Being the most

highly organized group of party members, they are also the most consistent in voting in terms of primary group behavior. Among those in
the sample that voted like their families, 16 percent voted for religious
parties; among those who voted differently from their families, 6 percent voted for these parties. The pattern of loose party ties that characterizes the dominant party is reversed in the case of the religious
parties. Moreover, Gahal's pattern of party ties is more likely that of
the labor parties, though it enjoys neither their effective organizational efforts nor the advantages of being a dominant party.

The constituent parties of the Alignment have always been the single
most important political fact in Israel. Although no single list has ever
won a majority of the votes, Mapai (now Labor) dominates the entire
political system. Just as Labor occupied a centrist ideological position
in the left-of-center atmosphere of Israeli politics, and just as it is the
arithmetical center of all coalition calculations, Labor's support tends
to come from the center of the electorate. As voters move up and away
from the socioeconomic center that Labor dominates, their votes tend
to be fragmented among the other parties of the Israeli multi-party
system, rather than channeled into one of the stronger parties already
existing. If this pattern holds, Labor's position of domination should be
secure; the egalitarian trends in the economy and society are likely to
be associated with increased Labor strength at the polls, while those
who are more educated, younger, earn more, and are Israeli-born are dividing their votes among the smaller other parties.

Labor's domination puts it in a class by itself, both at the polls and in
Israeli politics. It is misleading to perceive Gahal as the antagonist to
the Labor hegemony. The interesting feature of Israeli politics will
continue to be coalition formation, for every indication is that the
pattern of stable election results will continue. The popular labeling of
Labor as the "thousand-year party" is probably grossly exaggerated,
but it has already been proved 5 percent correct.

III

It is quite obvious that many factors influence the voting decision in
Israel. The question of interest is which factors are more influential
than others. The answer to the question is likely to be very complex,

since the influencing factors are interrelated one with another. Education is influential in determining the party vote and so is place of birth, but both of these are related to one another, and so on.

One technique widely used to establish some kind of order among these interrelated variables is tree analysis.[16] This is a computerized procedure whose objective is to explain as much as possible of the variance in the dependent variable.[17] The sample is partitioned into a series of categories, which are defined by the independent variables, through a sequence of binary splits, starting with the division of the sample into two parts. Each step constructs a new part of mutually exclusive combinations of characteristics specifying the two groups to be formed. Before a split is actually decided upon, all existing groups and the entire list of independent variables are explored in order to find the group division that will contribute most to the reduction of the proportion of unexplained variance in the dependent variable. The independent variable chosen for a given split is dichotomized in the optimal way, and then the program proceeds to the next split.

In the application of tree analysis to the data under discussion here,[18] the dependent variable was vote intent for the Alignment, and the independent variables were age, sex, education, place of birth, monthly income, year of immigration, marital status, Histadrut membership, social class, density of living conditions, political party involvement, religious observance, language spoken at home, father's place of birth, father's education, mother's place of birth, mother's education, spouse's place of birth, and spouse's education. The program considered only those respondents who gave a party vote preference.

The results of the tree analysis (see Figure 3.1) reveal that the two variables that most effectively explain the variance in the data are Histadrut membership and religious observance. Of those who reported a party vote preference, 64.5 percent (or 1,924 individuals) indicated the Alignment. Of all the independent variables, the one which provided the highest proportion of explanation in the dependent variable was Histadrut membership: 76 percent of the 1,299 Histadrut members in the sample vote Alignment, while only 40.6 percent of the 625 nonmembers do. The next splits follow from the respective Histadrut branches. In each case religious observance is the most explanatory variable. Of the 1,047 nonobservant Histadrut members, a very large

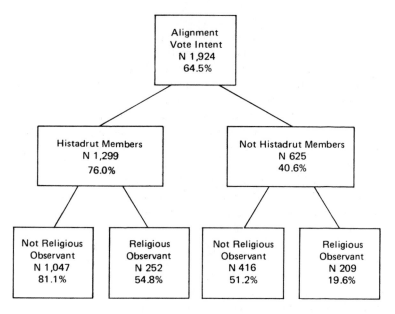

Figure 3.1 Tree Analysis

proportion (81.1 percent) vote Alignment, compared with 54.8 percent of the observant Histadrut membership. For the non-Histadrut members, the pattern is reversed. The Alignment is supported by 51.2 percent of the non-observant but by only 19.6 percent of the observant non-Histadrut. The splits in the branches of the tree continue, but the sizes of the cells become too small for meaningful analysis.[19]

The tree generated by the data presents a number of fascinating aspects. First is its symmetry. The fact that the split off the Histadrut membership and non-membership branches is identical indicates a high degree of structure within the data. Second, the tree provides a clear continuum of Alignment support. The highest and lowest Alignment supporters follow a congruent pattern regarding the Histadrut and religious observance. The labor-union non-observant support their party heavily; the observant non-labor-unionists do not. The other two permutations represent one group under cross-pressure from both Histadrut and religious networks and another group under the influence of neither of these networks. Third, this Israeli pattern is very similar to the European experience, where the socialists and clericalists have a long history of political competition and provide the outward manifestations of many social cleavages.[20] In Israel the contest between the two camps is modified, since electoral power is so lopsided in favor of the left, but it is evident from the tree analysis that the pattern of cleavage so widespread in industrialized states is also present in Israel.

The Histadrut has always been an important element in the functioning and dominance of the left. In that sense, the analyses offered here refer directly to the Histadrut as well. The role and public acceptance of religion, however, must be explained before the networks of social bases of Israeli politics can be considered. In the next chapter the former topic will be undertaken, and Chapter 5 will then return to the latter topic.

NOTES

1. The three religious parties were combined in these analyses. All are orthodox Jewish parties; in 1969, the National Religious Party (Mafdal) received 9.7 percent of the vote, Agudat Israel 3.2 percent, and Poalei Agudat Israel 1.8 percent.

2. See Seymour M. Lipset and Stein Rokkan (eds.), *Party Systems and Voter Alignments: Cross-National Perspectives* (New York: Free Press, 1967), "Introduction," pp. 1–64.

3. Maurice Duverger, *Political Parties* (New York: Wiley, 1963), pp. 308–9.

4. The analyses in the first two sections of this chapter are based on the third phase of the field work detailed in Appendix II. For previous empirical research on Israeli elections, see Judah Matras, *Social Change in Israel* (Chicago: Aldine, 1965), ch. 3.

5. David Butler and Donald Stokes, *Political Change in Britain* (London: Macmillan, 1969), p. 486 (questions 40a and 40d in the 1964 questionnaire) and p. 500 (questions 44a and 44c in the 1966 questionnaire).

6. Samuel H. Barnes, "Social Structure and Political Behavior in Italy," in Richard Rose (ed.), *Political Behavior in Industrial Society* (New York: Free Press, forthcoming), Table 18.

7. The Alignment has the power and good fortune to fortify this perception among the voters. Each party is represented by a Hebrew letter or a group of letters, and campaigning and voting are conducted using these letter-symbols. When voting, the citizen chooses the slip of paper with the letters representing the list of his choice on them and places the slip of paper into his election envelope, seals it, and deposits it in the ballot box. The choice of letters for each party must be approved by the Central Elections Committee, which tends to have a party composition which reflects the party strengths in the outgoing Knesset. The letter combination which the Alignment requested and was assigned was AMT-aleph, mem, taf. A good argument could be made for this combination, since the aleph (revealingly, the first letter of the alphabet) was traditionally the letter of Mapai, the mem the symbol of Mapam, and the taf that of Ahdut Haavoda, all of which were now in the Alignment. But this special combination of letters was more than a throwback to the days when the parties ran as separate entities. For AMT (pronounced "emet") means Truth in Hebrew. And who can be against Truth?

8. The "other" parties mentioned in phase 3 were Independent Liberals (2.4 percent), Haolam Haze (0.8 percent), Free Center (0.6 percent), Israel Communists (0.3 percent), New Communist List (0.1 percent), and assorted other lists (2.5 percent).

The Independent Liberal supporters are mostly older, tend to be female, have at least some high school education and were born in Europe-America. Those who expressed support for Haolam Haze tend to be younger, also female, with high levels of education and are largely Israel-born. Most of the Haolam Haze supporters were either born in Europe-America or had fathers who were.

9. This statement is true immediately before the election, as Table 3.1 shows. It should be modified, though, for periods much before the election. In phase two of the data collection (see Appendix II), conducted a month before the elections, 38 percent of the sample refrained from answering the question.

10. Voting results are from *Results of Elections to the Seventh Knesset and to Local Authorities* (Jerusalem: Central Bureau of Statistics, 1970), Special Series No. 309.

11. For an expansion of this point, see my *Ideological Change in Israel* (Cleveland: Press of Case Western Reserve University, 1968).

12. The notion that those who break with their former milieu are more committed than those for whom the issue is a matter of tradition or habit is familiar in the literature. See Georg Simmel, *The Sociology of G. Simmel,* translated and edited by K. Wolff (New York: Free Press, 1950), pp. 379–95; and Juan Linz, "Cleavage and Consensus in West German Politics," in Lipset and Rokkan (eds.), *Party System and Voter Alignments,* pp. 283–321.

13. Duverger, p. 312.

14. Political trend was ascertained by offering the respondent four alternative trends to choose from: left, moderate left, center, and right. 152 respondents volunteered the term "religious" to identify their trend; 360 respondents claimed that they identify with no political trend.

15. Duverger, p. 312.

16. See, for example, Klaus Liepelt, "The Infra-Structure of Party Support in Germany and Austria," in Mattei Dogan and Richard Rose (eds.), *European Politics* (Boston: Little, Brown, 1971), pp. 183–202; Klaus Liepelt, "Esquisse d'une typologie des électeurs allemands et autrichiens," *Revue Française de Sociologie,* 9 (1968): 13–32; Bo Särlvik, "Socioeconomic Determinants of Voting Behavior in the Swedish Electorate," *Comparative Political Studies,* 2

(1969): 99-135; and the contributions to Richard Rose (ed.), *Political Behavior in Industrial Society.* For a different manner of attacking the same problem see Arthur S. Goldberg, "Discerning a Causal Pattern Among Data on Voting Behavior," *American Political Science Review,* 60 (1966): 913-22.

17. John A. Sondquist and James N. Morgan, *The Detection of Interaction Effects* (Ann Arbor: Survey Research Center, 1964), Monograph No. 35. The program is called the Automatic Interaction Detector or AID.

18. The data for all three phases reported in Appendix II were used simultaneously. This was done to afford the program the largest number of respondents possible. It is justified theoretically since each sample was representative and empirically since the variation in response among phases was slight.

19. The Histadrut members-observant split by age: those under thirty-four support the Alignment at a rate of 36.8 percent; those above thirty-five at a 62.5 percent rate. The other groups split by place of birth and by mother's place of birth. The over thirty-five, observant, Histadrut members also split by mother's place of birth at the fourth branching. Some of the implications of these later splits are developed in Chapter 5.

20. See Lipset and Rokkan (eds.), *Party Systems and Voter Alignments,* and Seymour M. Lipset, "Political Cleavages in 'Developed' and 'Emerging' Politics," in Erik Allardt and Stein Rokkan (eds.), *Mass Politics: Studies in Political Sociology* (New York: Free Press, 1970), pp. 23-44.

CHAPTER 4

RELIGIOUS AND
POLITICAL BEHAVIOR

THE FACT THAT RELIGIOUS behavior is an important determinant of an individual's vote in Israel is especially noteworthy, since religion is one of the most complex and underplayed issues in the body politic. The role of religion in public life is potentially one of the most explosive of issues in Israel, and yet it has been successfully dampened by the politicians through a fascinating mechanism called the "status quo." There is very little correspondence between the machinations of the politicians in the sphere of religion and the religious behavior and attitudes of the population. The arrangements arrived at by the politicians often fill organizational and personal needs of the party leadership and of course have profound influence on the individual citizen. But these two separate spheres of behavior must not be confused. The religious "status quo" is a political device; religious behavior and attitudes on the part of the general population are an important aspect of the total culture of Israel.

Basically, the status quo agreement stipulated that ad hoc arrangements worked out before the founding of the state would not be altered in the future. This froze the situation: matters of personal status law, such as marriage and divorce, remained the province of the religious authorities. Institutions supported by public funds (the army, university, city-hall cafeterias, and the like) are obliged to observe the dietary laws and may not employ their workers on the Sabbath except by special permission granted by the Minister of Labor. Public transportation on Sabbath and holy days is almost nonexistent, except in areas that have a large non-Jewish population.

In a dynamic society arrangements made at least a quarter of a century ago may not cover all the contingencies. But innovation in response to changing conditions is denounced by the religious parties as upsetting the status quo. Secular groups argue that the conditions are

61

new and hence the status quo does not apply. The partisan debate may focus on a basic question, such as: Is television an extension of radio or is it something new and different? If an extension, then it can be transmitted on the Sabbath, since radio is. If new, it may not be used, since it was not covered in the original status quo agreement.[1] A reorganization of the Education Ministry will obviously affect religious education. Is this prohibited by the status quo, or will the reorganization have to be structured in a way acceptable to the religious parties? And so on. The very indefiniteness of the status quo furthers the partisans' arguments on the issue of religion and the state.

The status quo has become a fact of political life in Israel. Now and again issues arise that threaten the long partnership between the National Religious party and the dominant parties of the left, but somehow the issue always seems to be resolved short of confrontation. The status quo is reinforced by habit and by the political benefit both sides achieve from adhering to it. It must be recalled that the status quo agreement was made before the state's establishment and that political cooperation between Mapai and the religious parties stretches back to 1935. This is not an easy tradition to break. A dramatic reminder of this was provided in the coalition negotiations for the Tel Aviv municipality after the 1969 elections. Younger elements of the Tel Aviv branch of the National Religious party wanted to support Gahal and thus swing the majority of the municipal council to Gahal rather than to the Alignment. Moshe Chaim Shapira, the long-time leader of the party and Minister of the Interior, appeared before this group and reminded the young upstarts of the long tradition of cooperation Mapai and the party had enjoyed. "I was the first to sign an agreement with Mapai in 1927 regarding the Sick-Fund and I'm not sorry about it." He went on to explain that through forty years of cooperation they had achieved great things, all of which could be lost if the Tel Aviv branch formed a coalition with Gahal.[2]

In the face of the political detente worked out by the politicians, the citizen remains basically passive. He simply adapts to changes in the environment. When the Tel Aviv zoo charged for admission on Sabbath (when the use of money is forbidden), visitors were urged to buy tickets in advance. But for those who didn't, there were a number of distributors who sold tickets at regular prices about a block away from the zoo's entrance. The public went to the zoo, the religious tending to buy tickets in advance, the secularists a block away. The tickets were sold for the same price, so everything worked out well. As a part of the coalition agreement after the 1969 elections, the religious party had its suggestion approved that entrance to the zoo on Sabbath and holy days would be free. The public again accepted this with no trouble. At first the crowds were heavier, but they soon leveled off. The capacity of the Israeli to adjust to such situations is born of experience.

In matters of personal religious law the situation is similar. Most Israeli Jews follow religious law, since it is the path of least resistance—and the law of the land.[3] When there are difficulties (as in the case of a Jew marrying a non-Jew or a priest—*cohen*—wanting to marry a divorcée), a trip to Cyprus or a cooperative foreign embassy usually settles the problem. Occasionally voices are heard decrying violations of civil liberties and the existence of religious compulsion, but these have always faltered. Proposals for civil marriage have always been voted down for reasons of coalition stability.

Compliance with the religious law is a normal and acceptable feature of life in Israel. There are vocal opponents of the status quo arrangements; some demand total separation of religion and state, others the establishment of a theocracy. For many compliance is perceived as a privilege, for others a hardship. But the debate rarely takes place in the open. The role of religion in the state is a smoldering issue dampened by the politicians' agreement not to disagree.

Whatever their opinion on how public life should be ordered, individual citizens cannot avoid confronting the issue in everyday life. The one overriding feature of Israel is its Jewish nature. The return to the land, the building of a nation, the goals of Zionism, the revival of the Hebrew language are all uniquely Jewish acts. The in-group/out-group mentality in Israel is very strong. Most of the adults in Israel—and three out of four in the sample—were born abroad and have experienced a Gentile environment whether friendly or hostile. The security problems Israel faces heighten the feeling of friend and foe, us and them. The heavy emphasis laid on the Jewish history of tribulation also plays a part. A revealing incident was related by the father whose three-and-a-half-year-old son returned from nursery school puzzled. After his father asked what was worrying him, the boy replied that he had forgotten something. He remembered who the enemy is at Passover (Pharoah), who he is at Purim (Haman), and who it is at Independence Day (the Arabs). He even remembered who it is on Hannuka (the Greeks) and who it is on the 33rd day of Omer (the Romans). What he was puzzled about is who is the enemy on Arbor Day?

Two separate dimensions are of importance here. One is the individual's attitude toward the role of religion in the state. The other is his own personal religious behavior. Table 4.1 reports the distribution for two questions relating to each of these dimensions.[4] It is clear that religious behavior among the Israeli population generates a pattern very different from the one for attitudes about religion. The pattern for behavior shows that the largest groups are moderate in religious behavior: 36 percent report that they attend synagogue a few times a year,[5] and 48 percent that they observe only somewhat. Attitudes about religion, however, are much more extreme. The pattern of responses regarding the separation of the state and religion is almost a perfect U-curve. The answers to the question about the religious tradition in public life also shows the extreme tendency, with the two largest groups at either end—27 percent for and 42 percent against.

The intersection of these two dimensions provides a fascinating picture of religious behavior and attitudes in Israel. There are many for whom the two positions coincide—a pro-religious attitude and religious behavior, or vice versa. For some, less consistent combinations are found.[6] Consistent religious answers were provided by 21 percent of the respondents, consistent secular responses by 51 percent. Twenty-two percent reported that they personally observe but do not favor government action to ensure the religious tradition in public life, and five percent reported that they favored the religious tradition in public life but were not personally religious.[7] In other words, almost three out of four respondents are consistent, and almost half of the population is secularist by this definition.[8]

To approximate how matters of religion changed during the decade of the 1960's, these results can be compared with those reported by Antonovsky.[9] In one sense, things have been remarkably stable; in another sense, a very important change has taken place. Antonovsky reports that 22 percent of the sample provided a consistent religious response and 49 percent a consistent secular response. These results are

TABLE 4.1   RELIGIOUS BEHAVIOR AND ATTITUDES
(N 1,314)

"How many times a year do you attend services at the synagogue?"

Every day	5%
On Sabbath	13
A few times	36
On Yom Kippur	19
Never	27
	100%

"Do you observe Jewish religious law?"

To the letter	12%
Quite a bit	14
Only somewhat	48
Not at all	26
	100%

"What is your opinion about separation of religion and the state?"

Definitely do not separate	37%
Perhaps do not separate	12
Perhaps separate	12
Definitely separate	35
No answer	3
	99%

"Should the government see to it that public life be conducted in accord with Jewish religious tradition?"

Definitely	27%
Probably	16
Probably not	14
Definitely not	42
No answer	2
	101%

almost identical with the findings presented above. The change involves those who have inconsistent patterns: 19 percent reported that they are personally not religious but support the religious tradition in public life, whereas 6 percent said that they are personally religious and oppose the religious tradition in public life.

The consistent groups have not changed at all in the period since 1962. But the inconsistencies have reversed their previous pattern.

Whereas three out of four in 1962 supported the tradition in public life even though they were not personally religious, four out of five in 1969 opposed the tradition even though they were personally observant. We can speculate that this clear reversal reflects the poor public image the religious parties have presented during this period. Some of their leaders have been accused of misuse of public funds, of improper personal behavior, and of associating with questionable types. These instances are usually played up by the local—especially nonreligious—press. The religious party is often accused of political blackmail by conditioning its continued political support of the Alignment with demands that will further interests of the religious community. In normal times this might be perceived as shrewd politics. But in security-conscious Israel, where national unity is an important value, the religious parties raise issues that appear to be marginal to many and threaten the unity that is cardinal. Many feel that the religious parties use their balance-of-power role as consistent coalition partner with Mapai and Labor to secure legislation that does not have popular support. The power of the religious parties has not changed, but its public image has evidently declined.[10]

For most of the population religious behavior and attitudes about religion are closely related. And they in turn are closely related to socioeconomic factors (see Tables 4.2 and 4.3). Education and income are inversely related to religion in Israel. Asian-African-born are much more observant than European-American-born, but the Israeli-born children of the former are less observant than their fathers while the Israeli-born children of the latter are about as observant as their fathers. A different pattern presents itself regarding separation of religion and the state.[11] Respondents born in Asia-Africa are much more likely to oppose separation than European-American-born, but the rate for their Israeli-born children does not change appreciably. The Israeli-born children of European-American fathers, on the other hand, oppose separation more strongly than do their fathers. The Israeli-born children of fathers born in Israel are between the two other groups. An Israeli pattern seems to be forming on this question, somewhat below the Asian-Africans but above the Europeans.

When both education and place of birth are considered, the patterns are somewhat modified. For the Asian-African-born extreme obser-

TABLE 4.2 RELIGIOUS OBSERVANCE BY EDUCATION, INCOME, AND PLACE OF BIRTH

"Do you observe Jewish religious law?"

BACKGROUND	N	TO THE LETTER	QUITE A BIT	ONLY SOMEWHAT	NOT AT ALL
Education					
Elementary or less	379	20%	18%	46%	16%
Through high school	646	7	14	53	26
More than high school	282	10	10	38	42
Total	1307				
Monthly Income					
Under I£. 600	321	19	21	45	16
I£. 600–I£. 1000	440	12	17	49	23
Above I£. 1000	468	6	7	50	37
Total	1229				
Place of Birth					
Asia-Africa	297	19	25	42	14
Europe–America	641	10	11	48	31
Israel (father Asia-Africa)	89	5	17	63	16
Israel (father Europe-America)	214	11	8	45	36
Israel (father Israel)	69	10	16	52	22
Total/Averages	1310	12%	14%	48%	26%

vance falls off with increased education. For the European-American-born extreme observance decreases sharply between elementary and high school education and stays low for those with more than a high school education. For Israeli-born educational level does not affect extreme observance. At the other extreme, education is a secularizing agent regardless of place of birth. Between a third and a half of respondents with more than a high school education, regardless of place of birth, reported that they were completely secular.

The pattern regarding separation of religion and state by education and place of birth is very clear. European-American-born support separation more strongly than do those born in Asia-Africa or Israel, although the gap between the Europeans and the others diminishes with education. Education has a very powerful influence on attitudes toward

TABLE 4.3 SEPARATION OF RELIGION AND STATE BY EDUCATION, INCOME, AND PLACE OF BIRTH

"What is your opinion about separation of religion and the state?"

BACKGROUND	N	DEFINITELY DO NOT SEPARATE	PERHAPS DO NOT SEPARATE	PERHAPS SEPARATE	DEFINITELY SEPARATE	NO ANSWER
Education						
Elementary or less	379	56%	14%	7%	18%	6%
Through high school	645	35	13	14	35	3
More than high school	283	19	10	14	56	1
Total	1307					
Monthly Income						
Under I£. 600	321	53	13	10	19	5
I£. 600–I£. 1000	440	38	12	12	35	3
Above I£. 1000	468	26	12	14	46	2
Total	1229					
Place of Birth						
Asia-Africa	297	58	11	7	20	4
Europe-America	641	27	11	15	43	3
Israel (father Asia-Africa)	89	55	15	8	17	6
Israel (father Europe-America)	214	34	15	11	38	2
Israel (father Israel)	69	39	20	15	23	3
Total/Averages	1310	37%	12%	12%	35%	3%

separation, regardless of place of birth. The greater the education, the stronger the support for separation. The reverse of these statements is also true: the Asian-African-born oppose separation more strongly than Israeli-born, who in turn oppose it more strongly than European-American-born, regardless of education. And within each place of birth group, opposition to separation falls off as education increases.

Age does not affect report about observance consistently. Only for the very observant category is there a discernable pattern, and then only for males. Twelve percent of the 18 to 20-year-olds indicate that they are very religious, compared to only 2 percent for the 25–29 group. For the 30-year-olds it jumps to 13 percent, and it is 14 percent for the forty-year-olds and 17 percent for those above 50. Neither age nor sex strongly affects opinions about separation of religion and the state.

These data indicate that the population is severely split by the issue of religion in public life and that religious behavior is quite widespread. On the whole, support for religion and observance are related to social class; the lower the class, the higher the support and rate of observance. The interesting problem to the observer of the Israeli scene is why the religious parties do not fare better, considering the prevalence of attitudes and behavior which can be considered supportive of religion. Part of the answer has to do with the distinction between personal behavior and attitudes toward religion, on the one hand, and the activities and public image of the religious parties, on the other.[12] Behind this is a fundamental question: do the religious parties represent those who are religious? Evidently not. Some who are religious do not feel that separate political institutions are necessary. Others do not feel that the behavior of the religious parties and their leadership live up to the high standards these people set for a religious party. If a "religious" politician is just like any other politician, the argument goes, why support him just because I am also religious?

Whatever the reasons behind it, the fact is clear that the natural constituency of the religious parties in Israel is much larger than the percentage of the vote the parties actually win. Before attempting to estimate its actual size, it is instructive to consider how individuals with religious behavior and attitudes actually vote. The important finding in Table 4.4 is that individuals with religious behavior and attitude patterns are spread over all of the party-choice categories. While those who choose a religious party are much more likely to behave according to attitudes consistent with religious positions, there is no clear difference among the other party choice groups in this sense. Thirteen percent of Alignment supporters and 16 percent of Gahal voters attend synagogue at least once a week. Eighteen percent of the former and 27 percent of the latter report that they are observant. While 83 percent of those who choose the religious party definitely oppose separation of religion and the state, three of the other party choice groups generate a very neat U-curve pattern. Regarding the question of the religious tradition in public life, Gahal voters are closer to a religious position than support-

TABLE 4.4 RELIGIOUS BEHAVIOR AND ATTITUDES BY PARTY CHOICE

Worship

PARTY CHOICE	N	EVERY DAY	SABBATH	FEW TIMES	YOM KIPPUR	NEVER
Alignment	590	3%	10%	36%	23%	29%
Gahal	104	3	13	46	19	18
Religious	84	29	38	26	5	2
Others	51	4	10	27	18	41
No answer; not decided, etc.	482	5	13	35	16	31
Total/Averages	1311	5%	13%	36%	19%	27%

Observance

PARTY CHOICE	N	TO THE LETTER	QUITE A BIT	ONLY SOMEWHAT	NOT AT ALL
Alignment	590	7%	11%	52%	30%
Gahal	104	9	18	48	24
Religious	84	74	18	7	1
Others	51	8	18	33	41
No answer; not decided, etc.	485	8	16	51	25
Total/Averages	1314	12%	14%	48%	26%

Separation

PARTY CHOICE	N	DEFINITELY NOT	PERHAPS NOT	PERHAPS	DEFINITELY	NO ANSWER
Alignment	590	33%	13%	15%	37%	3%
Gahal	104	39	13	13	32	4
Religious	84	83	7	1	5	4
Others	51	27	6	12	50	4
No answer; not decided, etc.	479	37	13	11	35	4
Total/Averages	1308	37%	12%	12%	35%	3%

Public life according to religious tradition

PARTY CHOICE	N	AGREE	PERHAPS	PERHAPS NOT	DISAGREE	NO ANSWER
Alignment	590	19%	17%	15%	49%	1%
Gahal	104	29	19	14	38	—
Religious	84	88	5	6	1	--
Others	51	16	6	20	57	2
No answer, not decided, etc.	483	27	17	14	42	1
Total/Averages	1312	27%	16%	14%	41%	2%

ers of the Alignment and other parties, but even in Gahal the majority opposes the proposition.

The assumption that the religious parties should get the votes of the religiously oriented must be carefully qualified. Factors other than religion might well influence the voter.[13] Also, parties other than the religious ones make efforts to win the religious vote. Labor, the dominant party, which tries to be as all-inclusive as possible, is a good case in point. Gahal, and especially the Herut movement, is heavily supported by those of low education and income and the Asian-African-born. As we have noted, these groups also tend to be most religiously oriented.

To discount these influences of political party activity, it is useful to consider religious behavior and attitude in terms of political trend. This is especially rewarding, since only the first four responses in Table 4.5 were offered the respondents. Those who identified themselves here as religious were "self-selected," so to speak, having volunteered the information. Again we find that religious behavior and attitude is not the exclusive domain of any single political trend. Of course these attributes are concentrated among the self-selected religious identifiers, but in other groups their appearance is regular and shows no clear identifiable pattern. Between 15 and 25 percent of all groups among the left-right spectrum reported that they were observant. Political trend, then, obviously does not presume anything about religious stance. The openly secular (the "not at all" response in Table 4.5) also show a much narrower range of variation among political trends than might be expected. No more than one of three nor less than one of four of the respondents of the four political trend groupings claims no observance at all. At least for the respondents, it makes little sense to speak of Israeli political parties and political trends as clericalist or anticlericalist. As in the politics of coalition formation, so too in the response patterns of Israelis religion and politics are intimately combined.

Something closer to the expected pattern is evident when the question of separation of religion and state is considered. Moving from right to center to moderate left, support for separation increases and opposition decreases. But even here the picture is modified by the fact that two out of five moderate leftists oppose separation.[14] This is obviously not the militant, anticlerical left.

Given that religious observance is an important determinant of the

TABLE 4.5 OBSERVANCE AND SEPARATION OF RELIGION
AND STATE BY POLITICAL TREND

Observance

POLITICAL TREND	N	TO THE LETTER	QUITE A BIT	ONLY SOMEWHAT	NOT AT ALL
Left	80	11%	14%	43%	33%
Moderate left	245	5	10	53	32
Center	346	6	12	51	30
Right	215	11	14	52	24
Religious	80	75	23	3	—
No interest in politics	255	7	18	50	25
Other	10	10	40	30	20
No answer	83	10	16	49	24
Total/Averages	1314	12%	14%	48%	26%

Separation

POLITICAL TREND	N	DEFINITELY NOT	PERHAPS NOT	PERHAPS	DEFINITELY	NO ANSWER
Left	80	40%	16%	13%	28%	4%
Moderate left	245	26	13	16	44	2
Center	346	32	10	13	44	2
Right	215	38	11	14	35	1
Religious	80	90	4	1	4	1
No interest in politics	255	40	16	13	24	7
Other	10	40	30	—	20	10
No answer	83	37	17	2	34	10
Total/Averages	1314	37%	12%	12%	35%	3%

vote and is largely class-related, it is reasonable to expect the religious
parties to benefit from these regularities. The rate of success of the
religious parties can be estimated by applying these assumptions to the
data at hand. We know, for example, that one-third of the Jewish
school children in Israel attend government religious schools. And yet
the religious parties received in 1969 only 15 percent of the vote. While
part of the discrepancy may be attributed to the higher birth rates
among lower-class groups who tend to be religious, the gap demands
further exploration.

Twenty-six percent of the sample claims to be extremely or somewhat observant. If this is assumed to be the natural clientele of the religious parties, the norm for the religious parties would be 26 percent (a figure, incidentally, much closer to the third of the school children in religious schools). This assumption is reasonable in view of the fact that 92 percent of those who actually do choose a religious party report observant behavior. But the religious parties fall far short of this goal. Only 6 percent of the total sample were actually observant and reported a religious party choice. It might be suggested that many religious party supporters avoided answering the party choice question; even so, the figures do not change dramatically. Those who were observant and reported a religious party choice constituted only 9 percent of the respondents who offered a party choice.

The failure of the religious parties to attract their natural clientele is much more severe than even these figures would indicate. Even among those who are observant, the religious parties fall short of winning the percentage of the votes it is "entitled" to among the entire population. Among those who are observant, only 23 percent report a religious party choice.

To recapitulate, the line of reasoning presented here assumes that the religious parties are the most likely recipients of the votes of the observant (26 percent of the sample). However, these parties win only 15 percent of the actual vote, the support of only 6 percent of the sample and 9 percent of the respondents who indicated a party choice. Moreover, these parties are supported by only 23 percent of the observant.[15]

Whatever the reasons for their failure, it is clear that the religious parties have a tremendous political potential if personal observance can be translated into support at the polls. Their power might be released if the status quo agreement fails in the future. It may be that some of the natural clientele of the religious parties are attracted to other parties because of the platforms of these parties on secular issues. Should the "protection" which the status quo agreement affords fail, many of the potential religious parties' voters may vote for the religious parties as religious issues become politically salient.

NOTES

1. For an instructive, if somewhat polemical, introduction to the topic of religion and state in Israel see Ervin Birnbaum, *The Politics of Compromise: State and Religion in Israel* (Rutherford, N.J.: Fairleigh Dickinson University Press, 1970).
2. *Maariv,* Nov. 7, 1969.
3. Members of other religions are subject to their own religious courts.
4. Phase two, described in Appendix II, was used in these analyses. This phase provided most questions on the subject.
5. Synagogue attendance is only an approximate indicator of religious behavior, since women are largely exempted and private prayer is also permitted. Only a small number of prayers must be said in the presence of the congregation.
6. The second and fourth question of Table 4.1 were used. The first two categories of each question were considered religious answers; the third and fourth categories were considered to be secular answers.
7. One or both questions were not answered by 1.5 percent of the sample.
8. It should be clear that this procedure only gives us an approximation of religiosity or secularism. Especially problematic is the 48 percent who report that they observe the religious law somewhat. For purposes of these analyses, it is assumed that these respondents are traditionalists but lack deep religious commitment. But even if this is true, many of them may have very different attitudes from the members of the group that report that they observe not at all. Future research will have to try to measure these gradations more finely.
9. Antonovsky devised the questions and applied the cross-tabulation to data collected in 1962 by the Israel Institute of Applied Social Science in conjunction with a project run by Hadley Cantril and the Institute for International Social Research. The Israeli phase was directed by Antonovsky; the sample of 1,170 Jewish adults formed a representative cross-section of the population. Initial analyses of the data are found in Aaron Antonovsky, "Israeli Political-Social Attitudes," *Amot* (Hebrew) 6 (1963): 11–22.
10. Another explanation for this might be the popular notion that religious observance has increased since the Six Day War. But this

popular notion is not supported by the data. If anything, observance has decreased: in 1962 the percentages for the "to the letter" and "quite a bit" categories were 15 and 15; in 1969 they
were 12 and 14, respectively.

11. The question regarding the religious tradition in public life is ana-
lysed in a different context in Chapter 7. See Table 7.3 and the
relevant discussion.

12. Whereas supporters of religious parties have clear class characteristics, the religiously observant do not differ greatly in their patterns
of concerns from other groups. See Aaron Antonovsky and Alan
Arian, *Hopes and Fears of Israelis: Consensus in a New Society*
(Jerusalem: Jerusalem Academic Press, 1972), esp. Ch. 6.

13. See, for example, Chapters 3 and 6.

14. The respondents who answered left are misplaced on the continuum. From their response patterns in Table 4.5 and elsewhere it
is clear that they are more similar to groups much farther to the
right on the continuum. This left is certainly not the established
left; it appears to be comprised of lower class respondents.

15. The results of phase 3 of the survey described in Appendix II show
that while the figures are higher the pattern is similar. The comparable figures for phase 3 are: 96 percent of those who vote for
religious parties are observant; 36 percent of the observant vote for
religious parties; 12 percent of the party vote identifiers vote for
the religious parties; and 8 percent of the total sample vote for the
religious parties. The norm for the religious parties in phase 3 is 23
percent—the percentage of the sample that reports religious behavior.

CHAPTER 5

FOUR MAJOR BLOCS

THE ISRAELI POLITY has evidenced a high degree of consensus since its inception. The democratic consensus regarding the rules of the game is strong,[1] with the political elite probably more committed to it than the mass public for both ideological and instrumental reasons.[2] A homogeneity regarding patterns of concerns has developed among Israelis, despite their very divergent backgrounds and lifestyles. The Jewishness and smallness of the country play an important role in producing a high level of consensus in citizens' approach to life.[3] Although political issues obviously divide the population, these divisions are often either postponed or obfuscated.[4]

The broad base of political and social consensus provides the background for the sociology of Israeli politics. While it is important not to exaggerate the social cleavages and their impact on the polity, it is also important to realize that certain social networks are operative in influencing the electoral choice of the citizenry. From the results of the tree analysis reported in Chapter 3, two such major networks are apparent, the Histadrut and the religious. The former refers to organizational affiliation and has no necessary relationship with behavior; the latter is behavioral and does not necessarily receive organizational expression. Yet these two social networks are the most influential in determining political behavior.

The continuity of the Israeli experience with the European pattern in which the socialist and religious dimensions are determinant is striking. Liepelt has found this pattern operative in Germany and Austria, and Barnes has demonstrated a similar phenomenon for Italy.[5] There are of course many differences between Israel and these other countries, but the similarity in the findings suggests that Israel is undergoing processes familiar to industrialized countries of continental Europe. Israel was spared cleavages of region and language as well as those that resulted

77

from the early stages of the industrial revolution for historical reasons (if we refer only to the Jewish population), but it has the latent potential of developing a sharp cleavage along secular-religious lines.[6] It is because this cleavage tends to be reinforced by class and ethnic differences that it becomes potentially so dangerous for the society.

The Histadrut and religious networks are hardly precise descriptions of social reality. The Histadrut, formally a federation of trade unions, is in reality a major source of economic and political power. Its membership includes 62 percent of the Jewish population and 32 percent of the Arab Israeli population.[7] While its success among new immigrants appears to be waning, it still organizes a near majority of them. The figures on enrollment of immigrants reveal one of the sources of the Histadrut's strength and serve as an indicator of its success, especially in the pre-state and early post-state periods:[8] in 1969 two-thirds of the pre-state immigrants were Histadrut members, some 59 percent of the immigrants from 1948–60, and 47 percent of the immigrants after 1960.

The political composition of the Histadrut reflects and reinforces the power structure of Israel as a whole. The Histadrut General Convention is elected by members on a proportional representation basis. With the exception of the religious parties, those political parties that dominate the national scene also reign in the Histadrut. The left-of-center parties have lost steadily in the most recent elections, but their power is still unassailable. In the 1969 elections to the Histadrut Convention, the Labor-Mapam Alignment won 62 percent of the vote. In earlier elections the left-of-center parties had won as much as 85 percent of the vote. In the 1965 elections the Mapai-Ahdut Haavoda Alignment won 51 percent of the vote, while in the 1955 and 1959 elections the two parties, running separately, received about 72 percent of the total vote. The closest competitor in the 1969 competition, Gahal, won only 17 percent of the vote. None of the other nine lists won more than 6 percent of the vote cast.[9]

The Histadrut is the nation's largest employer, owning factories, construction companies, and other productive businesses. It is involved in transportation, farming, banking, publishing, cooperatives, and medical services. Some 90 percent of the eligible labor force belongs to the Histadrut.[10] It is obviously a powerful economic and social force in

Israeli life. Its political influence lies in the role it plays in the country's economy and also in its close relationship with the dominant party of the country. As the dominant party in the Histadrut and in the government coalitions, Labor has been able to use the Histadrut and its tremendous power in providing patronage and in determining the nation's economic policy in a manner that would aid the perpetuation of its own position. A good example of this power is the party activities tax, which Histadrut members are called upon to pay.[11] The income from the tax is to be distributed according to the proportionate strength of the various parties at the last Histadrut Convention elections. The rationale is that it is perfectly proper and desirable for parties of a labor union to tax its membership for purposes that will further the goals of the working class. The rub is that the dominant party benefits most and thus provides itself with yet another mechanism of power perpetuation.[12]

The interlocking dependency that a citizen might develop with the various branches of the party-Histadrut complex is formidable. Labor, as a party of democratic integration, channels much of its effort toward "integrating" the citizen through activities of the Histadrut. Newspapers, cultural activities, health services, sports clubs, banking services, insurance, and housing all help to make the Labor party and its efforts through the Histadrut the mass party that "can count on its adherents; it has taken over a good part of their social existence."[13]

The Histadrut and its activities are so comprehensive and all-encompassing that it is likely that many of its members join to benefit from its services rather than for more socialist ideological reasons. It is also probable that a considerable proportion of the Histadrut membership does not perceive the social network that the organization represents. The Histadrut—like the Labor party, which is its main component—benefits from its identification with national goals and achievements. If the researcher who tries to sort out the government, Histadrut, and Labor party institutions and personnel quickly becomes muddled in a three-dimensional organizational chart, there is no reason to assume that the average citizen is capable of more precise differentiation.

The Histadrut does not exclude non-secularists from its ranks; on the contrary, a Labor-affiliated religious list ran in the 1969 Histadrut elections and won 3 percent of the vote. A more practical arrangement, which was worked out long before the establishment of the state, provides the medical services of the Histadrut for the 100,000 members of the religious trade union federation. This allows some of the benefits of the Histadrut to the religious party members without exposing them to the complete range of the Histadrut social network.

While Histadrut membership is merely organizational and may have no behavioral implications, membership in the religious network is only behavioral.[14] The Histadrut member is likely to be confronted with formal or nonformal *group* pressures to identify with and vote for the dominant party. The person who identifies himself in the religious network may generate his *own* internal pressure to have his vote conform to his personal religious practice.

These two major social networks generate four blocs. Two are congruent in that individuals are in either the Histadrut or religious network but not in the other, the third consists of those individuals in both, and the fourth is made up of those in neither. More than half of the respondents are in the Histadrut network and not in the religious network, a little less than a quarter are in neither, about 12 percent are in the religious non-Histadrut bloc, and an additional 12 percent are in both the religious and the Histadrut networks.[15] The tree analysis in Chapter 3 showed that the rates of support for the Alignment vary greatly among these groups. The congruent blocs with respondents who are only in one network and not in the other either heavily support the Alignment or refrain from supporting it, depending upon whether they are in the Histadrut network or not (see Table 5.1). For those whose position is dissonant (exposed to both) or ambivalent (exposed to neither) the rate of support is about 50 percent. These cases are especially interesting since they will provide insight into the correlates of support or nonsupport for the dominant Alignment. The Histadrut non-religious bloc (HR) supports the Alignment heavily; the non-Histadrut religious bloc (HR) gives its support to the religious parties. Those who are in both networks (HR) give their support to both the Alignment and religious parties. Gahal gets about half the vote from the bloc that is affiliated with neither network (HR).

This distribution points to a fundamental feature of the Israeli political system and is a mark of the success of the parties of the dominant left. Of the two social networks identified, the parties of the left are the

TABLE 5.1 PARTY VOTE BY BLOC MEMBERSHIP[a]

BLOC	N	ALIGNMENT	GAHAL	RELIGIOUS PARTIES
H*R*	608	86%	14%	—
*H*R	144	15	15	71%
HR	150	50	15	35
*H*R	273	52	46	2
	1175			

a. Those who gave no party choice are omitted from this table to make it comparable to the tree analysis reported in the figure in Chapter 3. There, too, those who gave no party choice were ignored in the analyses.
The data here are from phase 3; see Appendix II.

most successful in gleaning potential voters; the other network, the religious, is less effective in retaining its natural clientele. Among those voters who are exposed to both the Histadrut and religious networks, the religious parties fare less well than the leftist parties. For those who are in neither network, the religious parties have virtually no attraction, while half of them go to the Alignment. Gahal is in an even worse position. Its only large gains are from those who are associated with neither of the two networks. But, and this is the significant political fact, it has no network of its own upon which to build. It is most successful in that bloc in which it can win by default. It does not have the requisite social bases of support that might sustain a bid for changing its status from the largest party of the opposition.

The secret of the dominant party is that it draws its strength from all sectors of the society. While it will obviously be stronger among some groups and weaker among others, its continued success depends upon its being generally accepted and its ability to prevent the opposition from mobilizing a sizeable segment of the population—that is, from developing a base of support within a social network. The experience of the Christian Democrats in Germany in 1969, when they fell from their previous status as the country's dominant party, can in part be explained by the fact that for political and ideological reasons they failed to mobilize the German working class and thus paved the way for the Social Democrats to emerge as a true competitor for government. As

Table 5.1 indicates, the Alignment does not seem to be making the same mistake.[16]

Having traced the votes of the four blocs, it is also of interest to know the sources of the parties' votes from among them (see Table 5.2). Many of the patterns noted earlier are again in evidence. The Alignment and religious parties get about two-thirds of their vote from their respective congruent network members. Half of Gahal's support comes from the no-network bloc and a third from H*R* bloc. Gahal's support, then, comes overwhelmingly from individuals outside of the religious network. Its support from the H*R* group can be explained in part by the fact that even Gahal is represented in the Histadrut; these individuals probably vote for Gahal in Histadrut elections as well. The very fact that it is in the Histadrut and must compete for votes from within the social network associated with the Alignment indicates the difficulty it would have in establishing an autonomous base for political competition.

Analysis by demographic characteristics presents a picture of relative consistency, with the H*R* bloc receiving the support of half the respondents in almost every category (see Table 5.3). The middle-aged, the Europe-American-born, and those with more than a high school education are most likely to be in the Histadrut non-religious bloc. In the bloc that has congruent religious individuals (*H*R), the old are especially evident. Asian-African-born and those with an elementary school education or less are very apparent in the bloc that is exposed to both the Histadrut and the religious networks. These are likely to be individuals who came from religious backgrounds but upon immigration to Israel were absorbed and socialized by Histadrut-related parties. This type of

TABLE 5.2   BLOC MEMBERSHIP BY PARTY VOTE

PARTY VOTE	N	H*R*	*H*R	HR	*HR*
Alignment	759	69%	3%	10%	19%
Gahal	256	34	8	9	49
Religious parties	160	—	64	33	3
No answer	517	51	13	11	25
Total/Averages	1692	52%	12%	12%	24%

TABLE 5.3 BLOCS BY DEMOGRAPHIC CHARACTERISTICS
(percentaged across)

BACKGROUND	N	HR	HR	HR	HR
Age					
Below 35	542	51%	12%	10%	27%
35–49	560	56	9	14	22
Above 50	584	48	17	14	22
	1686				
Place of Birth					
Asia-Africa	421	44	10	25	20
Europe-America	894	55	13	9	23
Israel	371	51	13	7	28
	1686				
Education					
Elementary or less	583	46	14	21	19
Through high school	795	53	11	8	28
More than high school	307	59	13	6	22
	1685				
Year of Immigration					
Before 1947	532	52	14	11	22
1948–54	606	52	10	15	22
1955 and after	157	50	13	16	22
Born in Israel	375	50	13	8	29
Total/Averages	1670	52%	12%	12%	24%

pattern was most prevalent after the founding of the state. Indeed, for those who immigrated after 1948, the likelihood of being in the HR bloc increases.

The respondents who are young, Israel-born, and have a moderate level of education are more prevalent in the no-network bloc than those of other age groups, foreign-born, or high and low education groups. This is the sabra generation, which was raised in the period of independence, when many of the functions that had formerly been filled by the party had shifted to governmental ministries. The army was depoliticized, the schools were deprived of much of their ideological character, and party-affiliated youth groups became less fashionable. The differences among the groups are not great, but the trend seems to be away from network exposure.

The information about how the various age, place of birth, education and immigration groups distribute themselves among the blocs can be used to analyze the composition of each bloc. The previous discussion suggested that the bloc exposed to both the Histadrut and religious networks would tend to be Asian-African-born and have low education. Table 5.4 provides dramatic confirmation of this suggestion and also indicates that those who are exposed to both networks also tend to be older and to have immigrated in the immediate post-state period. These are the immigrants who came with a religious background and were absorbed by the dominant Histadrut structures of the state.

Their pattern is quite different from those only in the religious network. The HR bloc is composed of members who tend to be older, have lower levels of education, and arrived before the establishment of Israel. They were exposed to a different pattern of absorption from the two-

TABLE 5.4   DEMOGRAPHIC COMPOSITION OF THE BLOCS
(percentaged down)

BACKGROUND	HR (N 870)	HR (N 209)	HR (N 209)	HR (N 398)
Age				
Below 35	32%	30%	26%	37%
35–49	36	23	36	31
Above 50	32	47	38	32
Place of Birth				
Asia-Africa	22	21	51	22
Europe-America	57	56	37	52
Israel	22	23	13	26
Education				
Elementary or less	31	40	59	28
Through high school	49	41	32	55
More than high school	21	19	9	17
Year of Immigration				
Before 1947	32	36	29	30
1948–54	37	30	45	34
1955 and after	9	10	12	9
Born in Israel	22	24	14	27

network bloc. Significantly, most of them were born in Europe and America.

The Histadrut network bloc shows significant strength in all of the categories. In fact, its success lies in its ability to draw its support within the HR category from each group in proportion to that group's size in the total population.[17] Thus, for example, the HR bloc is composed of the three age groups in almost equal size; this is the stuff of which a dominant party is made.

The bloc exposed to no network ($H\overline{R}$) also demonstrates this characteristic of drawing its support from across the entire population in relation to the size of the group in the population. The crucial difference is that the $H\overline{R}$ bloc members are organized and hence potentially exposed to the formal and informal pressure and cues that the Histadrut network can activate. The nonorganized are also the nonexposed. Their political power is undirected and splits, as we saw in Table 5.2, between the Alignment and Gahal.

As noted in Chapter 3, the Alignment does better as age increases; this is especially true in the two blocs that are exposed to the Histadrut network (see Table 5.5). Among the bloc members who are exposed to neither network the opposite pattern holds: the younger tend to support the Alignment more. This is probably related to the identification of the Alignment with the state, especially for those who grew up in the period when direct party activity was less obvious.

Gahal's strength falls as age increases in all of the blocs except the non-Histadrut religious. In the latter bloc, Gahal receives 10 percent of

TABLE 5.5 ALIGNMENT VOTE BY BLOCS AND AGE[a]

BLOC	BELOW 35	35–49	ABOVE 50
HR	52%	59%	68%
HR	6	12	11
HR	24	34	46
$H$$R$	37	33	28

a. Figures are the percentage of the Alignment vote in a given age group within a given bloc. For example, 52 percent of the 277 respondents below the age of 35 in the HR bloc reported an Alignment vote. Each percentage is based on a different N (see Table 5.3); hence neither the rows nor the columns add up to 100.

the vote of each age group. In the *H*R bloc the religious parties have their strength, and it is especially effective among the young. The percentages of support for the religious parties in that bloc are 62, 48, and 41, respectively, from youngest to oldest age groups. If these patterns continue and are projected into the future, the Alignment will receive less of the vote of the members of the two blocs that are exposed to the Histadrut but will pick up votes from the undifferentiated *HR* bloc. The religious parties and Gahal, on the other hand, will increase their share of the vote if they can retain the relatively high rates of support of the young as they advance into the older age groups, and if the pattern of greater support among the young can be maintained. There is the counter-possibility that with age people will abandon the religious and Gahal choice made earlier in their lives and choose the dominant party, just as most of the older population has done in the past.

If the average educational level of the society also continues to increase, the Alignment is likely to be less effective in forestalling the loss of some of its present strength (see Table 5.6). For those who are exposed to the Histadrut network and are not in the religious network, the effect of higher education is slightly in the Alignment's favor. But for those in the no-network bloc, the decline of support for the Align-

TABLE 5.6 PARTY VOTE FOR THE H*R* AND *HR* BLOCS BY EDUCATION LEVEL

BLOC	ELEMENTARY OR LESS	THROUGH HIGH SCHOOL	MORE THAN HIGH SCHOOL
H*R*	(N267)	(N423)	(N181)
Alignment	59%	59%	62%
Gahal	12	10	7
Religious parties	—	—	—
No Answer	29	31	31
HR	(N111)	(N222)	(N68)
Alignment	38%	38%	25%
Gahal	32	31	31
Religious parties	2	1	—
No Answer	28	30	44

ment with higher education is steep. Numerically, of course, this is not likely to cause a change in governments, but it is a pattern that could have political consequences in the future. The fact that so many of the highly educated respondents in the *H*R bloc refrain from reporting party choice may indicate that they will choose none of the parties discussed here but will give their votes to small, marginal parties, thus perpetuating the fragmentation of the party system.

In the *H*R bloc, the European-American-born and the Israeli-born are most consistent in giving their vote to the network to which they are exposed. Only 14 percent of the former and 16 percent of the latter report that they vote for the Alignment or Gahal (see Table 5.7). The

TABLE 5.7 PARTY VOTE FOR THE *H*R AND HR BLOCS BY
PLACE OF BIRTH

BLOC	ASIA–AFRICA	EUROPE–AMERICA	ISRAEL
*H*R	(N43)	(N117)	(N48)
Alignment	26%	6%	6%
Gahal	14	8	10
Religious parties	33	51	59
No Answer	27	35	25
HR	(N105)	(N76)	(N27)
Alignment	33%	39%	33%
Gahal	14	8	7
Religious Parties	23	28	26
No Answer	30	25	34

Asian-African-born, on the other hand, are much less likely to vote their network: only one-third of them vote for the religious parties, with 40 percent voting for the Alignment and Gahal. This represents a serious gap and an unexploited opportunity for the religious parties. Evidently many of the Asian-African-born in the religious network are not exposed to organizational pressures from the religious parties, even though they have no contact with the Histadrut either. For those who are exposed to both blocs, voting patterns are rather similar, regardless of place of birth. The Alignment and religious parties do somewhat better in winning votes among the European-American-born, and Gahal is more effective with the Asian-African-born in this bloc; but, in contrast to the HR bloc, the patterns are consistent. Those in the HR bloc are likely to vote for the religious parties unless born in Asia-Africa, in which case they are likely to give the Alignment a sizeable share of their vote. Those in the HR block consistently favor the Alignment over the religious parties in dispersing their votes, regardless of place of birth. This indicates the difficulty of competing with a dominant party.

Similar patterns are found for these two blocs when level of education is controlled. Those with medium and high education in the HR are loyal in delivering their votes to the religious parties. Those with an elementary education or less, on the other hand, are much less loyal; 21 percent of them vote for the Alignment. Within the group exposed to both networks, 25 percent vote for the religious parties regardless of level of education. But the Alignment support is less consistent: 35, 45, and 16 percent vote for the Alignment within the respective low to medium to high education groups. A very high 47 percent of the latter withdraw from the cross pressures of the two networks to which they are exposed and refrain from offering a party choice.[18] The appeal of the Histadrut network over the religious network among individuals exposed to both is strongest with lower and especially with medium levels of education.

For the two blocs that are not exposed to the religious network (HR and HR), the findings presented in Table 5.6 about educational level support the place-of-birth findings as well. Two-thirds of the European-American-born and about half of the Asian-African-born and Israeli-born in the HR bloc vote Alignment, with Gahal winning 17 percent of the Asian-African-born vote, 15 percent of the Israeli-born and only 6 percent of the European-American born. For the no-network bloc, both the Alignment and Gahal win about a third of the Asian-African vote, while for the European-American-born the figures are 39 and 29 percent, respectively, and for the Israeli-born, 26 and 35 percent, respectively. Gahal is relatively successful, then, in both blocs among the Asian-African-born and the Israeli-born, the Alignment among the European-American-born.

The picture is completed by examining the contribution of each of the blocs to the various parties controlling for the demographic characteristics. The question is: What characterizes the supporters of each party from among the various blocs? We find, for example, that among those who support the Alignment there is a direct relationship between age and support within the HR group. That is, while only 6 percent of the group below 35 and 10 percent of the 35–49 group are from the HR bloc, 13 percent of the above-50 group are. Gahal supporters from the HR bloc are especially concentrated in the younger age groups, while 61 percent of the oldest age group comes from the HR bloc. Gahal's appeal seems to be differentiated, with the older groups coming from the no-network bloc and the younger from the Histadrut network. This probably is connected with Gahal's relatively recent entry into the Histadrut as a party of competition, or it may reflect a protest vote against the Alignment by individuals who are in the HR bloc. The religious parties receive consistent support from all age groups within the two blocs exposed to the religious network, with the HR bloc receiving two-thirds of the votes and the HR one-third.

Among Alignment voters, support grows from the HR bloc as education increases (see Table 5.8). The converse holds for Gahal: within its

TABLE 5.8 BLOCS BY EDUCATION LEVEL WITHIN PARTY
VOTE GROUPINGS

BLOC	ELEMENTARY OR LESS	THROUGH HIGH SCHOOL	MORE THAN HIGH SCHOOL
Alignment	(N259)	(N365)	(N133)
HR	61%	68%	84%
*H*R	7	1	1
HR	16	8	2
*H*R	16	23	13
Gahal	(N87)	(N130)	(N39)
HR	37%	33%	31%
*H*R	7	8	10
HR	16	5	5
*H*R	40	54	54
Religious parties	(N64)	(N68)	(N26)
HR	1%	–	–
*H*R	47	72	81
HR	48	24	19
*H*R	3	4	–

voters support falls from the H*R* bloc as education increases. Gahal
support increases with education, however, in the *HR* bloc. Among
Gahal voters who are in the two blocs not exposed to the religious
network, Gahal is more successful among those exposed to the Histadrut of lower education level; with no exposure to the Histadrut,
Gahal does better as education increases.

For voters for religious parties, a similar pattern is found for the two
blocs exposed to the religious network (*H*R and HR). Those who are
exposed to the Histadrut as well as the religious network are less likely
to support the religious parties as education increases. Those who are
not exposed to the Histadrut and are in a congruent bloc (*H*R) are more
likely to vote for the religious parties as education increases. The religious parties are more successful with individuals exposed to the Histadrut network (HR) the lower the level of education. With no exposure
to the Histadrut, the religious parties do better as education increases.

Place of birth follows a similar pattern. For those who support the
religious parties, 35 percent of the Asian-African-born, 71 percent of
the European-American-born, and 80 percent of the Israeli-born are
from the *H*R bloc. In contrast, the parallel percentages for the religious
parties voters from the HR bloc from the three place-of-birth groups are
60, 25, and 20. In the case of the religious parties we seem to be witness
to two simultaneous phenomena: for those who are in the congruent
*H*R bloc, identification with the party becomes stronger the more "modern" the voter (higher education, European, Israeli-born). This "modernity" may impart to the voter the necessary strength to vote his bloc.
For the religious party voters from the dissonant HR bloc, a second
process is at work. Increased "modernity" facilitates the weakening of
the traditional, religious ties when confronted with the competing
Histadrut network. The more "modern" he is, the less likely is the
member of the dissonant bloc (HR) to vote his bloc. Higher levels of
education and European-American-Israeli birth rather than Asian-
African reinforces the pattern of religiosity for those in the congruent
bloc (*H*R) and weakens it for those in the dissonant bloc (HR). For the
Gahal voters the case is different, as they lack a social network in which
to place their vote. The Gahal voter who is exposed to a politically
displeasing message (we may assume that by his voting Gahal, the Histadrut network member indicates that he finds the Alignment message

displeasing) reacts to the dissonant situation he is in as his level of "modernity" increases; hence, Gahal voters from the HR bloc decline as education level increases. The mechanism for achieving consistency may be leaving the Histadrut network, or, over time, changing his vote. Looking at just this one point in time, however, it is clear that those Gahal voters in a dissonant condition decrease in percentage as "modernity" increases. On the other hand, Gahal voters who are exposed to neither network are much more likely to increase as modernity increases.

The analysis of the four major blocs has indicated the overwhelming forces at work in the society in favor of the Alignment and its HR bloc. The Histadrut network effectively reaches out in the entire society and influences many of its citizens. Only those in the religious network and not exposed to the Histadrut (HR) are relatively shielded from its effects. The HR bloc is successful in picking up support from many groups within the society. The HR group is disproportionately drawn from the less modern (low education, Asian-African-born) elements. With "modernity," the movement toward consistency grows as the percentage of moderns in dissonant vote-bloc combinations falls. As a corollary to this, the vote and the bloc become more consistent as "modernity" increases in the HR bloc. These two separate processes lead to an ever increasing consistency with modernity.

The no-network bloc (HR) members are really the prime targets of the Israeli election campaign, with the Alignment getting slightly more than half of them and Gahal slightly less. Given the lack of a network base for Gahal, it is likely that the Alignment will continue to do well among this group if only because of the pervasiveness of the Alignment appeal and the Histadrut network. The Alignment does best among the HR young, while its greatest success within its natural clientele (the HR) bloc is among the old. This indicates that the Alignment is successful in diversifying its appeal in its attempt to ensure its own perpetuation in power.

NOTES

1. See Chapter 2.
2. Regarding the American experience, see Herbert McClosky, "Consensus and Ideology in American Politics," *American Political Science Review,* 58 (1964): 361-82.
3. See Aaron Antonovsky and Alan Arian, *Hopes and Fears of Israelis: Consensus in a New Society* (Jerusalem: Jerusalem Academic Press, 1972).
4. See Chapter 7.
5. Klaus Liepelt, "The Infra-Structure of Party Support in Germany and Austria," in Mattei Dogan and Richard Rose (eds.), *European Politics* (Boston: Little, Brown, 1971), pp. 183-202; Samuel Barnes, "Social Structure and Political Behavior in Italy," in Richard Rose (ed.), *Political Behavior in Industrial Society* (New York: Free Press, forthcoming).
6. For a discussion of the cleavages which have characterized modern European history see Seymour N. Lipset and Stein Rokkan, "Cleavage Structures, Party Systems, and Voter Alignments: An Introduction," in Lipset and Rokkan (eds.), *Party Systems and Voter Alignments* (New York: Free Press, 1967), pp. 1-64.
7. These figures include the families of the members. Data are from *The Histadrut Society,* a Hebrew mimeographed publication of the Dues Office of the Histadrut, Tel Aviv, September, 1970, Tables 1 and 2.
8. These figures are members only, excluding children. Since the two sources on which these data are based did not use identical cut-off points, the figures represent only approximations. The data were constructed from *The Histadrut Society,* Table 10, and the *Statistical Abstract of Israel 1969* (Jerusalem: Government Printer, 1969), p. 44.
9. See *Report to the Eleventh Histadrut Convention* (Hebrew), 1969, p. 43; and *The Histadrut Annual* (Tel Aviv: Havaad Hapoel), 2 (1966): 344.
10. Nadav Safran, *The United States and Israel* (Cambridge, Mass: Harvard University Press, 1963), ch. 9; Ferdynand Zweig, "The Jewish Trade Union Movement in Israel," *Jewish Journal of Sociology,* 1 (1959): 23-42.
11. The tax is now voluntary but plans are under way to make it compulsory.

12. Similar procedures are used in national politics. Radio and television campaign time and finances for campaign purposes are allocated in proportion to the strength of the parties at the last elections. This is detailed in Alan Arian (ed.), *The Elections in Israel–1969* (Jerusalem: Jerusalem Academic Press, 1972).
13. Sigmund Neumann, "Toward a Comparative Study of Political Parties," in Sigmund Neumann (ed.), *Modern Political Parties* (Chicago: University of Chicago Press, 1956), p. 405.
14. As used here the religious network is only behavioral. Obviously the religious network is organized in a complex manner but that organization is not tapped here. The question used to determine religious network affiliation refers to religious behavior. See Chapter 4.
15. The data are from phase 3; see Appendix II.
16. See Alan Arian and Samuel H. Barnes, "The Dominant Party System: A Neglected Model of Democratic Stability," *Journal of Politics,* forthcoming.
17. See Table 5.3 for group sizes.
18. This discussion is informed by the considerable literature on cross-pressures and dissonance. See for example Georg Simmel, *The Sociology of G. Simmel,* translated and edited by K. Wolff (New York: Free Press, 1948), 2nd edition; Bernard Berelson, Paul F. Lazarsfeld and William N. McPhee, *Voting* (Chicago: University of Chicago Press, 1954); Leon Festinger, *A Theory of Cognitive Dissonance,* Evanston, Ill.: Row-Peterson, 1957); Seymour Martin Lipset, *Political Man* (Garden City, N.Y.: Doubleday, 1963), Part II.

CHAPTER 6

THE DETERMINING FACTOR

ONE OF THE MOST FASCINATING aspects of the vote is the very complexity of the factors which influence it. There are the socioeconomic categories with which voting for one party or another is associated. There is the historical moment, the mood of the times. The structure of the society, the role of the parties, the character of party organization are all influential. The citizen's orientation to his political world, to the state, and to the elections themselves also plays a part in determining his ultimate decision. The candidate's place on the ballot, the weather, and the citizen's psychological disposition are all important. The interaction of all these factors—and many many more—finally manifests itself in the single solitary act of choice between competing candidates or parties.

To bring some kind of order into this mass of influence impinging on the voter, it is necessary to limit the field of concentration. The literature refers to three political symbols as the most influential on the voter's decision.[1] These are the party, the candidate, and the platform, program, or ideology of the party or candidate. Which of these three factors will be most important in influencing the voter's decision depends, in no small part, on the structure of the political system in which the elections are taking place. In a two-party system electing under a single-member district arrangement, the candidate and/or the party are likely to be more important than the platform or ideology of either. This is because of the limited scope of choice open to the voter and the intrinsic pressures within the system on both parties to adopt centrist, rather than extreme, positions. The most rational position for the party or candidate in a two-party system will allow him to capture a majority of the vote. He will want his position to be sufficiently differentiated from his opponent's and yet moderate enough to attract the middle voters. Since the opponent is likely to adopt a similar strategy, the

95

ideological or programmatic differences between the candidates tend to be less important and the party label or the personality of the candidate more influential.

If the campaign does not stir up public excitement, the results may be determined by long-held orientations toward the various party labels. If the campaign arouses interest and the exposure of the candidates is good, personality appeal might become more important. With the increased use of mass media in political campaigns and perfected methods of "selling" candidates, the importance of the candidate in determining the vote increases. However, on a long ballot in which many officials are elected, the importance of the candidate may be paramount in the major contests while party identification continues to determine the less prominent ones.

Two partly apochryphal stories illustrate these points. One immigrant to the United States is said to have learned how to read only one word in English in her forty years of citizenship in that country. The word was Democrat. On election day she would dutifully go to the polls and make the appropriate mark beside the name of every candidate that was followed by her English word. Identifying the party, not the issue and not the candidate, was all that mattered. The other story refers to a resident of an old-folk's home who was interviewed before the 1960 election for president of the United States. When asked for whom he would vote (Nixon and Kennedy were the major candidates) the reply was classic: "For Roosevelt, who else?" For this citizen, there was only one candidate who was—or, evidently, in his mind, ever would be—president.

In a multi-party system the situation is different. Again, this depends on the electoral arrangements. In Israel, with a party-list proportional representation system, the role of the candidate has traditionally been played down. It is true that the parties are often identified by the personalities who head the party list, but the connections of the citizen with the party are likely to be strong regardless of the first-place candidate. The party is active on many fronts, and the citizen may identify with its historical role in a symbolic, emotional sense. In addition, some may depend on the party for their livelihoods. Because of the electoral arrangements and the overwhelming importance of them in many spheres of life, parties can be expected to be important determining factors in the vote decision.

Many parties in Israel have historically conceived of themselves as something much more than groups of citizens competing for votes and political power. Many conceive of themselves as social and political movements whose activities range far beyond the scope of typical election-oriented organizations. These parties are concerned with the whole range of social and political existence. In a sense, power is the tool and not the goal. The ultimate objective is the transformation of society in the image of the party's ideology.

Politics in Israel is ideological in that public discourse is often carried on in ideological terms. But this discourse is certainly not as passionate as it once was, and there are many signs of a more pragmatic approach to political problems.[2] For the voters themselves, the ideological preference and the voting decision are not identical: voters tend to vote to the left of their ideology.[3] The folklore of Israeli politics has it that voters make their decisions in ideological terms; this reasoning is one of the major justifications for the continuation of the proportional representation party-list system. The advantages of being able to identify and support an ideology, a way of life, a movement are heralded as opposed to the single-member district system, for example, in which such relatively minor matters as the candidate's personality and the representation of a smaller geographic area are maximized.

Observing Israeli elections does not fortify the evaluation that ideology is the major determining factor of the vote. In earlier elections organizational efforts to cash in on the citizen's dependency on the party apparatus were obvious. Especially in the 1969 election, when the issues were never clearly brought out into the open, and where the facade of national unity was painstakingly maintained, ideology appeared to be eclipsed by the personalities of the candidates. Television was used for the first time, and new means of exposure were employed. The mass rally and the excitement and potential for ideological stimulation that accompany it were replaced by the relatively low-profile selling of the television tube.

Many thought that the candidate would be the key to the 1969 elections, especially during the months immediately before the elections.[4] At the time, Dayan was being pressured by his former Rafi colleagues to leave the uneasy coalition with Mapai and break the ranks of the Labor party, created at the beginning of 1968 by the merger of Mapai, Rafi, and Ahdut Haavoda. The polls showed that a sizeable portion of the population would shift their vote if Dayan left to form a separate list, and there was even talk that he would switch camps and enter the type of rootless alliance that could be born only of the frustration of trying to crack the dominance of a party that had ruled for all of his adult life. There were hints that Gahal and the religious party would sponsor Dayan as their candidate for the Prime Minister, thus offering a real alternative to Labor. After Dayan decided to remain within Labor's ranks, the importance of his candidacy was still stressed by the State List, the renegade Rafi group that refused to return to Labor in 1968. They used his pictures in their campaign, pointing out that they knew that he belonged outside the Labor party and running with them even if he did not. They made him their candidate for Prime Minister even though he was in a different and competing party. These posters were forbidden by court order. Meanwhile, other candidates such as Allon, Eban, Sapir, and of course Mrs. Meir herself were being discussed as if the voice of the people would determine who would be the next prime minister.

Unfortunately, we are not in a position to know what actually was the determining factor in forming the vote, but we can know what the voter *reports* to be the determining factor. Reports of the determining factor confirm the folk wisdom: 39 percent of the sample reported that the party's program "was the most important factor in making your decision about which party to vote for." Only 21 percent said it was the candidate, 17 percent identified the party label, and 8 percent were concerned with whether the party is in the government or the opposition.[5] The importance of the candidate was eventually defused by Dayan's refusal to leave Labor, but the timing of the question evidently does not make that much difference in structuring the pattern of response.[6] We will gain some insights into the relative importance of these factors by considering them more fully. Unfortunately, we are not dealing with discrete variables: there is obviously much overlap between party identification and party platform. But since most voters managed to answer the question, they can speak for themselves.

DETERMINING FACTORS

Some voters viewed the development of a candidate-oriented campaign as a sign of progress and maturity toward a more responsive electoral

system. They felt that this movement away from the extended domination by party apparatuses offered hope for the emergence of a truly
competitive political system with frequent rotation of parties in power.
The data, however, fail to support this interpretation. The groups that
are least "modern" (those with only an elementary education and those
born in Asia and Africa) reported that the candidate was the important
factor in the vote decision at a higher rate than did other groups (see
Table 6.1). The "modern" with more than a high school education and

TABLE 6.1 DETERMINING FACTOR BY EDUCATION, PLACE OF
BIRTH, AND YEAR OF IMMIGRATION

BACKGROUND	PLATFORM	CANDIDATE	PARTY	GOVERNMENT OPPOSITION	NONE	OTHER NA	N
Education							
Elementary or less	25%	24%	15%	10%	18%	8%	379
Through high school	37	22	19	7	8	7	646
More than high school	52	15	17	6	6	5	283
Total							1308
Place of Birth							
Asia-Africa	25	27	13	11	18	6	297
Europe-America	41	18	18	7	10	7	642
Israel (father Asia-Africa)	39	21	15	6	12	6	89
Israel (father Europe-Amer.)	43	22	22	7	3	4	214
Israel (father Israel)	35	23	17	6	9	10	69
Total							1311
Year of Immigration							
Before 1947	35	16	22	6	11	9	358
1948-54	34	25	13	10	13	6	433
1955 and after	48	19	10	7	12	4	137
Born in Israel	40	22	19	6	6	6	372
Total/Averages	37%	21%	17%	8%	10%	6%	1300

from a Western background is much more likely to indicate that the
party's platform is central in his vote choice. This is especially true in
the education category, where more than half of the respondents who

have more than a high school education indicate platform as the determining factor, as compared with only 25 percent of those with less than
an elementary education.

As education increases, the importance of the party's platform rises.
The candidate's role, on the other hand, is inversely related to increased
education. The very high percentage of the highly educated who reported that their voting decision was based on the party's platform
gives the impression of a high level of citizen rationality in Israel. The
problem is that the platform of many of the parties on crucial issues is
far from crystal-clear. Were the educated reporting the actual process
whereby the voting decision is made, or the way the vote decision
would—or should—be made if they had the information?[7]

It is interesting that party identification is most important among
pre-state immigrants and among citizens of European and American
backgrounds (even for first-generation Israelis). It is likely that in both
a material and symbolic sense a party was much more important in the
personal experiences of the members of these groups. After independence, many of the functions that were previously provided by parties
were provided by the state (although the importance of the parties
remained strong). While party was the key factor even in the post-
independence era, the administration of the state introduced another
buffer between the citizen and the party. This often diminished the
visibility of the party.

The determining factor is strongly influenced by the respondent's
political trend and party choice (see Table 6.2). Moving from moderate
left through center to right, the importance of the platform decreases
and that of the candidate increases. This corresponds with the historical
stresses placed by the various parties along the continuum. The moderate left has tended to stress ideology and movement, while the right
has been less ideological and more leadership-oriented. The left generates a pattern closer to that of the right. The extreme left in Israel in
the late sixties and seventies has tended to resemble the right—both
demographically and structurally—more than it has the dominant, organized moderate left. Those who identify with the religious trend
provide the highest rates for both the platform and party identification
as determining factors and the lowest rate of any group for the candidate.

TABLE 6.2 DETERMINING FACTOR BY POLITICAL TREND
AND PARTY CHOICE

	PLATFORM	CANDIDATE	PARTY	GOVERNMENT OPPOSITION	NONE	OTHER; NA	N
Political Trend							
Left	34%	30%	18%	5%	9%	5%	80
Moderate left	46	17	20	7	5	4	245
Center	41	21	17	8	9	5	346
Right	30	29	21	9	7	4	215
Religious	50	9	23	5	10	4	80
None	28	22	10	10	22	9	255
NA	34	17	13	5	8	23	83
Total/Averages	37%	21%	17%	8%	10%	6%	1304
Party Choice							
Alignment	33	27	19	7	7	6	590
Gahal	39	20	15	15	4	6	104
Religious	45	8	31	6	6	4	84
Other	56	21	17	2	2	2	52
No decision; no vote	35	19	10	8	20	8	345
No answer	45	10	17	5	11	12	138
Total/Averages	37%	21%	17%	8 %	10%	7	1313

Certain discontinuities are evident when party choice is compared
with political trend. These discontinuities can be explained by the
nature of the 1969 campaign. The Alignment voters, caught up in the
possible withdrawal of Dayan from the Labor party, accorded the
candidate a higher rate than did the members of any other party. Gahal
voters, many of whom were anxious about expressing their opposition
to retreat from territories occupied in the 1967 war, indicated that the
platform was the determining factor. The religious voters (consistent
with the religious trend identifiers) ignored the candidate almost completely and stressed the importance of party identification and the
party platform.

It is reasonable to expect that the choice of the determining factor
would be influenced by the extent of participation in party politics.
And, indeed, this is the case (see Table 6.3). Except for the paid officers (and this is a very small sample), the importance of party identifi-

TABLE 6.3 DETERMINING FACTOR BY PARTY INVOLVEMENT

RELATION TO PARTY	PLATFORM	CANDIDATE	PARTY	GOVERNMENT OPPOSITION	NONE	OTHER; NA	N
Paid officer	44%	13%	25%	0%	13%	6%	16
Unpaid officer	15	17	49	8	4	7	53
Member	40	14	27	9	6	4	170
Sympathizer	43	22	16	7	8	4	491
Unaffiliated	34	23	12	8	15	8	570
Total/Averages	37%	21%	17%	8%	10%	7%	1300

cation increases with greater involvement in party affairs. The more involved one is, the more one seems ready to accept the party at face value. The unpaid officers are especially uncritical of the party's candidates and platform.

In summary, platform is the determining factor for about twice as many respondents as are party identification or the candidate. It is especially relevant for high education and citizens of European-American extraction. The moderate left rates platform high; the right rates it relatively low. On the other hand, the candidate is more important for the right than for the left. As to party choice, Gahal was especially concerned with platform and much less with candidate; the Alignment—probably for reasons peculiar to the 1969 campaign—stressed candidate (relatively). The religious voters and trenders ignore candidate and stress party identification and platform. Party involvement is directly related to choosing party identification as the motivating factor.

With these general lines drawn, the picture can be completed by concentrating on the issues, candidates, and parties that competed in the 1969 election. Each respondent was presented twice with a list of ten issues. First he was asked to identify the major issue which he felt faced Israel. The second time he was asked to identify the issue that motivated his determining the party for which he would vote.

Admittedly the issues as presented are vague and are not of equal weight. But only a very small fraction of the sample had difficulty in choosing one of the issues offered. The response rate is shown in Table 6.4. The most interesting features of this listing are the great predomi-

TABLE 6.4 RESPONSE RATES FOR MAJOR
ELECTION ISSUES (N 1,311)

	MAJOR ISSUE	MOTIVATING ISSUE
Peace in the area	58%	38%
Economic independence	13	8
Military strength	11	6
Relations with world powers	8	3
Immigrant absorption	6	5
Religion in the state	1	6
Labor relations	0	5
Relations with Arab population	2	2
Relations among ethnic groups	1	2
Israel's image in the world	0	1
Other	1	1
None	0	9
No party choice	0	13
No answer	0	2
	101%	101%

nance of the "peace in the area" response *and* the sharp decline of "peace in the area" responses from the major issue to the motivating issue. While the difference between the major issue response rate and the motivating issue response rate for the next three issues is only 5 percent each, the difference for the "peace in the area" issue is 20 percent. This is fascinating, for it hints at the possibility that the party platform might not be as important in determining the vote as was previously indicated. A 20 percent difference is large; for these people the party's stand on the issue they consider central is not the issue that determines their party choice. This difference is stable over level of education groupings. As education increases, "peace in the area" is mentioned as the major issue by 54, 58, and 63 percent, respectively. As the motivating issue, it is mentioned by 31, 41, and 41 percent, respectively. The overall percentage difference between the major and motivating issue is 20 percent; for the lowest education category it is 23 percent, for the middle group 17 percent, and for the highest group 22 percent.

The lack of consistency between the choice of major issue and motivating issue is even more pronounced in Table 6.5. The number of

TABLE 6.5 MOTIVATING ISSUE BY MAJOR ISSUE

MAJOR ISSUE	MOTIVATING ISSUE											
	1	2	3	4	5	6	7	8	NONE	NO PARTY	NA	N
1. Peace in the area	48%	6%	4%	2%	3%	6%	5%	5%	8%	12%	2%	760
2. Economic independence	22	22	4	5	4	5	5	5	10	16	1	165
3. Military strength	22	11	20	3	4	4	7	5	10	13	1	139
4. Relations with world powers	28	6	7	11	7	5	7	8	6	12	3	110
5. Immigrant absorption	28	10	4	3	15	5	4	12[a]	7	8	4	74
6. Religion in the state	0	0	0	0	0	100	0	0	0	0	0	11
7. Labor relations	14	0	0	0	0	14	14	43	0	14	0	7
8. Others	25	10	6	0	10	6	0	13	13	13	3	31
DK, NA	14	0	0	0	0	0	7	7	21	36	14	14
Averages/Total	38%	8%	6%	3%	5%	6%	5%	6%	9%	13%	2%	1311

a. This includes 10 percent who answered "relations with the Arab population."

consistent responses can be ascertained by calculating the number of people who fall on the diagonal—that is, who identified an issue as both the major and the motivating one. Of the 1,266 respondents (97 percent of the sample) who identified a major issue, only 465 of them (37 percent) were consistent. The other 63 percent evidently chose their party in terms of an issue other than the one they believed to be the major problem facing the country. Only 48 percent of those who considered "peace in the area" the major issue chose their party in terms of that issue. And yet about a quarter of those respondents who identified the next four most mentioned issues reported that "peace in the area" was what motivated them to choose their party. Only the eleven people who identified "religion in the state" as the major issue consistently chose it also as the motivating issue, although a relatively high 6 percent of the sample identified it as the motivating issue.

Obviously a process of issue fragmentation is under way. While party platform might be important to the voter, the issue that motivated his vote might not be the one he reports as the central problem facing the country. This problem might have been especially acute in 1969, when the parties' positions on the major issue of "peace in the area" were blurred by the considerations of internal party and coalition politics. It seems likely, however, that the explanation of issue fragmentation on the part of the voters is also associated with the historical dominance of one party in the political system. Labor, being as large and dominant as it is, has taken on many of the characteristics of a pluralist party in a two-party system. Many demands can be made and met in this type of party. Some voters who considered peace as the major issue may have had explicit faith in the country's leadership in the handling of foreign policy and decided their vote in terms of some other, perhaps internal, issue. Voters of other parties, not optimistic about winning a victory that would afford them government leadership, may have been content to stress some pet issue even while they assessed a different issue to be major. These considerations seem to diminish the actual—as opposed to the reported—importance of platform in determining the vote.

There is little difference between the party choices of the groups who identified various issues as motivating them in their choice of party (see Table 6.6). Gahal did better among those who mentioned economic independence, and the religious parties were very successful among

TABLE 6.6 PARTY CHOICE BY MOTIVATING ISSUES

	ALIGNMENT	GAHAL	RELIGIOUS	OTHER	NO DECISION OR NO VOTE	NA	N
Peace in the area	52%	8%	4%	4%	22%	10%	492
Economic independence	47	14	2	8	14	15	111
Military strength	53	11	0	1	27	9	78
Religion in the state	13	3	59	6	14	5	78
Immigrant absorption	60	8	5	5	9	12	60
Labor relations	59	7	6	0	23	4	68
Total/Averages[a]	49%	9%	8%	4%	19%	11%	887
Total/Averages	45%	8%	6%	4%	26%	11%	1310

a. These totals are for the party choices of the 887 respondents who mentioned the six motivating issues that received at least 5 percent of the sample total.

those who identified religion in the state as the motivating issue. On the whole, however, the Alignment was successful in all issue-identifying groups.

When the other direction—motivating issue by party choice—is considered, some differences are noted. Of the Alignment supporters, 44 percent mentioned peace, as compared to 38 percent for Gahal and 23 percent for the religious. The economic independence issue was mentioned by 15 percent of the Gahal supporters, 9 percent of the Alignment voters, and 2 percent of the religious parties voters. Religion in the state generates the same pattern, evident in Table 6.6. Religious party members mentioned it at a rate of 49 percent, while only 2 percent of both Alignment and Gahal supporters did so.

CANDIDATE

In an openended question the respondent was asked to identify the candidate of his choice. Only five names received more than 2 percent of the responses: Golda Meir (32), Moshe Dayan (19), Menahem Begin (6), Yigal Allon (4) and Moshe Chaim Shapira (2). Since Israeli politics are not built on popular elections either within the electorate or within the party, these figures do not have much significance. Perhaps more important is the fact that three of the five are from the dominant Labor party; only Begin (Herut) and Shapira (National Religious party) are outside it.

It is unreasonable to analyze this question in terms of a popularity contest since Israeli politics are not structured in that way. Nor can we take into account the many changes that have occurred since the question was asked (including the passing away of Shapira). It will be more helpful to analyze this question in terms of the light it sheds on the relative importance of the candidate in the voter's calculations in determining his vote.

The vast majority of all of the respondents were loyal to the candidate's party (see Table 6.7). The three Labor candidates received unusually large rates of no decision, no vote, and no answer responses from among their supporters. In the case of Dayan, this is evidently associated with his lack of decision regarding the party list he would join before the election. His followers were waiting to know.

TABLE 6.7 PARTY CHOICE BY CANDIDATE CHOICE

	ALIGNMENT	GAHAL	RELIGIOUS	OTHER	NO DECISION OR NO VOTE	NA	N
Meir	78%	2%	2%	2%	14%	3%	415
Dayan	67	5	2	2	8	16	247
Begin	3	81	6	0	8	3	80
Allon	72	5	4	0	16	4	57
Shapira	4	0	84	8	4	0	25
Total/Averages[a]	64%	11%	5%	2%	13%	5%	824
Total/Averages	45%	8%	6%	4%	26%	11%	1313

a. These totals are for the party choices of the 824 respondents who mentioned the five candidates who received at least 2 percent of the sample total.

Candidate choice varied by motivating issue (see Table 6.8) but not enough to lead to the conclusion that candidates were chosen to expedite the handling of a specific motivating issue. Golda Meir was the candidate of those motivated by the peace and immigration issues. For those concerned with military strength, Meir and Dayan were tied. In

TABLE 6.8 CANDIDATE CHOICE BY MOTIVATING ISSUES[a]

	MEIR	DAYAN	BEGIN	ALLON	SHAPIRA
Peace in the area[b]	39%	21%	5%	5%	1%
Economic independence	30	22	12	5	1
Military strength	31	31	9	7	0
Religion in the state	10	6	18	0	5
Immigration absorption	40	13	8	7	3
Labor relations	29	35	6	2	0
Total/Average (N1,311)	32%	19%	6%	4%	2%

a. Candidates who were mentioned by at least 2 percent of the sample and motivating issues that were identified by at least 5 percent of the sample are included here. Five percent of the sample claimed that they could not name any candidate, and an additional 13 percent responded that they had not yet decided how they would vote and hence could not name a candidate. The rows do not total 100 per cent, since the minor candidates and the various non-answers are not reported.

b. The size of the sample that mentioned each motivating issue is found in the previous tables.

the group motivated by labor relations, he was the more frequent choice.

VOTE STABILITY

What would have happened if a party had changed its platform on the issue central to the voter's concern or if a candidate had been denied a prominent position in the party's list? These questions were probed by asking the respondent to anticipate his behavior if the platform or candidate were changed. The results are instructive. If the platform of the voter's party choice should change, 40 percent said they would shift their vote; 27 percent reported that they would continue to vote for the party even in the face of a platform change on the issue most central to the voter. In contrast, only 16 percent reported that they would shift their vote if the candidate of their choice were not given a choice place on the party's list, as opposed to 49 percent who indicated that their vote for the party of their choice would be stable regardless of the fortunes of the candidate.

In effect, these data provide a test of the saliency of platform and candidate. Obviously the platform is much more central in the electorate's calculations. This pattern is clearly affected by level of education (see Table 6.9). A voter is much more likely to change his vote in the light of platform change if he has a higher level of education. The lower the level of education, the more likely the voter to retain party loyalty in the event of either platform or candidate change. Education is associated with a more cognitive process in making the vote choice; the lack of education is evidently more closely associated with affective and symbolic processes.

Those who identify the platform as the determining factor are much more likely to change their vote in the event of a platform change than are others. Respondents who claim party identification to be the determining factor are, understandably, least likely to do so. Most of those who identify the candidate as the determining factor also report that they would switch their votes in the event of a platform switch by their chosen party (see Table 6.9). Regarding a hypothetical candidate change, all categories, regardless of determining factor, reported that their vote would remain stable. It is true that those who identified

TABLE 6.9 STABILITY OF VOTE BY EDUCATION AND
DETERMINING FACTOR[a]

| | VOTE IF PLATFORM CHANGES | | | VOTE IF CANDIDATE CHANGES | | |
| | | | NO | | | NO |
	STABILITY	CHANGE	PLATFORM	STABILITY	CHANGE	CANDIDATE
Education						
Elementary or less	32%	31%	24%	52%	14%	22%
Through high school	26	41	21	49	17	20
More than high school	22	50	17	46	16	21
Determining Factor						
Platform	23%	53%	14%	50%	15%	21%
Candidate	28	40	25	47	30	13
Party	40	36	17	62	8	18
Government/opposition	31	38	22	52	15	19
None	19	18	40	36	7	39
Total/Average	27%	40%	21%	49%	16%	21%

a. The sizes of the independent variables are found in earlier tables. The rows do not add up to 100 percent, since those who claimed they would not vote and those who did not answer are not reported.

candidate as the determining factor generated the highest rate of change reported, but more than half again as many respondents in even that category reported their intention not to change their vote. Those who identified party were stable in this hypothetical situation to an unusual degree. This reflects the intensity of the importance of party identification for them and their disdain with the practice of placing individual (candidate's) good above the general (party's) good.

Table 6.2 revealed a pattern of inconsistency between the determining factor by political trend and by party choice. For the former, platform was seen to be most important from moderate left through center to right, and candidate was reported as determining from right through center to moderate left. For party choice, on the other hand, candidate was more important for the Alignment (moderate left), platform more important for Gahal (right). Probably both patterns are partially correct: the political trend findings represent a long-term tendency, the party choice findings a situation specific for 1969. Table 6.10 provides a different perspective for the discussion by examin-

TABLE 6.10 STABILITY OF VOTE BY POLITICAL TREND
AND PARTY CHOICE[a]

| | VOTE IF PLATFORM CHANGES | | | VOTE IF CANDIDATE CHANGES | | |
| | | | NO | | | NO |
	STABILITY	CHANGE	PLATFORM	STABILITY	CHANGE	CANDIDATE
Political Trend						
Left	39%	35%	15%	60%	20%	5%
Moderate left	31	44	12	58	16	12
Center	27	47	19	55	17	19
Right	27	49	15	51	21	16
Religious	23	60	8	48	11	31
None	21	21	44	35	10	41
NA	25	29	22	36	7	17
Total/Averages						
(N 1,304)	27%	40%	21%	49%	16%	21%
Party Choice						
Alignment	38%	39%	13%	71%	17%	5%
Gahal	32	45	18	58	30	4
Religious	26	58	6	59	7	26
Other	23	51	17	57	20	16
No decision; no vote	9	34	40	18	10	60
No answer	17	42	23	20	12	11
Total/Averages						
(N 1,313)	27%	40%	21%	49%	16%	21%

a. See note to Table 6.9.

ing the stability of the vote by the political trend and party choice categories.

Party identification is a more important factor as one moves from right to left on the Israeli political continuum. Whether platform change or candidate change is examined in association with political trend or party choice, the stable vote is higher for the left and falls off consistently to the right. In other words, even if the platform is changed and the party stand on the issue the voter regards as central is altered, even if the candidate of his choice is dumped or lowered on the list, the voter of the left is more likely to remain loyal to the party of his choice than is the voter of the right.

Alignment voters are clearly the most loyal of any other group (see

Table 6.10). In the event of a platform shift, almost even numbers of Alignment supporters will remain stable and change their votes. The other party grouping will lose a good deal more proportionately should they alter their platforms. On the other hand, Alignment voters reported that they would be most stable even if the candidate of their choice is shifted. The data of Table 6.10 provide evidence that the party identification, especially in the case of Alignment voters, is a powerful factor. If either platform or candidate changes, their vote will remain more stable than the vote of any other party group.

The Alignment's loyal voters are most noticeable among the respondents who named Golda Meir as their candidate (see Table 6.11). Only

TABLE 6.11 STABILITY OF VOTE BY CANDIDATE CHOICE[a]

	VOTE IF PLATFORM CHANGES			VOTE IF CANDIDATE CHANGES	
CANDIDATE	STABILITY	CHANGE	NO PLATFORM	STABILITY	CHANGE
Meir	39%	35%	16%	76%	16%
Dayan	23	51	14	60	34
Begin	34	46	15	64	33
Allon	32	49	14	75	23
Shapira	32	52	12	88	8

a. See note to Table 6.9.

in her case is the percentage of stable voters greater than the percentage of changing voters in the case of platform change. Her supporters are very loyal to the party even in the eventuality of her being deprived of a prominent position on the list. Even among the supporters of Dayan (whom many tried to portray as a charismatic leader regardless of his party affiliation), 60 percent would remain loyal to the party in the case of his withdrawal or removal. Loyalty to party rather than candidate is especially pronounced for Shapira's supporters, 88 percent of whom would have remained with the party had he been demoted.

Party involvement is clearly related to vote stability. The higher the involvement, the more likely the vote will be stable in the case of platform change. In the event of a candidate change the pattern is less clear, but for all groups except the unaffiliated at least 60 percent will remain loyal to the party even in the face of candidate change (see Table 6.12).

TABLE 6.12 STABILITY OF VOTE BY PARTY INVOLVEMENT[a]

RELATION TO PARTY	VOTE IF PLATFORM CHANGES			VOTE IF CANDIDATE CHANGES		
	STABILITY	CHANGE	NO PLATFORM	STABILITY	CHANGE	NO CANDIDATE
Paid officer	69%	13%	6%	63%	6%	13%
Unpaid officer	45	36	11	74	13	6
Member	31	44	9	60	12	14
Sympathizer	30	46	13	60	17	10
Unaffiliated	21	36	34	36	16	35

a. See note to Table 6.9.

Candidate change threatens less voter change than does platform change (see Table 6.9). Almost 80 percent of the respondents will remain a stable vote in the face of candidate change, while only 18 percent of them will shift votes. In contrast, only 32 percent will remain stable in the face of platform change, as against 46 percent who reported that they would shift their vote. But how many of the respondents reported that they would remain stable in any event, and how many that they would change in any event? The answer is provided in Table 6.13. Some 24 percent of the respondents reported that they would remain stable in the face of platform and candidate change; these are certainly the hard core party faithfuls. Another 11 percent were candidate-platform-oriented: they would shift their votes in the event of either platform or candidate change. About 4 percent were candidate-oriented only: they would remain stable in the face of platform change but shift in the face of candidate change. The largest single group was platform-oriented: candidate change would not affect their vote, but a change in platform would.

Even the 12 percent of the respondents who failed to report about one of the hypothetical situations of voter stability strengthen the conclusion that platform change is potentially more costly to Israeli parties

TABLE 6.13 REPORTED VOTING STABILITY AND VOTING
CHANGE RELATED TO CHANGE IN PARTY
PLATFORM AND CANDIDATE (N 1,025)

	VOTE	STABILITY	CANDIDATE CHANGE		TOTAL
			CHANGE	NO CANDIDATE	
Platform	Stability	23.7%	3.9%	4.0%	31.6%
Change	Change	26.2	11.2	8.2	45.6
	No Issue	8.8	3.2	10.7	22.7
	Totals	58.7	18.3	22.9	99.9

$$x^2 = 10.791 \quad d.f. = 4 \: p < 0.5$$

than candidate change. Of that 12 percent, 8 percent claimed they
would shift parties if the platform were altered. On the other hand, 8.8
percent claimed that they would remain stable if the candidate
changed.

The Israeli voter believes that platform and ideology are central in his
calculations regarding the voting decision. This analysis has provided
much corroboration for that position. However, there is apparently a
downgrading of the importance of party identification as a determining
factor in the vote and an emphasis of the candidate. I would argue that
these two factors are not equal in influencing the voter, despite the
impression given by the data in Table 6.1. In the Israeli system, the
importance of previous identification with a party (or movement) far
outweighs the momentary popularity of a particular politician.

This argument must be hedged considerably, since the categories are
obviously not mutually exclusive. A respondent who identifies with the
labor movement might express his position by talking about socialist
ideology or the party platform rather than the party itself. But support
for the proposition that party identification is more influential than the
marginals indicate is provided by computing the rates of trend choices
in party vote categories controlling for the determining factor. Of the
Alignment voters who identify with a left or moderate left political
trend, 47 percent claim platform as the determining factor. The comparable figure for those who claim that party identification is determinant is 46 percent, while only 30 percent of the left-trending Align-

ment voters identify the candidate as the determining factor. This would suggest that both platform and party identification are more important than candidate.

The evidence adduced for the importance of one determining factor as opposed to another was based on the aggregate responses of the sample as a whole. This is clearly an unsatisfactory method of dealing with the influences on individuals. But the analyses do provide a method of estimating the relative importance of the various determining factors. Coupled with the behavior and organization of Israel's political parties, they lead to the conclusion that party identification is probably more important than indicated, the candidate much less. The platform, even if it does not reflect accurately the chances of the party to gain power or the behavior of the party when in power, is believed to be the determining factor by a large portion of the sample. This perception, even if inflated, is an important political and social fact.

NOTES

1. The work of the scholars at the Survey Research Center at the University of Michigan is especially relevant. See, for example, Angus Campbell, Gerald Gurin, and Warren E. Miller, *The Voter Decides* (Evanston, Ill.: Row, Peterson, 1954); Angus Campbell, Philip E. Converse, Warren E. Miller, and Donald E. Stokes, *The American Voter* (New York: Wiley, 1969); Campbell, Converse, Miller, and Stokes, *Elections and the Political Order* (New York: Wiley, 1966); and David Butler and Donald Stokes, *Political Change in Britain* (London: Macmillan, 1969).

2. See my *Ideological Change in Israel* (Cleveland: Press of Case Western Reserve University, 1968).

3. *Ibid.*, ch. 2.

4. The responses of phase 2 are used in the analyses in this chapter; see Appendix II.

5. Another category, "the party's being in the government or opposition," was also added. There was some feeling that the fact that Labor had been in power since before independence in 1948 would work against it and that many would vote against Labor in order to provide rotation of power. As the election results showed, this was not a major theme in the elections as Labor retained power; 8 percent of the sample indicated this as the determining factor. An additional 10 percent claimed that there was no determining factor, and 6 percent gave a different answer or refused to answer the question.

6. In phase 3 (see Appendix II) conducted after Dayan had decided to stay in the Labor list, the same question was asked again. The results are very similar: platform 39 percent, party identification 21 percent, candidate 18 percent, and government opposition 13 percent.

7. For a discussion of issues in the 1969 campaign see the articles by Efraim Torgovnik and Ernest Stock in Arian (ed.), *The Elections in Israel–1969* (Jerusalem: Jerusalem Academic Press, 1972).

CHAPTER 7

STABILITY AND CHANGE IN PUBLIC OPINION AND POLITICS

VOTING IS SOMETIMES CONCEIVED to be a good indicator of public opinion. There are, however, obvious differences between a referendum or a survey, on the one hand, and casting a ballot, on the other. The citizen is confronted with a dilemma[1] when his single ballot, called upon to express many things, is necessarily ambiguous. Moreover, the literature records the importance of influences other than a citizen's position on policy issues on his voting decision.[2]

In the Anglo-American system, under which each district elects one representative, the ballot must indeed convey many messages. Proponents of proportional representation have suggested that this electoral system, widely used in Europe, increases the sensitivity of the election results to the distribution of opinion in the polity. The proposition that proportional representation tends to lead to many independent, ideologically distinct, and rigid parties[3] supports their suggestion: theoretically, the more parties, the wider the spectrum of opinion on any given issue.

Unlike American parties, which must fight for the vast middle of the electorate, parties operating under proportional representation must stake a clear claim to an opinion position and defend it vigorously. Their major opposition comes from parties ideologically adjacent to them and not from parties diametrically opposed to them. The assumed ideological mobility of voters is never more than one or two parties from his original one. This analysis admittedly elevates the opinion factor to one of supreme, and probably unwarranted, importance in the voter's decision-making process.[4]

Israel's 120-member Knesset (parliament) is elected under a list system of proportional representation in which changes in public opinion are not reflected in the voting results. As the theoretical literature leads us to suspect, Israel has a large number of independent political parties. All attempt to establish independent ideological positions, and they are generally more conscious of the positions of ideologically adjacent parties than they are of parties further removed from them on the spectrum. The expectation that the party system is sensitive to changes in public opinion, however, does not appear to be fulfilled. There seem to be two major reasons for this. First, the issue universe of Israeli politics is complex, and different issues are handled in different ways. For example, a high level of consensus exists on the issue of the economic structuring of the society, while disagreement is obvious on the question of the proper role of religion in public life. Second, the parties in the Israeli political system vary in size and political power, and the larger ones tend to behave in ways more characteristic of large, pluralistic parties. They diverge from the behavior anticipated by the model of parties operating under proportional representation. In Israel the Labor party (made up of Ahdut Haavoda, Mapai, and Rafi) has made the greatest efforts to become a majority party and has come closest to that goal. In 1969 it won 46 percent of the vote, almost twice as much as its nearest rival. Labor's behavior as a near-majority pluralistic party goes a long way to explain why the election results are less than sensitive to shifts in public opinion.[5] The party accommodates such changes by altering its coalition-formation strategies *after* the election results are in.

The three major dimensions along which Israeli parties and the public array themselves are security policy, economic ideology, and religion.[6] This chapter examines the differences between major parties on these dimensions in 1969 and the pattern of public opinion on these issues in 1962 and in 1969.[7]

In the 1969 Knesset elections, sixteen lists were presented to the electorate. Of these, thirteen achieved representation in the House. (The minimum needed to win a seat is 1 percent of the total vote cast.) Here I shall deal only with the three most successful lists. Among them they won 77.6 percent of the total vote, with the other thirteen lists sharing the rest (see Table 2.1). These parties are the Alignment, a joint list of the Israel Labor party (Ahdut Haavoda, Mapai, and Rafi) and Mapam, which won 46.2 percent of the vote; Gahal, a joint list of the

Herut movement and the Liberal party, which won 27.7 percent; and the Mafdal, the National Religious party, which won 9.7 percent. None of the other parties won more than 4 percent of the total votes.

SECURITY POLICY

Some points of difference between the parties are evident in the following selections from the platforms on security policy which they presented for the 1969 elections.

ALIGNMENT

> The strengthening of the Israel Defense Forces will continue to be the number one priority. Every effort will be made to promote research and to quickly broaden independent production within the military and aeronautical industries so that our dependence on foreign sources will be limited.

> Until peace comes, our forces will remain on all the cease-fire lines.

> Israel will never return to the armistice lines used before the Six Day War. The State's boundaries must be strategic boundaries, as is needed to insure the State's survival.

> Steps will be taken to strengthen, to fortify, and to raise the level of preparedness of border settlements, even in the face of prolonged aggression. Additional settlements will be established in the border areas.

> In order to meet the security demands and to perpetuate normal conditions, the use of human and economic resources must be planned in full coordination with the needs of the economy.

GAHAL

> As a result of our nation's right to the land of Israel, the national sovereignty of the State must be extended to the liberated areas of the country.

> We seek peace with the Arab nations. Peace means making

peace treaties which can be achieved only by direct negotiations between the parties. Our security requirements in peace treaties with Arab states, stemming from our experience, demand our ruling in areas which served as the basis of our enemies' aggression.

Large-scale Jewish settlement, urban and rural, in Judah, Samaria, Gaza, the Golan Heights and Sinai must be given priority in the development plans of the state.

Terrorist groups are nothing but the continuing instrument of aggression of the Arab states. Those states from whose territory these gangs operate must be held fully responsible for acts of murder and sabotage.

MAFDAL

With complete and unshakable faith in the Divine promise given by the prophets of truth and justice concerning the return of the nation of God to the inheritance of its forefathers . . . in order to establish a kingdom of Law and commandments, we see the political and security developments in the last generation as a process and as a step on the road to the complete salvation of the people of Israel in the land of its fathers.

Peace treaties will be achieved by direct negotiations between the parties. The representatives of Israel will be guided by the following basic principles in negotiation:

(1) The religious and historical right of the Jewish people to the land promised by the God of Israel, (2) The desire for lasting peace, (3) The establishment of agreed security borders.

The Mafdal will work for continued large-scale, speedy urban and rural settlements in the liberated areas.

The most striking feature of these positions is their similarity. In a sense, Mafdal's is the middle position, while both the Alignment and Gahal platforms are straining toward the middle. Within the Labor party there was considerable difference of opinion regarding security policy, Eban and Sapir supposedly being much more dove-like than

Dayan, Allon, or Golda Meir. As if these differences were not enough, the platform committee had to attend to the demands of Mapam, the group farthest to the left in the Alignment. That the final document turned out as tough as it did caused much ill feeling among many Mapam members. The possibility of returning territory (the word "re‑ treat" is never used) is only mentioned in a positive form: "Until peace comes, our forces will remain on all the cease-fire lines." But the next sentence, "Israel will never return to the armistice lines used before the Six Day War," quickly recovers the momentarily lost initiative of the most hawk-like.

It used to be possible to identify an individual's political position by whether he talked about the "conquered territories" or the "liberated territories." Both Gahal and Mafdal use the phrase "liberated terri‑ tories." The Alignment's statement is a classic use of terminology by a pluralistic party made up of hawks and doves, ideologues and prag‑ matists: it speaks only of the "territories." When discussing settlement, it cannot even bring itself to use that term; instead, it gives what must be considered one of the weakest clarion calls ever issued by a political party: "Additional settlements will be established in the border areas."

Gahal's platform also strains a bit to the center, but not nearly as hard. It is a relatively straightforward declaration, and those looking for the statement, "Not one inch of land will be returned," will search in vain. This line was deleted in deference to the more centrist Liberal party, many of whose leaders became uncomfortable when categorical language was used.

Undoubtedly the mass of Israeli opinion tended to be hardheaded about security policy. While the argument over the ordering of the security and peace priorities persisted, most Israelis took the view that the argument was largely irrelevant since no Arab leader was willing to sit down to talk, and that "the typical Arab" respects only force and probably can't be trusted to keep his word anyway. The type of con‑ sensus generated by the issue was demonstrated by the response to the question, "To what extent would you agree to an aggressive policy toward the Arab states?" (see Table 7.1).[8] On a simple agree-disagree basis, an overwhelming portion of the Israeli population answered posi‑ tively (some 72 percent). When the agree and disagree categories were broken down into more extreme and more moderate positions, an un‑

TABLE 7.1 OPINION ON AGGRESSIVE POLICY TOWARD ARAB STATES BY EDUCATION AND PLACE OF BIRTH, INCOME, AND POLITICAL TREND

"To what extent would you agree to an aggressive policy toward the Arab states?"[a]

BACKGROUND	N	DEFI-NITELY	SOME-WHAT	NOT TOO MUCH	NOT AT ALL	DK NA
Education and Place of Birth						
Elementary or less						
Asia-Africa	239	60%	18%	13%	9%	b
Europe-U.S.	244	41	35	16	8	
Israel	92	58	30	8	4	
Through high school						
Asia-Africa	164	52	34	12	2	
Europe-U.S.	478	33	36	21	10	
Israel	194	48	36	11	5	
More than high school						
Asia-Africa	20	25	40	25	10	
Europe-U.S.	202	21	39	15	25	
Israel	114	22	53	11	14	
Total/Averages	1747	40%	34%	15%	10%	
Monthly Income						
Under I£. 600	473	48	25	15	9	4
I£. 600–1000	737	43	32	14	9	3
Over I£. 1000	537	26	42	17	12	3
Total/Averages	1747	39%	33%	15%	10%	3%
Political Trend[c]						
Left	77	40	23	10	25	1
Moderate Left	374	29	33	22	15	2
Center	403	36	36	15	10	4
Right	303	47	33	11	6	3
Religious	152	42	36	13	7	2
No trend	360	43	34	16	5	3
Total/Averages	1669	39%	33%	15%	10%	4%
1962 Results[d]	1170	17	22	20	32	9

a. See note 8.

b. This response was unavailable for this table. The number of respondents in each group who did not answer can be ascertained approximately by comparing the sample size of each group in this table with those in Table 7.3, since the no answer rate there is very low.

c. See note 9.

d. See note 7.

usual distribution of opinion arose: linear, with the extreme agreement position containing almost four times the number of respondents as the extreme disagreement position. Together—and this gives a feeling of the intensity of the issue—the two extreme positions accounted for about half of the respondents. This contrasts sharply with the distribution in 1962, when the agree-disagree split was 39–52, the extreme agree-disagree split 17–32, and the extreme-moderate split 49–42. The contours of this issue in public opinion have taken on entirely different proportions, especially since the 1967 war.

Place of birth had a strong influence on the distribution of responses. The extreme statement was supported by 56, 43, and 33 percent of the Asian-African, Israeli, and European-American born, respectively. Personal memories and greater assurance of the accuracy of the assumptions—born of personal experience—on which the analyses were based may explain this trend. Educational level is clearly associated with agreement with the extreme position: the percentages are 51, 41, and 21 from low to high levels of education.

Increased level of education moderates the rate of support which the extreme statement enjoys in each of the place-of-birth categories (see Table 7.1). Overall support for the aggressive policy decreases with education for the Israeli-born and the European-American born. Within each educational achievement level, the Asian-African born consistently take the most extreme position, followed by the Israeli-born and then the European-Americans. When the two agreement positions are considered jointly, the Israeli-born seem to take the lead from the Asian-Africans. Those who have studied beyond high school are most supportive of the extreme disagree position in each of the place of birth categories.

Social class, as measured by monthly income, was not a very effective indicator of response to the question. The lowest income group had the highest rate of extreme agreement and the highest group the lowest rate. This high rate of extreme position by the lowest income group was mitigated, however, by the fact that the middle income group had the highest proportion of overall positive response.

Political trend made considerable difference. Looking only at the moderate left, center, and right,[9] the pattern was very neat and consistent. Both the total positive responses and the extreme positive responses increased from left to right. The inverted J-curve generated by the moderate left straightened out and became steeper as the right was approached. The religious group and those who identify with no trend presented a pattern similar to the right.

The Israeli consensus of 1969 clearly called for a tough policy regarding the neighboring Arab states. This was reflected in the platforms of the major parties and was true of most segments of the population. Political party leaders who dragged their feet on this issue felt the consequences: the "professors' peace list" got less than 1 percent of the vote; Mapam was carried along by organizational needs to acquiesce in a harsher platform than it might have wished. While Mapam agreed to go to the polls with Labor, it refused to become a full member of the coalition with Labor when Gahal participated on a programmatic basis. Mapam was being dragged along by the current. It did not seem to have the strength to try to swim upstream.

ECONOMIC IDEOLOGY

Excerpts from the three parties' economic planks follow.

ALIGNMENT

> In the last two years, our national product has grown by an average rate of 12 percent per year, and our competitive position in the world's markets is improving.

> The value of our agricultural production will soon reach two billion Israeli pounds.

> All this has been achieved while protecting full employment, and a steady rise in the standard of living.

> In the future the Alignment will protect full employment, a proper increase in the standard of living—especially for the underprivileged strata—a just distribution of the national income, decreasing social disparities and building a progressive society in Israel.

> The policy of eliminating poverty and distress will be implemented. . . .

The system of insurance and pensions will be expanded, and will gradually be extended to the entire population.

GAHAL

The goal of our economic policy is to develop the national economy and to make it more efficient in order that it may be self-sufficient.

The economy must be liberated from the constant dependence on the authorities; restricting regulation and bureaucratic rigidity must be eliminated; conditions for the development of free enterprise in all areas of production must be encouraged.

A tax system will be introduced which assures the individual a just share of the fruits of his labor, his enterprise, and his capital, and which encourages effort and willingness to save and to invest. Sectoral and political discrimination in tax regulations will be done away with.

MAFDAL

The efforts to strengthen the economy and to increase the national product must continue in spite of the heavy demands made by defense.

The National Religious Party demands the continued growth of the economy on a scale which will assure full employment and which will allow filling the requirements of defense expenditures and immigrant absorption.

The Alignment was in its ideological element when it discussed its economic positions. There were those who argued that the Alignment had abandoned its position as a socialist party, but there could be little doubt that it still represented the center of ideological gravity on economic matters in Israel. The socialist ideology it represented had undergone change since its elements had been implemented as government or Histadrut policy. But the accepted verbal formulas were still those of the old socialist leadership. The ideals of equality, cooperation, and the importance of the public sector continued to be the dominant ideology of the country.

Mapai's (Labor's) coalition behavior was a good indicator of its increasing flexibility on economic ideology. In 1952, when the "bourgeois" General Zionists entered the government coalition, this was considered a significant swing to the right. The fact is that the General Zionists had jumped from seven to twenty mandates between the 1949 and 1951 elections. The inclusion of the General Zionists in the coalition was an effective way of coopting the big winner of 1951 and of introducing a more "pragmatic" economic program in closer tune with public opinion.[10] The first crisis of that government, interestingly, did not concern economic matters at all. It occured on May 23, 1953, when the four ministers representing the General Zionist party resigned over the display of the Red Flag and the singing of the Internationale in government-run schools on May Day.

In the 1969 government, the General Zionists (now the Liberals) were represented as a segment of the Gahal list. While the rationale of the broad coalition was to present a united front to the world on security matters, the inclusion of such a broad array of parties also reduced the amount of public sniping at government economic policies. There were inevitable costs associated with this tactic. The price of bringing Gahal into the coalition as a full-fledged member had been that Mapam entered the coalition with limited responsibility only. Mapam's leftist influence in government circles dropped, leading to increased influence by the elements of the right represented by Gahal.

While some of Gahal's statements sound far to the right of the Labor party, the party accepted and demanded many features of the welfare state. In addition to the demands listed above, Gahal's platform also called for full employment, a fair minimum wage, freedom of laborers to organize, the right to strike, national health insurance, a government pension plan, and grants to newly married couples and families with many children. The major area of disagreement between Labor and Gahal—besides the general ideological differences reflected in the quotations—referred to labor-management relations. Gahal called for compulsory arbitration when strikes threatened essential services; the Labor party rejected this out of hand. As is evident from its platform, the religious party was not about to take up sides.

The response to the question, "Concerning the economic arrangements in Israel, are you more in favor of the capitalist method or the socialist method?" justifies the conclusion that a socialist theme characterized the dominant ideology (see Table 7.2). Some 60 percent indicated socialist, 31 percent capitalist, and 10 percent gave no answer. While the strength of the extreme group was not very large (7 percent answered definitely capitalist, 20 percent definitely socialist), the extreme socialists outnumbered the extreme capitalists three to one. Together, however, the extreme responses accounted for less than 30 percent of the total. Positions on the economic issue were distributed in the society in favor of the socialist method but with a relatively low degree of intensity. The pattern appears to be very stable; no considerable shift had occurred since 1962.

Education is also important: the lower the educational level, the higher the support for the socialist method. This is especially true for extreme support of socialism, with 28, 21, and 16 percent support from low to high education. The pattern holds for all place of birth categories (see Table 7.2). By level of education, the Asian-Africans are most supportive of socialism (extreme and moderate responses combined), followed by the European-American-born and then the Israeli-born. The Israeli-born with more than a high school education presented the pattern of an almost perfect inverted U. Only in their case did more than half of the population identify with the capitalist method.

The experience of other countries would lead us to expect economic orientation to be associated with level of income. The expected relationship was very tenuous in Israel. While it is true that support for socialism decreased as income increased, 54 percent of the upper income bracket supported the socialist method.

The political trend variable distinguished very nicely between economic orientations. As further evidence of the dominance of the socialist ideology, however, note that only 43 percent of the rightists identified with capitalism, and 23 percent of them were extreme socialists.

The economic debate had been tempered by more pressing national demands, by political and administrative necessity, and by dealings with capitalist investors from abroad. But it would be a mistake to conclude that the socialist camp was on the run. On the contrary, the institutions and style of the country were indelibly stamped with the red mark of

THE CHOOSING PEOPLE

TABLE 7.2 ECONOMIC IDEOLOGY BY EDUCATION AND PLACE OF BIRTH, INCOME, AND POLITICAL TREND

"Concerning the economic arrangements in Israel, are you more in favor of the capitalist method or the socialist method?"

BACKGROUND	N	DEFINITELY CAPITALIST	MORE CAPITALIST THAN SOCIALIST	MORE SOCIALIST THAN CAPITALIST	DEFI- NITELY SOCIALIST	DK NA
Education and Place of Birth						
Elementary or less						
Asia-Africa	183	9%	18%	40%	33%	a
Europe-U.S.	235	6	20	50	25	
Israel	85	15	26	32	28	
Through high school						
Asia-Africa	154	10	21	43	25	
Europe-U.S.	460	5	29	48	18	
Israel	184	9	28	40	23	
More than high school						
Asia-Africa	19	5	32	47	16	
Europe-U.S.	197	6	31	45	18	
Israel	115	8	43	38	10	
Total/Averages	1632	7	27	44	22	
Monthly Income						
Under I£. 600	473	6	20	39	21	15
I£. 600–I£. 1000	737	6	22	41	24	7
Over I£.1000	537	8	30	41	14	7
Total/Averages	1747	7	24	41	20	9
Political Trend[b]						
Left	77	5	16	46	31	3
Moderate left	374	4	15	57	22	2
Center	403	7	31	42	15	6
Right	303	10	33	29	23	5
Religious	152	8	16	32	27	17
No trend	360	5	26	37	17	16
Total/Averages	1669	7%	24%	40%	20%	10%
1962 Results[c]	1170	7	19	39	15	19

a. See note b, Table 7.1

b. See note 9.

c. See note 7.

the socialist leadership which had been at the forefront of the state's strivings. The results presented in Table 7.2 display the continued dominance of their ideological position.

RELIGION

Finally, we consider political positions and public opinion on the religious issue.

ALIGNMENT —

GAHAL

> We are for legislation of a constitution which will insure democratic government and civil liberties, will set forward the political and social rights of the citizen, will separate the branches of government and define their authorities, will guarantee freedom of conscience and of expression and the equality of all citizens before the law, regardless of race, origin, sex, religion, ethnic group, or belief, and will establish the primacy of the law. The constitution will be altered only as a result of a special majority of the Knesset. No law will contradict the constitution.

MAFDAL

> The Mafdal sees legislation as the proper way to settle disputed issues in the social and public spheres and rejects violence and derogatory remarks.

> The Mafdal promises that no law will be legislated in the state of Israel which is not in accord with the Law (Torah).

> The party will also work in other ways to promote legislation based on Torah law and the tradition of Israel. The party will initiate activities whose purpose is to increase the awareness of the importance of basing life in Israel on the principles of Jewish law.

Considering the fact that the Mafdal had always been an important factor in Mapai's (Labor's) coalition calculations, what could the Alignment say? In fact, what could anyone add? The lines were drawn, sharp and clear. The one side demanded, in effect, a theocracy, the other a liberal constitutional state.

Issues of religion crisscross other issues in a haphazard yet penetrating manner. Now and again specific clashes between secular and religious camps have electrified the public atmosphere. There has been much expressed anxiety that fissures might widen and explode onto the political scene with ideological and partisan fury. The key political phrase regarding religion is "status quo." All political parties, with greater or lesser degree of tongue-in-cheek, have, since the early years of the state, proclaimed that it is preferable to accept the situation as it is today in order to avoid a *Kulturkampf.* But just what "today" is and how new issues are to be handled are matters of intense dispute. No Israeli political party—at least no party when in the government coalition—admits to attempting to change the status quo in religious matters. This "status quo" gives the religious authorities jurisdiction over personal law (marriage, divorce, etc.) and assures an independent, state-supported religious educational system, which about a third of the nation's school children attend.

The population was more evenly divided on the religious issue than on any other issue considered (see Table 7.3). In response to the question, "Should the government see to it that public life is conducted in accord with Jewish religious tradition?" 37 percent said yes and 62 percent no. The particular form which the distribution takes is quite unusual in survey research: the responses projected a U-shaped curve, with both sides quite intense.[11]

Comparison with the 1962 data shows some deterioration of the agreement position and a concommitant strengthening of the extreme disagreement position, but the pattern remains.[12] Asian-African-born were especially supportive of the position and especially intense, followed by the Israeli-born and then the European-American-born. Education tempers support for the extreme agreement position, with the percentages dropping from 30 to 19 to 15. The opposite effect obtained for the extreme disagreement statement: support rose from 37 to 53 to 65 percent as education increased. For this issue education is not a moderating factor; it merely tends to place the respondent in a different extreme position.

In each place-of-birth group, overall support for the statement de-

TABLE 7.3 OPINION ON GOVERNMENT IN RELIGION BY
EDUCATION AND PLACE OF BIRTH, INCOME, AND
POLITICAL TREND

"Should the government see to it that public life is conducted in accord with
Jewish religious tradition?"

BACKGROUND	N	DEFINITELY	PROBABLY	PROBABLY NOT	DEFINITELY NOT	DK NA
Education and Place of Birth						
Elementary or less						
Asia-Africa	245	37%	18%	17%	28%	a
Europe-U.S.	253	25	16	13	46	
Israel	91	25	22	13	40	
Through high school						
Asia-Africa	165	22	19	15	44	
Europe-U.S.	490	18	13	13	57	
Israel	194	20	13	15	52	
More than high school						
Asia-Africa	20	30	5	5	60	
Europe-U.S.	209	14	10	9	67	
Israel	120	13	15	11	62	
Total/Averages	1787	22	15	13	50	
Monthly Income						
Under I£. 600	473	29	19	14	37	1
I£. 600-I£. 1000	737	22	13	13	51	1
Over I£. 1000	537	16	12	12	59	1
Total/Averages	1747	22	15	13	50	1
Political Trend[b]						
Left	77	21	12	12	53	3
Moderate left	374	13	13	16	58	1
Center	403	13	14	14	58	1
Right	303	23	18	15	45	0
Religious	152	76	14	5	6	0
No Trend	360	16	16	13	54	
Total/Averages	1669	22%	15%	13%	49%	1%
1962 Results[c]	1170	23	20	16	37	4

a. Unavailable for this table.
b. See note 9.
c. See note 7.

creased with education. This was also true for the extreme support given by the European-American and Israeli-born (see Table 7.3). Within each education grouping, the Asian-African born were consistently most supportive, the European-American born consistently most opposed, for both extreme and overall support and dissent, respectively.

It is quite remarkable to see how effective income level was in structuring the responses to this question, especially after its relative failure regarding the economic question. But here the pattern is clear: level of income was inversely related to support of the statement and to the extremeness of the responses given.

It was difficult to explain an individual's stand about government in religion in terms of his political trend. Again there is a high degree of polarization for each political trend (except, understandably, the religious). At least two-thirds of each group adopted an extreme position, indicating that, regardless of political trend, the issue was emotionally charged and potentially divisive.

POLITICS AND PUBLIC OPINION

Basically different patterns were evident in the relationship between the three ideological issues and the background variables used in these analyses. Positions on the security issue were explained well by both place of birth and the political trend; opinions regarding the role of government in religion, by income level. Thus there are clear indications of the forces working in the society that influence the nature of partisan debate.

Economic ideology was not closely related to prime variables such as income or place of birth. In these groups the distribution of response was rather similar. Political trend—itself a complex variable associated with factors such as the year an immigrant arrived and the political movement that was instrumental in absorbing him—provided a better explanation of the distribution of opinion on economic matters. Both political trend and position on economic ideology were influenced by factors that had been working on the respondent for an extended period of time. This helps explain the staying power of the socialist cast of the dominant Israeli ideology and the stability of voting behavior of the electorate. An increase in income or educational level is not sufficient to overcome the effects of this long-range process of identification with an ideology and a trend.

Most of the left-of-center parties avoided taking a controversial position on the religious question. The status quo was quite acceptable to them. The rightist Herut movement, in alignment with the bourgeois Liberal party, took a liberal position on the issue. Liberal constitutionalism was well in keeping with the ethnic background and patterns of religious observance of the bulk of support of the Liberal party. But much of Herut's support came from lower-class, oriental areas, whose residents tended to be more traditional. The importance of political trend on the religious issue was neutralized by the abstention on the part of the moderate left trend and by the conflicting position of the center and right. On an issue that had been withdrawn from the political context and which was rooted in memories of home and father, other, more basic variables seemed to come into play. Social class—life style—was the most important of these. Personal religiosity persisted, but climbing up the social ladder seemed to lead increasingly to the liberal position on this issue.

The security issue was most affected by the widespread acceptance of the tough policy line. Identification with this position was accelerated if the respondent was of oriental origin or identified with a more rightist political trend. On the security issue, as on the economic but not the religious issue, the importance of political trend was obvious. This reflects the process whereby the immigrant or the youngster was absorbed into an ideological position regardless of ethnic origin or previous condition of belief. (On the security issue, ethnicity remained more important because most Asian-Africans came from Arab nations.) The left-of-center parties, having established hegemony over the political and economic structures of the state years before its formal establishment, defined the dominant ideology and perpetuated it among all groups in a manner that minimized the importance of other background variables and maximized the consensual atmosphere of the country.

The relationship between public opinion and party representation is obviously more complex than is assumed by those who expect proportional representation to reflect accurately the division of opinion among the voters. The political history, party structure, and leadership characteristics, among others, must also be considered; in Israeli politics, for example, it appears that the government-forming stage rather than the election itself demonstrates sensitivity to public opinion. In the case of security policy a clear change occurred in the structure of public response to the issue, but the election results were amazingly stable. After the election, however, Gahal, more militant on security policy than the Alignment on the whole, was granted full membership in the government coalition.

One of the secrets of success of the dominant elite of the ruling Labor party has been its sensitivity to the structuring of opinion among the public, its awareness of which issues could be introduced into the political system and which might best be deferred. This quality has demanded a good deal of flexibility on the part of the party and has opened it to the charge of unfaithfulness to principle and political opportunism. Labor has resembled the pluralistic party of a two-party system more than the type of party usually associated with proportional representation. But it is clearly the dominant party and has no effective opposition. Part of its secret of success is its desire to stay in step with public demands and to remain in power.

Proof of Labor's flexibility on issues and in political maneuvering was provided by the handling of the security issue. Increasingly, this issue took on aspects of the debate over the role of religion in the state. It was easier to concentrate on the day-to-day matters of maintaining the status quo than to discuss the intricacies of the dilemma. The avoidance of certain hard decisions on the defense issue stemmed from the same belief held by many regarding the religious issue: any fundamental decision outside of the existing status quo would split the population into two extreme camps. On the religious issue, this had been avoided by adopting a policy of mutual coexistence. The government's security policy, on the other hand, represented the broadest umbrella covering the largest number of major points of view.[13] Certainly the future disposition of the territories was as divisive an issue as religion and would lead to the same U-shaped distribution that was found for the religious issue. The potential cleavage that the religious issue introduced into the society had been mitigated by the politician's agreement to disengage. It was, of course, more difficult for the statesmen to ignore the issue of the boundaries than it was for the politicians to ignore the issue of religion.

Labor's flexibility on issues was paralleled by its flexibility in coalition formation. Although other factors were also important, Labor invited Gahal into the coalition to provide a broad base of national unity in dealing with the security and foreign policy issues. The religious party was appeased by legislation favorable to its conception of the answer to the question, "Who is a Jew?" and agreed to stay in the government. Government policy was characterized by common-denominator consensus, with the security issue overriding all others, thus allowing Labor to maintain its dominant position in Israeli politics and still be responsive to changes in public opinion.

1. A succinct statement of this dilemma is found in Charles E. Lind-blum, *The Policy-Making Process* (Englewood Cliffs, N.J.: Pren-tice-Hall, 1968), pp. 55-57.
2. For example, see Donald Stokes, "Some Dynamic Elements of Contests for the Presidency," *American Political Science Review,* 60 (1966): 19-28, as well as many of the articles in Angus Camp-bell, Philip Converse, Warren Miller, and Donald Stokes, *Elections and the Political Order* (New York: Wiley, 1966).
3. See Maurice Duverger, "Electoral Systems and Political Life," in Roy D. Macridis and Bernard E. Brown (eds.), *Comparative Politics* (Homewood, Ill.: Dorsey, 1961), pp. 251-63.
4. Israelis think that ideology is important in determining their vote. See Chapter 6.
5. For forms of distribution of opinion and their impact on the politi-cal system, see Robert A. Dahl, *A Preface to Democratic Theory* (Chicago: University of Chicago Press, 1956), ch. 4.
6. Cf. Arian, *Ideological Change in Israel* (Cleveland: Press of Case Western Reserve University, 1968), and Aaron Antonovsky, "Clas-sifications of Forms, Political Ideologies, and the Man in the Street," *Public Opinion Quarterly* 30 (1966): 109-19.
7. The 1962 data were collected by the Israel Institute of Applied Social Science in conjunction with a project run by Hadley Cantril and the Institute for International Social Research. The Israeli phase was directed by Aaron Antonovsky; the sample of 1,170 Jewish adults comprised a representative cross-section of the popu-lation. Initial analysis of the data is found in Antonovsky, "Israeli Political-Social Attitudes," *Amot* (Hebrew), no. 6, 1963.
   The 1969 data are from phase 3; see Appendix II.
8. The use of the word "aggressive" undoubtedly introduces an ele-ment of bias. In the Hebrew, the meaning is closest to "militant" and "hawkish." That so many people answer affirmatively despite the bias leads me to wonder if the positive positions would not have been even more strongly supported if a more neutral word had been used. In 1962 the wording was "activist" rather than "aggressive." By 1969, with a changed security position and new problems facing the state, the milder term "activist" was no longer part of the everyday vocabulary.
9. Asking directly about voting behavior is unrewarding in Israeli sur-vey research. First, a substantial proportion (38 percent) refrain

from answering the question by reporting that they have not yet decided, they do not know if they will vote, or they will not tell. Second, even those who reply with the name of a party are arrayed over sixteen lists, so that most cells are very small. Political trend was therefore used rather than voting intention.

Political trend was ascertained by offering the respondent four alternative trends to choose from: left, moderate left, center, and right; 152 respondents volunteered the term "religious" to identify their trend; 360 respondents claimed that they identify with no political trend.

The patterns of response for the "left" political trend are similar to the right. This is consistent with their demographic characteristics as well.

The background variables used in these analyses are of course related. The closest relationship is between income level and place of birth. European and their children are best off, Israeli-born next, and Asian and African-born lowest on the income scale. Relations with political trend are less clear.

10. See Amitai Etzioni, "Alternative Ways to Democracy: The Example of Israel," *Political Science Quarterly* 74 (1959): 166-214.
11. Cf. Arian, Table 2.10 (p. 56), and Chapter 4 in this volume.
12. In phase 2 (see Appendix II) the distribution was 27, 16, 14, 42. The marginals are probably influenced by current events; for example, the issue of allowing television on the Sabbath was being debated during phase 3 leading to a considerable popular uproar. For a discussion of the earlier findings see my "Consensus in Israel," in the General Learning Political Science List, 1971.
13. Until the decision in the summer of 1970 to accept the peace plan put forward by Secretary of State Rogers. Then the umbrella constricted as Gahal resigned from the Cabinet. But clearly, the security issue was explosive long before Gahal walked out of the Government.

CHAPTER 8

VOTING AND MODERNIZATION

I

ISRAEL PROVIDES a special case in considering the relationship between modernization and politics. The usual model of development does not seem to apply, since the historical base from which Israel began is so different from those experienced by most modernizing states.

Political development, most authorities agree, is initiated after basic social and economic transformations have occurred within a society.[1] In a geographic area where a vast portion of the population achieves a subsistence living in agriculture, where illiteracy, poverty, illness, and squalor are commonplace, the modernization process is complex, and achievement heartbreakingly slow. Small, imperceptible changes begin and gain a certain momentum: a radio is introduced into the village, a factory, a clinic are established nearby. Patterns that have been maintained for centuries change subtly until urbanization and industrialization dovetail with the spread of the revolution in communication to usher in the myriad dilemmas of modernization.

At a certain point in this process, depending on the strength and development of the urban elite and the proximity and visibility of models of modernization, the social and economic changes that have been wrought in the society are translated into political terms. One of the results of the increased literacy, urbanization, and industrialization is increased participation in the political processes of the state. Another is the institutionalization of the political process and of the organizational arrangements constituting that process.[2]

By many social and economic criteria, Israel is somewhere near the

139

middle of the developing-developed continuum.[3] A new state, it has
made mighty and impressive strides toward industrialization since 1948.
But it deviates in many important ways from the prototype of the society on the verge of modernization and hence becomes an interesting
limiting (if not deviant) case to attempts to theorize about modernization. By way of establishing the differences between Israel and other developing countries before searching for similarities in political behavior,
three points must be made.

First, the collectivity of Jews who established the State were largely
immigrants. Though Jewish settlement in Palestine has been continuous
throughout history, large-scale settlement commenced in the modern
era during the last part of the nineteenth century. The community that
evolved was autonomous from the Arabs living in Palestine at the time.
Both were under the aegis of the Turks and then, after the first World
War, under the British mandate. The Jews in Palestine desired, planned,
and moved for a separate national identity. This in fact was one of the
chief motivating factors that led them to the land of Israel in the first
place. Zionism—Jewish nationalism—was the ideology, and it assumed
political consciousness and national identity to an extent many today
would call modern.

The second *aliya* (wave of immigration), which arrived between 1904
and 1914, was part of the general exodus of Jews from eastern Europe.
Coinciding with the nationalist revolutions there and an upsurge in
anti-Semitic activity, Jews left for west Europe, America, and Palestine.
Those who arrived in Palestine formed by far the smallest group and
had to contest with the most severe economic, social, and climatic
conditions, compared with the other groups. Although many of this
second *aliya* subsequently left, the political leadership, ideological
force, and experimental social forms that characterized the Jewish settlement in Palestine emerged from this group. Only later, with the
ascendency of Nazism in Germany, did sizeable numbers of west European and transplanted east European Jews immigrate.

Many of the political institutions and arrangements that characterize
modern Israel have their roots in the period dominated by the second
aliya. The pioneering spirit and ideology of these settlers provided a
degree of self-sacrifice which was to stand the community in good stead
in the future. In very broad terms, it may be argued that the political
elite of the country arrived *before* the masses they were to lead.

After the first World War, with the establishment of the British mandate and the arrival of the third *aliya,* an important phase in Israeli political development was reached. In the 1920s the basis of Mapai—the major political party of the country—was formed, as well as the Histadrut—the powerful labor federation—and the Jewish Agency, an arm of the World Zionist Federation, which served as a preparatory government. The institutionalization of the major political forces long preceded the mass immigration that took place in the 1930s, and 1940s, and 1950s.

The masses that peopled this drama of nation building were very different from the masses generally found in the new nations. This is the second distinguishing factor between Israel and other new nations. First of all, there were not that many of them. At independence, there were about 650,000 Jews in Israel. This figure increased sharply with added immigration, so that by 1968 there were some 2.5 million Jews in the country. A fourfold increase in population is a formidable challenge and, while Israel does not face a population explosion from the usual sources, integrating this new population was a major social and economic task.

The Jewish population of Israel at the time of independence was overwhelmingly from European background (see Table 8.1). This pattern changed with increased immigration from Asian and African countries, but during the period of the institutionalization of Israeli political organizations and processes, and through independence, most of the population was born in (or had parents who were born in) "modern" European countries. They were hardly illiterate peasants. More than 95 percent of second *aliya* members, according to one study, came from

TABLE 8.1 JEWISH POPULATION BY CONTINENT OF BIRTH

	1948	1954	1968
Israel	35.4%	31.4%	44.0%
Asia	8.1	19.0	12.8
Africa	1.7	7.9	14.4
Europe-America	54.8	41.7	28.8
N	716,678	1,526,009	2,434,832

Source: *Statistical Abstract of Israel, 1969* (Jerusalem: Government Printer, 1969), p. 44.

east European towns and cities.[4] These individuals had been exposed to modernity and represented a very different population base from those in many developing nations.

One of the major elements of the pioneering ideology was a *return* to the land. As is well known, one of the characteristics of development is large-scale movement of the population from the rural to the urban areas. But, ideologically at least, this condition was reversed in Israel. Having been denied the right to own land throughout much of Europe, the Jews who returned to Palestine reasoned that no nation exists without deep roots in its own land. And these roots, they went on, could best be sunk by becoming pioneering farmers. This agricultural orientation is still honored in many ways. One of the most fascinating is revealed in the occupations listed for the members of the Knesset. Many of them still list "farmer" as their occupation, although this reflects neither what they do all day nor the division of power or the economic priorities of the country.[5] But this symbolic identification with the land and with agriculture persists.

The pull to the land is especially significant since Jews in Israel have always been an urban group. This is the third distinguishing feature. Even at independence, when the pioneering-defense functions of agricultural settlement were the most obvious, only one in five Jews lived outside of cities. The dominant ideology of the country, and especially that of the socialist-Zionist parties, stressed the liberating qualities of physical labor and the Tolstoian romanticism of "returning to the soil." Many of the political parties were dominated by the rural-oriented collectivist kibbutz movement and the cooperative moshav movement. Ideologically, agriculture was so important that Israel is sometimes characterized as having undergone an "agrarian revolution." But from a demographic and political point of view, this is simply not the case.

In Israel political participation and institutionalization preceded—both chronologically and developmentally—social and economic development and improvement in the standard of living. The primacy of the political is the nation's outstanding feature. By the advent of statehood, relatively stable political patterns had been worked out, with the socialist-Zionist labor movement occupying the dominant position in the system. The socialist-Zionist parties always won a plurality of the votes, but never a majority. They consolidated their power and their organizational machinery and have continued to dominate without interruption ever since the formation of the state. They have always been at the arithmetic center of coalition calculations and they are the major representative of the left-of-center political ideology. Decisions which they inspired—or at least backed—determined the rate and nature of investment in industrialization, the establishment of new towns or settlements, and the tax structure and relative egalitarianism of the country.

The leadership of the dominant socialist-Zionist parties has changed little in its ethnic and ideological composition over the last fifty years. The first-line political leadership now tends to be from the third *aliya;* only because of natural biological processes (aging and death) was the leadership of the second *aliya* replaced. These leaders of the early *aliyot* —east European-born pioneers—and their children are dominant. Their importance is explained by and is a monument to their dedication. On the whole, they placed the accumulation of political power for their movement and themselves ahead of purely social or economic rewards.[6] And in election after election their strength is reasserted by the electorate. Amazingly, even when dramatic demographic changes were occurring in the composition of the electorate (see Table 8.1), the voting results remained stable.

At the time of independence, well over half the population was of western origin; twenty-three years later most Jews in the country were of sephardic-oriental ancestry. While there are of course differences within the oriental and western categories in terms of modernity, on the whole it is reasonable to think of Asian-African-born and their children as less modern than the immigrants from Europe and America and their children. Levels of personal modernity are generally associated with place of birth.[7] Since the mass immigration of orientals into the country in the first years of the 1950s, the gap between the two groups has probably closed, but on every socioeconomic indicator—and probably on modernity as well—Israelis of western background still rank above orientals.

Since their arrival, orientals have been exposed to the western-style culture of the European-born Israelis. The orientals were strongly pressured to fit into the mold which the dominant Europeans, and subsequently their children, had formed. In this experience, as well as in their contacts with other public and governmental administrative units, the immigrants were exposed to a series of benefits and demands that put a premium on internalizing the values and behavior patterns of the veterans. Flexibility and accommodation with the new patterns were the surest means to moderate success in the new country. These socializing experiences—serving in the army, using the language, getting along with a civil servant—were often transferred to that segment of the population that was not directly exposed to Israeli society and culture by those that were.

The orientals began with an initial disadvantage which has not been overcome. Tending to be more traditional than the dominant European Jews, their large families, lack of formal education, and minimal financial resources made it more difficult for them to provide their children with the cultural or financial backing to break out of the cycle of non-modernity. While the welfare and wage policies and the tax structure of Israel worked in their favor, they were still relatively disadvantaged in comparison to the more modern European immigrant.

Improving living conditions and providing educational opportunities were stated objectives of the government. On the whole, these policies were applied even-handedly, although obvious advantages accrued to those living in the large cities. While the concepts of tradition and modernity are relevant for the Israeli population in a certain sense, they must be understood in terms of the special conditions of the Zionist ideology, the military threat of the neighboring Arab states, and the socialist commitment of the government.

Especially interesting here is the relationship between social and economic development on the one hand and political modernization on the other. As the Israeli Jewish population experienced a process of social and economic modernization that was preceded by political development, the immigrants—many traditional—were placed in a system that was essentially modern. Social and economic processes, subordinate to political decisions, were fostered or hampered according to the ideological orientations of the political elite of the dominant parties. It follows, then—and this is the key to the analyses that follow—that levels of modernity are not necessarily related to political participation or institutionalization.

The modernization induced in Israel was spasmodic in two important senses. First, it had differential impact within the society, since various

individuals and groups began from different levels. Second, modernization often influenced form but not necessarily content. It is evidently
this latter factor that is warned against by those who decry the possible
Levantinization of Israeli society. It is, they argue, easier to assimilate
the outward forms of modernity—the dress, language, and mannerisms—
than the cultural and ethical bases of modernity.

In a society characterized by induced and spasmodic modernization,
political participation and institutionalization are little influenced by
changes in social and economic level of modernity. On the contrary,
one indication that the society has undergone induced and spasmodic
modernization will be the lack of any such relationship. In the Israeli
case, two historical processes are associated with the lack of association
between socio-economic modernization, on the one hand, and political
development, on the other. The first is the emergence in Israel of a
one-party dominant political system in which the leftist socialist-
Zionists established their position of political supremacy years before
the founding of the state. The second is the primacy of party politics in
all aspects of Israeli social and political life.

As was the case throughout much of Europe, in Israel the left was
much quicker and more adept at organizing politically than were the
right and center. While the most important organization of the right
(Herut) considered itself a movement (significantly, not a party) and
the center fashioned itself as the *General* Zionists so as to be free of
ideological bickering, the left busied itself with establishing tight, hierarchical party organizations. It had a tremendous advantage once it had
organized and systematically taken over the leadership of many of the
national institutions of the organized Jewish community in Palestine
and of the international Zionist movement, and the transition to statehood brought it into the seats of power. The left's dominance reached a
peak in the period of independence. It well fit Duverger's description:
"A party is dominant when it is identified with an epoch; when its
doctrines, ideas, methods, its style, so to speak, coincide with those of
the epoch."[8] The left was identified with independence and has retained its position of dominance ever since.

The Israeli left, however, has never been monolithic—again, as is true
of much of Europe. Its history has been a kaleidoscope of splits, sub-
splits, alignments, and mergers. Political competition was intensified

because of these organizational changes. The very nature of its organization and ideology led to intense identification with the cause. Had the left merely had to face an unorganized center and a loose-knit right, it might have seemed less militant. But when division and dissension in the ranks were found to be common, party organizational efforts were intensified not so much against the right and center as against other parties of the left. The organizational behavior of the parties of the left was probably as much a reaction to intra-bloc pressures as it was to competition from other groups.

The left has always dominated but has been fragmented. Dissidence within the left has complicated the task of governing and of forming a solid coalition. One mechanism which allowed the left to dominate and yet permitted the individual leftist parties to retain their relative strength compared to one another was the party "key," which is of utmost significance to the discussion of immigrant absorption and power perpetuation. Its major feature was the distribution of resources for immigrant absorption in a manner proportional to the strength of the various Zionist parties at the polls. Thus it institutionalized a pattern in which the parties became the major agents for absorbing and socializing immigrants to the new country. Welcoming the immigrant to a cooperative village organized by the party or its affiliate and providing him with lodging, medical aid, a job, schooling, a newspaper—all of this may have been done by individuals explicitly identified with a certain political party although financed by communal funds. The atmosphere of the country, the youth groups available for his children, and his dependent position regarding housing, welfare, and employment all led to the reinforced importance of the party to the immigrant. Considering that the resources were distributed proportionally according to existing party strength, it is hardly surprising that the distribution of political strength was reproduced from election to election even while the composition of the electorate changed substantially.

The pattern began early in Zionist history and for the most part was kept out of the written record. But by 1950 the competition for new immigrants had become so intense both in Israel and abroad that the Zionist Executive Committee passed the following resolution:

> In order to ensure the necessary complete coordination among the various departments in matters concerning repre-

sentatives abroad, the Executive Committee decides that all
representatives who are sent abroad by any department
must have the prior approval of the Representatives' Department of the Executive. The Executive Committee further decides that the agreed upon key for representatives'
activities which assures participation of all branches of the
movement in proportion to their strength, shall be applica-
ble equally to all departments of the Executive.[9]

Giora Josephtal provides a revealing insight into the process when he
relates:

> On Friday, a ship arrived with 80 immigrants from North
> Africa. They demanded that we take them to Shaar Haaliya
> [the plan was to settle them in a moshav in Hevel Lachish]
> on the grounds that their relatives lived there. They also
> added that they did not receive accurate information about
> Israel. The argument was not between the moshav move-
> ment [affiliated with Mapai] and Hapoel Hamizrahi [a left-
> leaning religious party] but rather between the immigrants
> and all the movements at once. They [the immigrants]
> immediately felt they were worth more, that they were
> important and that we had to give them whatever they
> requested. . . . I wanted them to claim that they were from
> Hapoel Hamizrahi so that no one would say that the Mapai-
> bosses decided to get them into Mapai by force.[10]

The supremacy of party politics and the domination of the leftist
parties make Israel a special case in development. Identification with a
political party often occurred even before the first physical contact
with Israeli society and has remained immutable over the years, despite
changes in the voter's social and economic condition. Israel has well-to-
do private entrepreneurs who still identify with and vote for left-of-
center—even Marxist—parties. For many immigrants, party identification began abroad before reaching Israel. Many were identified with and
active in youth movements or Zionist political parties. On the whole,
these identifications seemed to have been retained regardless of the
disparity between one's socioeconomic condition abroad and in Israel.

II

Some of these assertions regarding the relationship between political modernization and social and economic development can be tested empirically. To do this, five different groupings of the Israeli electorate will be used:

(a) The Jewish settlements. In 1969, about 86 percent of the population lived in settlements which were overwhelmingly Jewish. These settlements are divided into urban and rural categories. The first category includes cities and urban settlements,[11] the second, villages and the moshav and kibbutz movements.

(b) The forty-four largest urban settlements in Israel. Among them, in 1969, they accounted for 71.7 percent of the total population and 78.5 percent of the vote. While there are some Arabs and Christians in some of these cities, the overwhelming majority of the population is Jewish.

The size of these units varies widely, from 211,056 voters in Tel Aviv in the 1969 elections to 4,788 in Rosh Haayin in 1969.

(c) In order to recheck patterns which might exist for the Jewish community but which are lost because of the variations in size of the units used in (b), the patterns for Tel Aviv will also be studied. This is the country's largest city, with close to half a million residents. The analyses will be based on Tel Aviv's twenty-four sub-precincts. The distinctions among sub-precincts are sharper than the distinctions among cities in (b). The Tel Aviv data base should reveal differences that might have been averaged out when using the less refined data base of the forty-four cities.

The urban Jewish settlements are likely to lead to inconclusive findings in light of the special circumstances in Israel. The rural Jewish areas will highlight this non-association; the minorities sector will illustrate that different processes are at work there.

(d) The kibbutz and moshav movements. These rural settlements are organized by and affiliated with various political parties. These settlements accounted for 76.7 percent of the Jewish population living in rural areas in 1969. The practice of political affiliation of rural communities has its roots in the history and ideology of the pre-state period, when parties or their affiliates were instrumental in setting up and aiding agricultural settlements. Both the kibbutz (collective) and moshav (cooperative) settlements are voluntary. They have wielded considerable power in various leftist political parties, and they are still over-represented in party inner circles in comparison with their actual contribution to party strength at the polls.

The "Israeli pattern" of nonassociation between socioeconomic development and political development should be most clearly seen for these rural settlements. Party affiliation precedes all other considerations.

(e) The non-Jewish sector shows evidence that Israel is not immune to the regularities of political development. While special provision is probably needed for the Jewish sector to fit Israel into development theory, the non-Jewish sector of the Israel electorate is likely to be more consistent with regularities observed in other areas of the world.[12] For the non-Jewish population has many of the prerequisites demanded by the model of modernization that the Jewish community lacks. Indigenous to the country for centuries, they fit many of the descriptions of the traditional culture prevalent in the literature. The non-Jewish voters comprise 8.6 percent of the electorate. It is possible to analyze their voting behavior since they live, on the whole, in separate cities, towns, and villages.

For the data bases in the Jewish sector, five political dependent variables will be employed. All voting data are from the 1969 elections.[13]

(a) Rate of voting participation

(b) Domination—the percentage won by the dominant Alignment. In 1965 the Alignment was composed of the left-of-center Mapai and Ahdut Haavoda parties. In 1968 these two parties merged together with Rafi (a split-off from Mapai before the 1965 elections) to form the Labor party. In the 1969 elections the Alignment consisted of the Labor party and the leftist Mapam party. These various parties have dominated the Israeli political scene since at least the 1920s. Mapai (the Labor party) has always been at the center of power, being the party of every prime minister the country has had. The dominant left is the party that is "in" and always has been. Its appeal has been strong throughout the electorate.

(c) Competition. The most consistent competition to the dominant Mapai (Labor) has come from the Herut movement, a movement with strong nationalist sentiments. Before the 1965 elections, Herut aligned with the bourgeois Liberal party to form Gahal. The measure of competition is the percentage won by the Alignment less the percentage won by Gahal. This allows additional information about the dominance of the left.

(d) The religious vote. Three religious parties represented orthodox Jewry in the 1969 elections.

(e) Fractionalization. The index of fractionalization measures the extent of concentration or dispersion of votes in a given group of voters. The formula for the calculation of fractionalization is:

$$Fe = 1 - \left(\sum_{i=1}^{n} Ti^2 \right)$$

where Ti is equal to any party's decimal share of the vote.[14] The closer the index approaches unity, the greater the dispersion of the vote; the closer the index is to zero, the more concentrated the vote. In a one-party system the index would be zero. The index will approach unity to the extent that the votes are spread among the competing parties.

For the minorities sector,[15] four political dependent variables will be considered.

(a) Rate of voting participation

(b) Domination—the vote won by the two minorities' lists affiliated with the Labor party. These are not parties in that they have no continuing program of organization. They appear before each election, supported by the Labor party, and have traditionally dominated in the Arab sector since they were close to the ruling party.

(c) Competition. The New Communist List has made substantial gains within the Arab community, especially among the young. It split off from the Israel Communist party before the 1965 elections and has since been identified with Arab nationalism, even though it is headed by a Jew.

(d) Fractionalization

For the independent variables, indicators reflecting the generally accepted measures of modernity will be considered: urbanization, literacy, industrialization, and living conditions. In addition, ethnic composition will be studied.

When political development is conceived as a consequence of social and economic modernization, the hypothetical relations between the two variables were clear: as modernization increases, so do political participation and political institutionalization. More people vote, the position of the traditional dominant party is threatened, and competition increases. The vote is less concentrated as modernity advances, and fractionalization increases.

But in Israel, as we have noted, the process was reversed. Political institutionalization preceded development; only after the political structures were established did the waves of mass immigration arrive. The dominant parties were associated with progress and modernity. The opposition parties offered a traditional and nationalistic alternative, which tended to appeal to nonmoderns. The organization of the dominant parties was very strong in the rural areas—kibbutzim, moshavim, and villages—and in these areas they are likely to retain their advantage. In the new settlements, with the introduction of a sizeable number of religious-traditional immigrants, the fortunes of the religious parties are likely to improve. Competition in the rural areas is not affected by immigration, since Gahal was never active there.

Dominance is likely to be a phenomenon of the middle strata in urban Israel. Nominally, the dominant parties are socialist, but, more to the point, they are dominant. They are likely to win the vote of the established strata of the Israeli society, which have achieved a certain degree of social and economic stability. The ideological content of their vote is probably less important than the conservatism it reflects. The vote is conservative in that it seeks to perpetuate the power of the dominant Alignment. Voting for a religious party and voting for Gahal are likely to decrease with modernity. In other words, with modernity the competition gap should increase.

POLITICAL PARTICIPATION

Participation rates in the elections are uniformly high in Israel. For all types of settlements among Jews and minorities, the participation rate is above 80 percent. Only among Bedouin tribes did the 1969 rate fall to 72.3 percent of those eligible to vote. While that low rate is associated with a low level of development, the level of 72.3 percent is very high compared with traditional groups in other societies.

In a society as developed as Israel's, it is perhaps unreasonable to

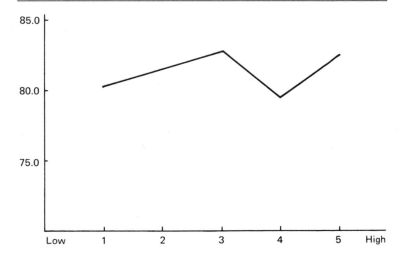

Source: Local Authorities in Israel 1968/69 (Jerusalem: Central Bureau of
Statistics, 1970), p. 85.

Figure 8.1. Participation and Percentage of 20-29-Year-Olds in Universities for
44 Urban Settlements

expect the association between literacy and participation to hold. Illiteracy is not widespread and participation rates are high. To test the association, the forty-four urban settlements were considered. In place of literacy, the measure used was the percentage of the 20–29 year-old population enrolled in universities. In a technological society this might be the functional equivalent to literacy in a nonmodern one. No connection was found (see Figure 8.1).

POLITICAL INSTITUTIONALIZATION AND URBANIZATION

Twenty-one years after independence, the 1969 elections results clearly reflected patterns that were established before the founding of the state. The parties that made up the Alignment in 1969 tended to be very strong in the rural areas, although in an absolute sense the cities provided them with most of their votes. The opposition was concentrated in the cities and had very little influence in the hinterland. With the advent of statehood and the influx of new waves of immigrants, these patterns were somewhat altered. Since many of the immigrants, many of whom had traditional backgrounds, were channeled to rural settlements, the fortunes of the religious parties rose in rural areas. The opposition Gahal—and especially the Herut movement—did relatively well among these new immigrants in the cities, since its nationalist message could easily be phrased in religious-traditional terms.

These patterns are clear from an examination of Figures 8.2, 8.3, and 8.4. There the variables of political institutionalization are computed for veteran and new settlements separately.[16] The patterns are especially important because they demonstrate the organizational ability of the dominant parties, their ability to perpetuate their strength in veteran settlements, and the tendency in the new settlements for the traditional voters to vote for the religious parties. The political organization and system of rewards established in the veteran settlements were extended to the post-independence era. After the establishment of the state, the National Religious party became very active in immigrant absorption, especially in the rural areas. They were aided by the traditional values held by many of the new immigrants.

The dominance of the Alignment is clearly related to type of settle-

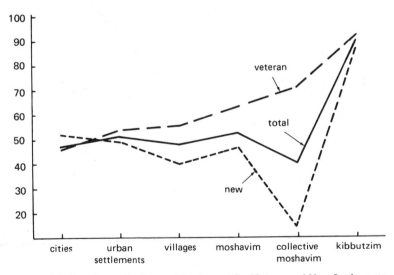

Figure 8.2. Dominance by Type of Settlement for Veteran and New Settlements

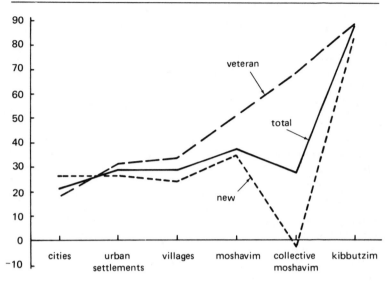

Figure 8.3. Competition Gap by Type of Settlement for Veteran and New Settlements

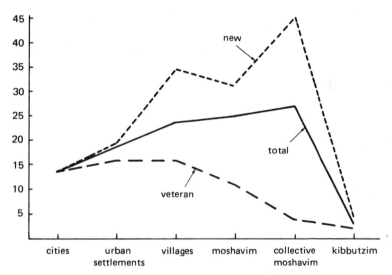

Figure 8.4. Religious Vote by Type of Settlement for Veteran and New Settlements

ment among veteran settlements (see Figure 8.2). The parties of dominance developed the rural sector for ideological, defense, and economic reasons. The rural sector—and especially the kibbutz movement—was an important political resource, since the movement could allow its members leaves of absence (supported by the kibbutz!) to work in party matters. This was a luxury that other parties, which had to depend on the good will and material belongings of their members, could not afford.

The dominant parties were strongest in rural areas. Development theory would argue that this is a result of the parties' harnessing the grievances of the traditional masses or exploiting their search for a dynamic, charismatic leader. In Israel the reverse held. The rural areas were the best organized politically and represented the political vanguard of the country. When the large-scale immigration began after 1948, the kibbutz movement was notoriously lax in absorbing new immigrants; those who settled in rural areas took up residence in moshavim and the new towns that were inaugurated in the 1950s. The rural sector as vanguard was especially marked before independence; as Figure 8.2 clearly indicates, the introduction of large numbers of Asian-African-born in the new settlements altered this pattern.

The cities of Israel are most competitive politically. This follows directly from the organized nature of rural Israel and the urban-bourgeois nature of the competitor, Gahal (see Figure 8.3). In addition, Gahal's nationalism appeals more strongly to those who have had first-hand experience with the Arabs by virtue of the fact that they lived in Arab lands. Such traditional, African-Asian-born individuals make up a larger portion of the lower class and unskilled worker group than does any other ethnic group. Since they are lowest on the economic and social ladder, there is a strong possibility that their vote for Gahal is also a call for a change in their conditions or a protest against the dominant parties.

Urbanization in Israel is strongly associated with political competition, but for unusual reasons. The rural areas are dominated by the Labor movement, and the rural settlement movement is dominant in the left-of-center parties. Competition occurs in the cities because only there has the opposition been active.

The religious parties, like the leftist parties with whom they have joined as partners in forming government coalitions since the pre-state era, are also relatively stronger in rural areas than in the cities. But, unlike the left, which has its strength in organization and in support concentrated in the veteran settlements, the religious parties excel in the new settlements (see Figure 8.4). This is a result of the fact that so many of the new immigrants who were channeled into new settlements were traditional in religious matters. The religious parties—especially the National Religious party, which ran the Ministries of the Interior and Welfare—could effectively look after the interests of its newly arrived supporters. The coalition gave the largest of the religious parties, the NRP, an effective means of recruiting and maintaining the support of many smaller settlements and new towns. Considering the fact that the Ministry of the Interior has jurisdiction over local government and the fact that a large percentage of the moshavim and new towns were inhabited by traditional individuals, the relative support of the religious parties in the rural areas is understandable.

The fractionalization measure supports this description (see Figure 8.5). For the veteran communities fractionalization increases with urbanization. For the new communities this effect vanishes, and all rates are high, except for the kibbutz movement. The left's dominance

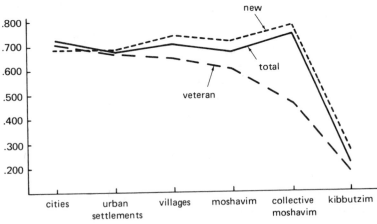

Figure 8.5. Fractionalization by Type of Settlement for Veteran and New Settlements

in the rural areas is strongest for the veteran settlements but is weakened in the rural areas by the success of the religious parties. This phenomenon is not connected with competition, however, since both the leftist and the religious parties retain strength in their respective settlements with little competition between them in a given rural settlement. The pattern provided by the new settlements reflects the establishment of the strength of the religious parties in the rural area, an area which was largely dominated by the leftist parties in the veteran settlements. The high degree of fractionalization in urban areas stems from competition there between the Alignment and Gahal.

JEWISH URBAN SETTLEMENTS

Within the Jewish urban settlements themselves, which in 1969 contained 71.7 percent of the country's population and 78.5 percent of the voters, few patterns are discernable. Israel is a very small country, and political forces are very important. Opening a new factory to employ a few hundred workers might well turn a city into one of the most industrialized in the country, using percentage of the population employed in industry as the measure. To open a factory of that size generally needs the blessing—in the form of loans, tax allowances, and so on—of the government, and that blessing is not regulated solely by economic considerations. In the highly centralized way in which the Israeli economy and polity are run, political considerations sooner or later enter the discussion and often determine the outcome. Since the development of the country is influenced—if not planned—by the hierarchical structure of decision making, no clear patterns link levels of modernization and political institutionalization.

Figure 8.6 indicates the problems involved in associating modernization and industrialization in Israeli urban areas. For the lowest level of industrialization, dominance is lowest, and the competition gap indicates that Gahal does relatively well in those communities. This is consistent with what has been said about Israeli politics and voting. But for the other four levels of industrialization, no clear pattern emerges. Part of the explanation is that the politics of each community affect the fortunes of the various parties differently. A popular Gahal mayor can significantly swing the Knesset election results, overshadowing the importance of social or economic indicators. In short, many considera-

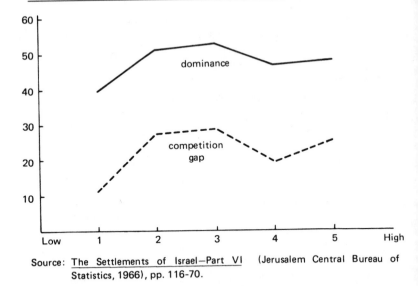

Source: The Settlements of Israel—Part VI   (Jerusalem Central Bureau of
        Statistics, 1966), pp. 116-70.

Figure 8.6. Dominance and Competition Gap in Jewish Urban Settlements by Industrialization

tions ignored by the hypothetical relationship between modernization and institutionalization are important.

When the communities are ranked in terms of their European-American-born contingent, the dominance factor is unaffected, but the vote for the religious parties shows strikingly that European-American birth is inversely related to religious vote (see Figure 8.7). African-Asian-born tend to be traditionals and, as such, to vote for the religious parties. But no connection is found between ethnic composition of a community and support of the dominant party, since it is successful among all the groups.[17]

In urban Israel, differences in modernization are not associated with varying rates of institutionalization. Variables that are more political in nature—the stability of the Labor party leadership, the party of the mayor, the importance of the community (Jerusalem for symbolic reasons, Tel Aviv because of size, and Haifa because it is the strongest Labor party base), and so on—are crucial in determining political institutionalization. Since the sizes of the communities vary greatly, as do

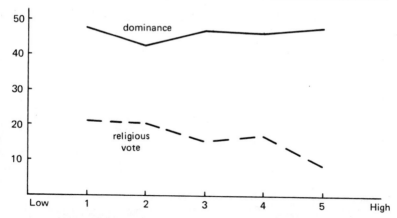

Source: <u>Local Authorities in Israel 1968/69</u> (Jerusalem: Central Bureau of Statistics, 1970), pp. 12-13.

Figure 8.7. Dominance and Religious Vote in Jewish Urban Settlements by European-American-Born Composition

their political experiences, close examination of only one of them will limit the number of factors that might interfere with the search for patterns between the two variables.

Tel Aviv is Israel's largest city and is almost completely Jewish. Non-left parties dominated in Tel Aviv even while the leftist parties were consolidating power in the rural areas and in the national government. In the 1959 elections the left won the Tel Aviv plurality and has held it ever since, winning it in the 1969 municipality in elections by only 3.2 percent. The city is highly diversified in its economy and in the background and living standards of its population. Its sub-precincts provide the units for this analysis of Tel Aviv's political institutionalization and its social and economic development.

The patterns generated for Tel Aviv are vaguely consistent with the notions about institutionalization and modernization discussed earlier, but the fit is far from complete. On the whole, the left's dominance is related to modernization, the competition gap widens with modernization, and the religious parties decline with modernization. But these rules are fairly often broken. As the percentage of the work force employed in industry increases, the support for the dominant left tends

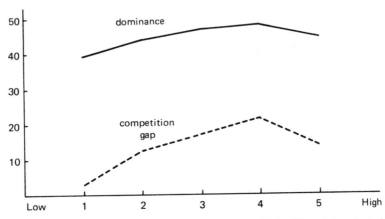

Source: <u>Population in Jerusalem, Haifa and Tel Aviv-Yafo</u> (Jerusalem: Central Bureau of Statistics, 1968), pp. 88-89.

Figure 8.8. Dominance and Competition Gap in Tel Aviv Sub-Precincts by Industrialization

to increase (see Figure 8.8). The competition gap widens as industrialization increases. The one exception is for the highest level of industrialization, where these generalizations do not hold.

Another effective measure of modernization in Israel may be the percentage of the working force employed in service industries. This is the step of modernization beyond industrialization. Figure 8.9 presents the dominance rates for Tel Aviv individually and for all forty-four urban settlements by employment in service industries. The pattern for Tel Aviv is similar to the one generated by industrialization: support for the dominant left as modernization increases with the exception of the highest level of service employment. For the forty-four urban settlements, however, no pattern is evident, although here too the highest category provides a very low rate of dominance support. The irregularity of the general curve is in part explained by the varying natures of the cities and their occupational compositions. Jerusalem, for instance, as the capital city, heavily populated by government clerks, also has a large oriental population and heavy concentrations of religious voters. A high rate of service employment—an indicator of modernity—coincides there with a high level of support for the religious parties—an

Source: The Settlements of Israel—Part IV (Jerusalem: Central Bureau of Statistics, 1964), pp. 94-95 and Population in Jerusalem, Haifa and Tel Aviv-Yafo (Jerusalem: Central Bureau of Statistics, 1968), p. 88.

Figure 8.9. Dominance in Tel Aviv Sub-Precincts and Jewish Urban Settlements by Employment in Service Industries

indicator of traditionalism. The tenuous relationship between modernization and the political indicators is demonstrated by Figure 8.10, which shows dominance, competition gap, and religious vote by ethnic composition in Tel Aviv. Only in a general sense are the expectations fulfilled.

In the rates of fractionalization in the Tel Aviv sub-precincts, an interesting pattern emerges. Most of the rates are arranged in a U-curve, with the highest and lowest of the sub-precinct groupings higher than the others. The patterns suggest that at both extremes of the rankings, the vote for the dominant left falls off, as already noted (see Figures 8.8, 8.9, and 8.10). The lowest levels of modernization generate high fractionalization rates, since competition at these levels is most intense. As modernization increases, the support for the dominant left also increases—up to a point. Before the extreme of the modernization scale is reached, votes tend to be dispersed among other parties. Usually the big gains are won by the Independent Liberals and the State List; only some of these votes go to Gahal. It is important to recall that one of the parties composing Gahal is the Liberal party—an urban bourgeois

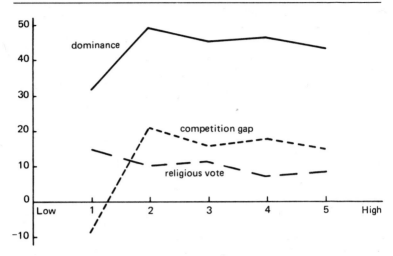

Source: <u>Tel Aviv=Yafo Population (1961-1965)</u> (Tel Aviv Municipality: Research and Statistical Department, 1967), p. 53.

Figure 8.10. Dominance, Competition Gap, and Religious Vote in Tel Aviv Sub-Precincts by European-American-Born Composition

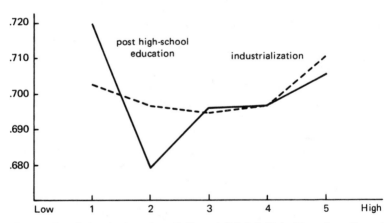

Source: <u>Population in Jerusalem, Haifa and Tel Aviv-Yafo</u> (Jerusalem: Central Bureau of Statistics, 1968), pp. 78–79, 88–89.

Figure 8.11. Fractionalization for Tel Aviv Sub-Precincts by Post-High School Education and Industrialization

party. Some of the most modern of the voters support the Liberal party (one of the units in Gahal) and vote Gahal. Herut (the other unit) wins wide support from non-modern, lower-class voters. Gahal wins support from the two extremes of the Israeli social and economic scale; the dominant parties tend to win support from the middle strata. The middle strata of Israeli society seem to be most inclined to support the dominant left; the most modern tend to spread their vote over many parties, and the fractionalization index is affected accordingly (see Figure 8.11).

RURAL SETTLEMENTS

The primacy of the political is most obvious for the Jewish rural vote. Levels of modernization are completely unimportant. The party with which the settlement is affiliated receives most of the vote. There are, of course, varying degrees of identification between the party and the settlement, but on the whole, the leftist parties and the religious parties are most successful in winning the votes of the settlers in moshavim and kibbutzim affiliated with their respective parties. [18]

The relationship between individual and party is complex. Especially in kibbutzim, a process of ideological self-selection takes place. One of the important motivations for joining the collective settlement might be identification with the ideology of the moment and, by extension, with the party with which the movement is affiliated. It is likely that those who join a kibbutz will have supported the party even before they become members. For those born and raised on the kibbutz, the process of political socialization is very successful. Out-voting in the kibbutz is very rare, as we shall see.

The symbiotic relations between individual and party and between settlement and party grow over time. Red tape might be cut by a party official, a loan might be arranged, disaster relief provided. The leadership of the settlement, be it cooperative moshav or collective kibbutz, recognizes that its organizational affiliation can be useful in special circumstances. The parties realize the importance of the rural settlements in terms of their historical and ideological role as well as their contribution to the economy and the defense of the country, and for the votes they deliver. The settlements and their members are loyal for both ideological and practical reasons.

There are six kibbutz federations. The three largest ones were affiliated with the three major leftist parties, Mapai, Ahdut Haavoda, and
Mapam. In 1969, with all three parties in the Alignment, the support of
the three largest kibbutz federations for the Alignment ranged from
89.8 percent to 96.9 percent. Two others are affiliated with religious
parties, and they supported these parties at rates of 97.4 and 93.0
percent. The next highest rate of support for the religious parties was
0.4 percent by the unaffiliated kibbutzim. The sixth federation is affiliated with the Independent Liberals, and the federation's members supported the party overwhelmingly.

The pattern of the moshavim is similar but less extreme. The moshavim are less intense ideologically, although they are as organizationally
committed as are the kibbutz federations. Of the eight moshav movements, two are affiliated with religious parties, one with Mapam, one
with the Labor party, one with Herut, and one with the Independent
Liberals, and two are unaffiliated. The pattern holds: regardless of
development level, the vote goes to the party of affiliation. Mapam gave
75.5 percent of its vote to the Alignment, the Labor party federation
gave 68.6 percent of its vote to the Alignment. By contrast, the religious parties won 90.5 and 85.0 percent from their movements.

It is obvious then that we are unlikely to find regularities when we
consider the dependent variables in terms of levels of modernization.
The participation rate is high, ranging from 79.5 to 86.2 percent for the
moshavim and 80.4 to 88.4 percent for the kibbutzim. Figures 8.12 and
8.13, which plot the Alignment vote against the percentage of the work
force in industry, clearly portray the power of the political party affiliation and the impotence of the modernization variable.

The kibbutz movements are politically more loyal than are the
moshav federations. The fractionalization measure for the kibbutz
movements ranges between .060 and .329. For the moshav movements
it ranges between .339 and .723. But both kibbutzim and moshavim
movements are less fractionalized than the urban settlements or the
sub-precincts of Tel Aviv. Again, this political dimension seems to have
nothing to do with modernization (see Figures 8.12 and 8.13).

The kibbutz and moshav movements, including 76.7 percent of the
rural Jewish population and 8.7 percent of the total Jewish population
in 1969, provide the key for understanding the lack of relationship

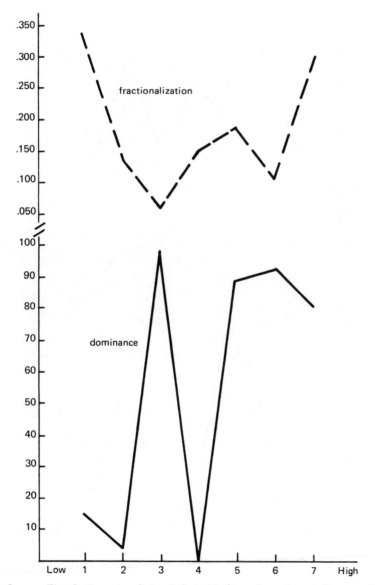

Source: The Settlements of Israel—Part VI (Jerusalem: Central Bureau of Statistics, 1966), pp. 110–11.

Figure 8.12. Dominance and Fractionalization in the Kibbutz Movement by Industrialization

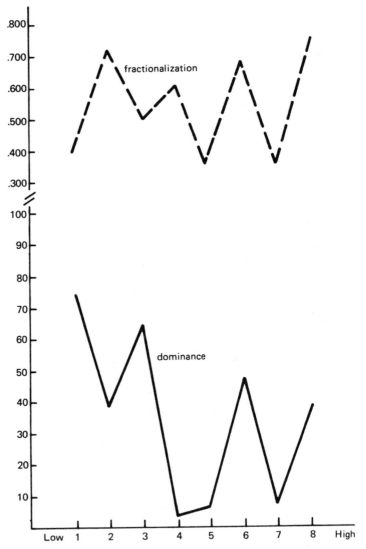

Source: The Settlements of Israel—Part VI (Jerusalem: Central Bureau of Statistics, 1966), pp. 110-11.

Figure 8.13. Dominance and Fractionalization in the Moshav Movement by Industrialization

between social and economic indicators, on the one hand, and political ones, on the other. Political organization and party affiliation precede social and economic development. The domination of the left was initiated and is perpetuated by the organizational forms that have developed. The rural settlements magnify processes that characterize the urban communities as well, although in the cities these processes are much more subtle and less extreme in scale. But the pattern of party identification, reinforced by ideological commitment and relations of dependency and habit, nullifies the effects of social and economic differences on political development.

THE MINORITIES SECTOR

The dominant left was quite thorough in establishing relations with the minorities in Israel. Usually this was accomplished through the local leader or head of the clan. In return for services supplied by governmental and Histadrut agencies, he was expected to deliver the vote. As anticipated, this arrangement worked best where pressures for tradition were strongest. The smaller the village, the more likely that the dominant parties would win handsomely (see Figure 8.14). With urbaniza-

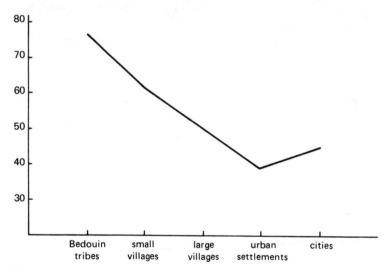

Figure 8.14. Dominance in the Minorities Sector by Type of Settlement

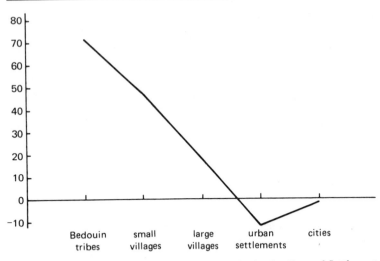

Figure 8.15. Competition Gap in the Minorities Sector by Type of Settlement

tion, this pattern breaks down, and non-establishment and even anti-establishment parties are supported (see Figure 8.15). In the cities traditional forces are weakest, and the pull of the nationalist New Communist List is felt.

In the minorities sector dominance is again associated with rural settlements, competition with urbanization. But the social bases of these processes are very different from those in the Jewish sector. There the rural areas provide vanguard leadership for the dominant left based on ideological and organizational grounds, whereas in the cities, where the level of political organization and dependence is *lower,* Gahal competes by appealing to bourgeois-nationalist feelings. In the minorities sector the reverse is true. Political awareness is lower in the rural areas, and considerations of proper traditional conduct provide the dominant parties with a substantial vote. In the cities awareness is higher, the bounds of tradition are broken, and the appeal of the nationalist move-ment—or a protest to the establishment—lead to support for the competition. Considering the bases of support for Gahal, we may say that urban Jewish competition is accelerated by the sizeable number of traditionals in the cities. Among the minorities competition is acceler-ated by the sizeable number of moderns in the cities.

In 1969, 67.8 percent of the minorities population was rural (to deal with aggregate data, we shall consider the population living in minorities rural settlements). Rural minorities composed 78.3 percent of that population.[19] The basis for our analysis is a study conducted on the modernization of the traditional Arab village. Using ninety-four villages (there are ninety-eight altogether), a "services scale" was developed to define the modernity of the village in terms of the services present. Established by multi-variate scalogram analysis, the scale comprised seven items: educational facilities, health services, labor exchange, local government, electricity, Histadrut institutions, and trade and business enterprises.[20] Once established, the development of a group of villages could be charted against the variables of political modernization.

Using the eight levels of modernization developed by the services scale, it is clear that political behavior is related to level of development (see Figure 8.16). As modernization increases, competition becomes more prevalent, even in the village. The more underdeveloped the village, the higher the proportion of the minorities lists of the two-party vote. With modernization the gap closes, and at the highest level of modernity, the New Communist List wins more of the two-party vote than do the minorities lists.

It is difficult to provide a more complete picture of the situation in the minorities sector. Information is scarce, and many live in Jewish settlements. From the few data at hand, however, it is clear that forces very different from those working in the Jewish sector are operative among the minorities. The population is largely rural, and urbanization tends to alter the traditional patterns of voting from support of the establishment to support of the anti-establishment parties. There seems to be no increase in participation with urbanization, since participation is at high levels even in the villages. A radicalization and polarization of politics are processes which are clear when one shifts from the village to the city. It is important—but difficult—to determine whether this behavior indicates genuine desire for a change or is simply a means of protest against the establishment.

Many parties compete for the minorities' vote. In addition to the minorities' lists and the New Communist List, many individuals support the dominant Jewish left and even the Jewish religious parties. For this reason, the fractionalization rate is uniformly high among minorities settlements. In the cities the high rate reflects competition among the

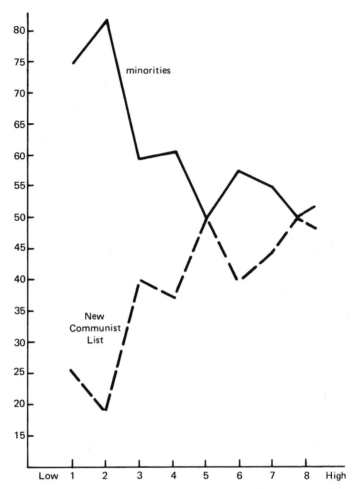

Source: Chaim Klaff and Chanoch Jacobsen, <u>Multi-Variate Analyses of Ninety-Four Arab Villages in Israel</u>, (Rehovot: The Settlement Study Centre, 1970), p. 38.

Figure 8.16. Share of the Two-Party Vote (Minorities and New Communist List) for 94 Arab Villages by Services Scale

establishment and anti-establishment parties. In rural areas the high rate reflects competition among various establishment parties.

III

The political system of Israel was highly institutionalized by the time the largest waves of immigrants arrived immediately before and after independence. This led to a situation which deviates from the expected relations between modernization and development. Figure 8.17 provides a summary of the expected relations between modernization and the political variables used in this study:

1. As modernization increases, political participation increases.
2. Dominance decreases with modernization.
3. The competition gap also decreases with modernity—that is, competition increases.
4. Religious parties' success decreases with modernization.
5. Fractionalization of the vote increases with modernization.

The results of this study show that the hypothesized relations hold for the minorities sector on the whole but do not hold for the Jewish sector. For the minorities the hypothesized relations are found for dominance, competition, and fractionalization. The religious party vote is irrelevant to that sector, and the relationship for participation only partially pertains.

For the Jewish sector, however, the hypothesized relationships only hold between the religious parties' vote and modernization. Participation in the Jewish sector is uniformly high. Dominance generates a sloping inverted J-curve in relation to modernization: the upper-middle strata tend to be most supportive of the dominant left, the upper strata slightly less so. In the rural areas no relationship between dominance and modernization exists, since the important consideration is the political affiliation of the rural settlement, not its economic or social characteristics.

The competition gap tends to widen with modernity; that is, the dominant party's strength continues to grow in comparison with the second largest list. Even at the upper levels of modernization, where the strength of the dominant left tends to fall off, parties other than Gahal are the major beneficiaries; hence the gap is unaffected. Again, in the rural areas the relationship is chaotic.

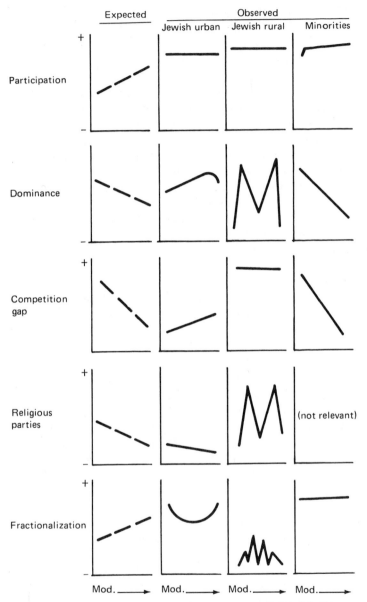

Figure 8.17. Expected and Observed Relations Between Political Indicators and Modernization in Israel

Fractionalization in Tel Aviv reflects a U-curve pattern. This is an extension of the relations observed between dominance and competitiveness. In areas of low modernization competition is strong; hence fractionalization is high. In the middle strata dominance is high and fractionalization low. In the most modern areas dominance falls off and the vote is highly fractionalized among many parties. In the rural areas, fractionalization tends to be low on the whole, since votes are concentrated for the affiliated movement. But the fractionalization rate has nothing to do with levels of modernization. In the minorities groups fractionalization is high regardless of level of modernization, since a number of establishment parties are in competition for the traditional vote and fractionalize it.

The vast majority of Jews in Israel live in cities; most non-Jews live in rural areas. Since most rural Jews live in settlements affiliated with political parties, their political behavior is highly predictable and consistent with their settlements' party affiliation. For the minorities rural population, traditional forces are associated with support of the dominant establishment.

Political organization and penetration have preceded social and economic development in Israel. All groups, regardless of level of development, participate actively in the electoral process. For the minorities population forces of modernization are associated with increased competition. For the Jewish urban population, however, forces of modernization are associated with strengthening the position of the dominant parties. This pattern, which is not usually found in developing nations, stems from the special history and conditions that exist in Israel.

NOTES

1. The literature on modernization and political change is vast. Many of the empirical tests presented in this chapter stem from the work of Samuel Huntington, *Political Order and Changing Societies* (New Haven: Yale University Press, 1968).

2. The notions of modernization, participation, and institutionalization are Huntington's. Roger Benjamin has been very resourceful at giving these concepts operational meaning in India and Japan. See Roger Benjamin et al., *Patterns of Political Development: Japan-India-Israel* (New York: McKay, 1972).

3. For a discussion of modernization in Israel see S. N. Eisenstadt, *Israeli Society* (London: Weidenfeld and Nicolson, 1967).

4. Yosef Gorni, "Changes in the Social and Political Structure of the Second Aliya (1904-1940)," *Zionism* (Hebrew) 1 (1970): 210, Table 6.

5. See Avraham Brichta's article in Alan Arian (ed.) *The Elections in Israel—1969* (Jerusalem: Jerusalem Academic Press, 1972).

6. A seminal study is Yonathan Shapiro, *The Dominant Party of Israel: The Formative Years of the Israeli Labor Party, 1919-1930,* forthcoming. For the pre-state period see D. Horowitz and M. Lissak, "The Yishuv as a Political Society," *Megamot* (Hebrew) 16 (April, 1970): 108-40.

7. See Leonard Fein, *Politics in Israel* (Boston: Little, Brown, 1967), ch. 4.

8. Maurice Duverger, *Political Parties* (New York: John Wiley, 1963), p. 308.

9. "The Meeting of the Zionist Executive Committee in Jerusalem," (in Hebrew), April 19-28, 1950 (Jerusalem: The Zionist Administration, n.d.), p. 163.

10. *The Life and Works of Giora Josephtal,* edited by Shalom Waram (in Hebrew), (Tel Aviv: Mapai Publishing, 1963), pp. 186-87. A careful study of a group of immigrants who do join a moshav is found in Alex Weingrod, *Reluctant Pioneers* (Ithaca, N.Y.: Cornell University Press, 1966).

11. Urban settlements have a population of 10,000 and over and include some smaller settlements that are not rural in nature. Rural settlements include all settlements with 2,000 inhabitants or fewer, and some larger settlements which are not urban. See *Statistical Abstract of Israel, 1969* (Jerusalem: Government Printer, 1969), p. xxiv.

12. Since a small portion of the non-Jewish population is Druze and not Arab, we shall use the official term "minorities" to indicate the non-Jewish population.
13. All election statistics are from *Results of Elections to the Seventh Knesset and to Local Authorities,* published by the Central Bureau of Statistics, Special Series No. 309 (Jerusalem, 1970).
14. Douglas Rae, *The Political Consequences of Electoral Laws* (New Haven: Yale University Press, 1967), p. 56.
15. See Jacob N. Landau, *The Arabs in Israel* (London: Oxford University Press, 1969); and his article in Arian (ed.), *The Elections in Israel.*
16. Veteran settlements were established before the founding of the state, new settlements after its establishment. *Statistical Abstract, 1969,* p. xxv.
17. Smith analyzes the voting behavior of citizens by level of wealth of the districts of Tel Aviv, Jerusalem, and Haifa and comes up with similar findings. See Herbert Smith's article in Arian (ed.), *The Elections in Israel.*
18. See my *Ideological Change in Israel* (Cleveland: Press of Case Western Reserve University, 1968), chs. 3 and 4, and Dorothy Wilner, *Nation-Building and Community in Israel* (Princeton: Princeton University Press, 1969).
19. *Statistical Abstract, 1969,* pp. 29–31.
20. See Chaim Klaff and Chanoch Jacobson, "Multi-Variate Analyses of Ninety-Four Arab Villages in Israel," Report No. 1 in the Modernization of the Traditional Arab Village Project, led by Emmanuel Yalan, Chaim Finkel, and Louis Guttman (Rehovot: The Settlement Study Centre, March 1970), mimeographed.

CHAPTER 9

SPLIT-TICKET VOTING*

IT IS BEYOND debate that the focus of political power in Israel is at the national level. Politically and administratively, local government is dependent on the political parties and the government ministries that operate from the center. Israeli politics, for historical and structural reasons, has always been dominated by national rather than local power. Since before the establishment of the state in 1948, an agrarian, virtually anti-urban ideology has dominated the important political parties. The relatively small size of the country and the newness of the settlers tended to prevent the establishment of regional sectional bases of cleavage. This lack of local autonomy coincided with the establishment of most of the Jewish settlements in Palestine, especially between the two World Wars, by such national institutions as the Jewish Agency and the Histadrut and, after independence, by the government itself.

Since the establishment of Israel in 1948, the institutional map of local government has changed considerably. In 1948 there were thirteen municipalities and twenty-three local councils, a total of thirty-six organized Jewish local authorities; by 1966 the total had jumped to ninety-eight Jewish authorities, with twenty-four municipalities and seventy-four local councils. By 1966, only 0.3 percent of the Jewish population was not organized under an elected local authority.[1]

In electing both his national and local representatives, the voter casts his ballot for a list of candidates proposed by a political party rather than for individual candidates directly. The party receives mandates in national and local elections in proportion to the total number of votes it obtains. Since it is unusual for one party to win an absolute majority in the elections, an intense process of bargaining to form the ruling coalition at both the national and local levels follows closely upon the publication of the election results. This bargaining process is usually

*The research reported in this chapter was conducted with Shevah Weiss.

very complex and again demonstrates the dependence of local government on the national parties: coalition agreements in municipalities and local councils are often dictated by the political needs of the national party. It is not unusual for the coalition deliberations concerning many local authorities to be held simultaneously, headed by the officials of the various parties responsible for municipal affairs. The arrangements that will affect the local government are often determined by functionaries of the national party, who bring to the bargaining table their perceptions of the interests of the national party. Thus, hypothetically, a concession might be made concerning the terms of the coalition in Tel Aviv in order to obtain a more beneficial arrangement in Jerusalem. The gains of the party at the local level are often traded off for political leverage at the center.

Although local government has undoubtedly been subordinated to the national center, it has developed its own political importance. Israelis are probably becoming increasingly aware of local issues and personalities. Even though a party-list ballot is used, the election at the local level often involves a dominant personality seeking office, an arrangement more usually found in a single-member district electoral system. The emergence of a popular vote-getter as local leader can influence the behavior of the national party and administration toward the local community and may well boost his own political career.

Some months before the 1969 elections, speculation was widespread that a new page was about to be opened in Israeli political history. Legislation was being prepared to provide for the *direct* election of mayors by the electorate. The Labor party had narrowly approved the move, and it appeared that a round had finally been won by those advocating change in Israel's election system.

Had the legislation been enacted before the 1969 election (it was not), it would have had far reaching effects on the election results. Instead of being elected by the members of the municipal council, who are themselves chosen in a number proportionate to the percentage of votes won by their parties, mayors were to have been elected by the people. The change in the election procedure would have altered the power relations among the political parties. But only in part would the formal change have affected the relationships; in fact, the proposal to change the electoral arrangements was itself a result of the emergence in the municipalities and local authorities of a new style of political leadership in Israel.

It is useful to conceive of the proposed change in the electoral arrangements both as a response to a process that was already underway in Israeli political life and as a mechanism to encourage its growth. Even though the proposal was not enacted before the 1969 elections, many local races tended to be characterized by contests between the popular leaders of the party lists. The campaign in many municipalities took on the characteristics of direct elections, with candidates facing off with one another for the mayor's office.

The tone of many municipal campaigns gave the impression that the direct election of mayors was the law of the land. This impression has been strengthened from election to election. Local governments and politics are the easiest and surest avenue of ascent for a young, ambitious leader. On the whole, the ranks of the national parties are much more difficult to penetrate, and the problem increases as one climbs higher up the power pyramid. Local politics, on the other hand, have seen the emergence of a series of dynamic leaders who have achieved status and power in a relatively short period of time.

The proposal to change the election law for mayors may, in part, have reflected the frustration of many about penetrating the political system, either because of the difficulties of being elected or because of the feeling that elected officials were not responsive to the wishes of the electorate. As is usual in debates about the relative merits of electoral systems, the discussion centered on the question of representation, with weighty ideological arguments expounded by both sides. But, behind this, personal and organizational needs were also being expressed. Those who supported the proposal tended to see in the direct election of mayors the creation of a more direct channel of expression for the electorate and the restructuring of the patterns of career advancement in Israeli politics. Those who opposed it tended to find in the present system an opportunity for the expression of a variety of views by many segments of the population and the continued dominance of program-oriented ideological parties. Small parties, especially the religious parties, feared their eclipse in a winner-take-all system. Larger parties hoped they could overcome the advantage of Labor's bargaining potential in the coalition discussions by offering attractive local candidates. The Labor party itself was seriously split on the issue, though when the final vote was held months before the elections in October, it voted to support the proposed legislation. Significantly, this vote was held under secret ballot; the party apparatus strongly opposed the proposal, realizing full well the price it would have to pay if it had to seek out popular—and not necessarily loyal—party members for mayoral contests. Even more significantly, the vote went against the party organization. Furthermore, it is extremely significant that the proposed legislation was not implemented before the October elections; the Labor apparatus was more effective in delaying the legislation than it was in securing the support of the Labor party Convention.

Not all municipal elections are characterized by contests between popular candidates. Often the major party candidates are loyal party machine members. In Tel Aviv, for example, Mayor Rabinowitz lacks charismatic appeal but, as a long-time ally of Pinhas Sapir, Labor party leader and Minister of the Treasury, he has a very strong power base within the party. Had the proposal carried, the loyal, lackluster party types would probably have been replaced by more dynamic and attractive candidates. This shift in the base of a mayor's power from the party to the people would have had obvious effects on the apparatus. In at least two cases, Rehovot and Hadera, attempts were made to put popular ex-army officers at the head of the Labor list. In Hadera the local branch and politicos defeated the attempt, and an apparatus candidate was nominated.

Electing the council under a system of proportional representation and then having it choose the mayor gave the parties obvious advantages. They could draw up the lists as they saw fit, restricting the effective choice given to the voters. They could enter into package deals, trading off gains in one locality for desired ends in another. Nevertheless, over time local leadership has managed to come to the front, and many mayors have been elected because of their personal popularity or because of local issues. At times this success was gained for candidates heading a regular party list; at others the candidate set up a local list unaffiliated with a national party.

The only meaningful opposition the dominant Mapai (Labor) party has faced in the political history of Israel had its power base in large urban centers such as Tel Aviv, Ramat-Gan, and Netanya. The General

Zionist party, which found its support primarily in the middle-class members of the country's cities, rose as an alternative to the ascendant left-of-center parties in the early 1950's. The first local election, held in November 1950—almost two years after the election of the First Knesset (parliament) in January 1949 and about eight months before the election of the Second Knesset in July 1951—was in effect a test of confidence of the new national government rather than an indicator of concern with local issues. Times were hard in November 1950—rationing, unemployment, and immigration were serious problems—and campaign platforms tended to stress solutions to national problems of the day. Following the local election of 1950, the General Zionists pressured for new national elections, arguing that the 1950 results indicated a vote of no confidence in the Mapai-led government. Whether or not this viewpoint was valid is debatable, but the General Zionists were certainly correct in assessing their own rise in popularity. In the First Knesset (1949) they won seven seats, while in the Second (1951) they were rewarded with twenty-two mandates.[2]

The General Zionists were restrained in their attempt to become a real opposition to the left-of-center parties for two reasons. First, they could never command sufficient seats in the Knesset to threaten government programs. Second, because they lacked power at the national level, the realities of Israeli politics prevented them from sustaining their appeal at the local level; being outside of the government coalition, they could not deliver benefits to the local authorities under their control as could the government parties. At least until the 1959 election, the General Zionists represented an effective opposition on the local level to Mapai; since then, as we shall see shortly, Mapai has tended to consolidate its strength in the large urban areas as well.[3]

In light of this background, it is interesting that voting turnout rates for both national and local elections are high. In 1965, for example, 83 percent of the eligible voters cast ballots in the national elections and 82.7 percent in the local contests.[4] Voters are evidently not deterred by the power gap between the national and local levels of government. Nor do they fail to vote in both elections even though it takes at least twice as long to vote in both elections as it does to vote in one. Israelis have gone to the polls to elect both national and local officials on the same day four times. In 1955, 1959, 1965, and 1969 they cast two ballots on election day, one for the Knesset and one for the governmental authority.[5]

The voter must go through identical procedures twice in order to cast ballots in both the national and local elections. He comes to the polling place, presents his identity card, receives an envelope, and enters the privacy of the polling booth. There he chooses a slip of paper with the name of the party of his choice and its symbol (consisting of one or two Hebrew letters) from the stacks of slips of the competing parties and places it in the envelope. He then deposits his sealed envelope in the ballot box and, if he wishes, begins the entire procedure again—identity card, envelope, party slips, casting the ballot—in order to vote in the other election.[6]

It is clear from the voting statistics that some voters split their tickets; that is, they vote for different party lists in the national and local elections. They may do this to reward a hard-working local politician or party or to punish a national party whose promises were not fulfilled. Perhaps the voter perceives that a party he would not vote for at the national level is more closely identified with local interests than is the party of his choice in the national contest. The party he prefers in the local election may not even appear on the national ballot. It may be that different types of factors motivate the voter in the two elections. The position of the Knesset as the central symbol of political legitimacy and the glamour and publicity of the contest between the national parties attract much attention at the national level. Locally, voters may tend to be more personality- and issue-oriented; the physical proximity of the campaign may have its own allure.

Notwithstanding the delaying tactics, the Labor party remains on record in support of the direct elections of mayors. The pressures in this direction on the local scene tend to increase. This is seen by noting the increased rate of split-ticket voting when the 1969 returns are compared with previous elections. Split-ticket voting appears to be on the rise in both an absolute sense and in terms of its impact on local politics in Israel. Although aggregate data will be used to test this proposition, the impression is that the rise in split-ticket voting between previous elections and 1969 reflects the increased importance of local issues in many municipalities and the trend toward voting in many local elections for the popular leader of a party list.

Three events since the 1965 elections probably encouraged this trend away from straight-ticket voting. First, the proposed legislation for the direct election of mayors initiated a widespread public debate on the subject. The debate itself, and the processes already underway at the local level, stressed the advantages of providing the voter with two direct and autonomous channels of communication to his elected officials, one at the national level and the other at the local. Second, there were some signs that the relations between the national centers of power and the agencies of local government were being regularized by law; this weakened the argument that a rational voter would not split his ticket, since effective local government demands good connections with the power center. Formalizing various regulations by law diminished the possibility that bureaucratic or political favoritism would determine the fortunes of a local council or municipality. A split ticket, then, became less irrational. Third, a split ticket might have been more legitimate by 1969. Gahal, the merged lists of the Liberal party and the Herut movement, had joined the national unity cabinet immediately before the 1967 war. For years a stigma had attached to the Herut movement, mostly because of its extreme positions and actions in the 1948 War of Independence. But twenty years later Herut was legitimized by being allowed to sit at the Government's table. Many voters may have felt that a new and important option—Gahal—had been opened to their electoral calculations.

On the whole, parties are as successful on the national level as they are on the local level (see Table 9.1). This is an overall judgement, as some parties do very well in the local elections in some communities and very poorly in others. In Ramat Gan, for example, Gahal received 39.6 percent of the vote in the local election but only 29.7 percent to the Knesset (see Table 9.3). But in Jerusalem, Gahal fortunes were reversed: there only 16.9 percent voted for Gahal in the municipal elections and 28.3 percent in the national balloting. These phenomena can be explained by pointing out the role of the party organization and electoral loyalties built by the long-time Gahal-affiliated leader in Ramat Gan and the popularity of the dynamic Jerusalem mayor. There are a number of causes of splits in various situations, but on the whole, as Table 9.1 indicates, local variations tend to be balanced out. However, the split seems to be rising.

TABLE 9.1 VOTING STRENGTH OF MAJOR JEWISH PARTIES IN NATIONAL AND LOCAL ELECTIONS OF 1955, 1959, 1965, AND 1969[a]

	1955		1959		1965		1969	
VALID VOTES[b]	NATIONAL 657,686	LOCAL 648,288	NATIONAL 816,710	LOCAL 821,257	NATIONAL 1,028,416	LOCAL 1,022,487	NATIONAL 1,196,809	LOCAL 1,188,615
Party								
Mapai	32.1%	30.8%	39.1%	34.7%	36.9% (Alignment)	33.6% (Alignment)	45.5% (Alignment)	39.9% (Alignment)
Ahdut Haavoda	8.1	7.0	5.5	5.6				
Rafi	–	–	–	–	7.9	8.0		
Mapam	5.8	6.1	5.5	5.9	5.3	6.1	3.1	1.7
State List	–	–	–	–	–	–	1.2	0.7
Communist	4.1	3.6	3.0	2.4	1.3	1.0	–	–
Religious[c]	14.2	13.5	14.7	15.1	14.1	14.1	15.0	14.7
Independent Liberal[d]	4.8	5.0	4.9	4.4	3.9	4.0	3.3	4.0
Liberal[e]	12.7	15.0	7.0	11.1	23.6 (Gahal)	21.9 (Gahal)	24.0 (Gahal)	21.9 (Gahal)
Herut	14.9	12.3	15.2	11.5				
Free Center	–	–	–	–	–	–	1.3	1.8
Others[f]	2.1	2.9	2.4	5.6	1.4	6.2	1.1	7.6

a. Adapted from *Results of Elections to the Seventh Knesset and to Local Authorities* (Jerusalem: Central Bureau of Statistics, 1970), Tables 1 and 3. Figures do not total 100 percent in the original.

b. The data presented in the table reflect the vote for the Knesset in those communities which also held local elections. Since local elected government has not yet been instituted in all communities, the total number of valid votes in the national elections is not the same as reported here. In 1955, the total number of valid votes was 853,219; in 1959 it was 969,337; in 1965 it was 1,206,728 and in 1969 it was 1,367,743. Only marginal differences are found when the party percentages of the national vote are computed on the broader base.

c. Including the National Religious party, Agudat Israel, and Poalei Agudat Israel.

d. Formerly the Progressive party.

e. Formerly the General Zionists.

f. These are Jewish ethnic or splinter parties. Not included in this table are the two parties which appeared in 1965 for the first time—the New Communist list and Haolam Haze—or the Arab parties. Excluding these parties from the table explains why the percentages do not total 100.

TABLE 9.2 DISTRIBUTION OF INDEX OF SPLIT-TICKET VOTING FOR 41 COMMUNITIES WITH MORE THAN 10,000 INHABITANTS (IN 1965) FOR THE 1955, 1959, 1965, AND 1969 ELECTIONS

NUMBER OF CASES[a]	1955 33	1959 39	1965 39	1969 41
0-4.9	48.5%	35.9%	23.1%	14.6%
5-9.9	15.2	10.3	10.3	14.6
10-19.9	21.2	30.8	23.1	22.0
20-49.9	9.1	12.8	28.2	14.6
50+	6.1	10.3	15.4	34.1
Totals	100.1	100.1	100.1	99.9

a. Eight of the 41 communities in 1955 and two each in 1959 and 1965 did not hold local elections on the same day that the Knesset elections were held; hence they were omitted from these calculations.

Analyzing split-ticket voting is most fruitful when the community results are studied. The statistics of the performance of the national parties in Table 9.1 are too gross for useful insights into the variations among communities. Aggregate data present the problem of reasoning about the behavior of the individual voter from the reported behavior of the group. But it is reasonable to assume that in the case of a party which received 35 percent of the vote to the Knesset and 30 percent of the vote to the municipality approximately 30 percent of the voters voted twice for the same party. It seems unlikely that the party in question received the votes (at least once) of some 65 percent of the electors. Most probably, 30 percent of the electorate voted for the party twice and 5 percent cast the ballot in the local election for a different party.[7] We shall use this assumption in the analyses that follow.

In order to compare the extent of split-ticket voting between communities in a single election or in the same community in more than one election, the following index will be used:

$$\text{Index} = \frac{\sum_{i=1}^{n} (x_i - y_i)^2}{n}$$

where x is the percentage of the vote won in the Knesset election by a

TABLE 9.3 ELECTION RESULTS IN JERUSALEM AND RAMAT GAN
FOR 1965 AND 1969

| | JERUSALEM | | RAMAT GAN | |
	KNESSET	MUNICIPALITY	KNESSET	MUNICIPALITY
1965 Election Results				
Alignment[a]	28.8%	23.5%	37.9%	28.0%
Mapam	3.3	3.7	4.9	5.3
Rafi	7.5	20.6	6.5	4.1
Religious Parties[b]	24.7	26.2	8.3	7.3
Gahal	28.3	17.2	29.2	38.7
Independent Liberal	3.8	3.0	5.3	4.8
Israel Communist	0.8	—	1.3	1.1
Others[c]	0.8	5.9	4.1	10.3
Split-ticket Index	44.1		29.2	
1969 Election Results				
Alignment[a]	35.0%	47.3%	46.3%	27.3%
State List	3.2	1.5	4.0	1.5
Religious Parties[b]	24.1	24.5	9.0	9.0
Gahal	28.3	16.9	29.7	39.6
Free Center	1.0	1.1	1.7	—
Independent Liberal	3.2	2.0	3.8	3.9
Israel Communist	0.9	0.6	1.5	0.9
Others[c]	3.3	6.0	3.3	17.7
Split-ticket Index	38.3		87.8	

a. The 1965 Alignment included Mapai and Ahdut Haavoda. By 1969 these two parties and Rafi had merged to form the Israel Labor party; the 1969 Alignment consisted of Labor and Mapam.

b. Including the National Religious party, Agudat Israel, and Poalei Agudat Israel.

c. These are Jewish ethnic or splinter parties. Not included are two parties that appeared in 1965 for the first time—the New Communist list and Haolam Haze—or the Arab parties. These exclusions explain why the percentages do not total 100.

given party, y the percentage of the vote won in the local election by that party, and n the total number of parties competing.[8] To compute the index of split-ticket voting for the entire country in 1969, for example, one takes the difference between the local and national percentages for the eight parties listed in Table 9.1, squares the differences so that signs will be positive, sums the squares, and divides by eight, the total number of parties. When these various operations are performed, the 1969 index of split-ticket voting for the eight parties listed is 10.1.[9]

To test the pattern of split-ticket voting in Israel, the index was applied to the forty-one Jewish communities whose 1965 population exceeded 10,000 inhabitants. These communities contained 76 percent of those Israelis who voted in the 1969 Knesset election. For the four elections considered (1955, 1959, 1965, and 1969), twelve communities' local elections were not held on the same day that the Knesset elections were held, leaving 152 cases whose indices were computed. Holon, a Tel Aviv suburb, recorded the lowest index, 0.7 in 1955; the highest index was recorded by Roah Haayin in 1965, with a phenomenal 387.9 (see Table 9.4).

It is hard to be certain that split-ticket voting is increasing. The impression is that it is, but since the aggregate data at hand do not tell us how the individual voted in either of the elections, we simply cannot know for sure. We can, however, test the frequency of split-ticket voting when the community rather than the individual is the unit of analysis. In these terms, the trend toward split-ticket voting is clear (see Table 9.2). In 1955, 48.5 percent of the communities considered had an index lower than 5, while in 1959 the percentage fell to 35.9; it reached 23.1 by 1965 and 14.6 in 1969. On the other hand, an index above 50 was recorded by only 6.1 percent of the communities in 1955; by 1959 the percentage had risen to 10.3, by 1965 to 15.4, and by 1969 to 34.1. The median index is certainly increasing: from 5.3 in 1955 to 10.7 in 1959 and 16.2 and 17.9 in 1965 and 1969, respectively.

Paradoxical as it seems, the number of communities whose index decreased from election to election is growing even while the trend of the index for the forty-one communities, as demonstrated in Table 9.2, is clearly up. Between the 1955 and 1959 elections, the index of only seven communities decreased with the rest increasing (see Table 9.4). Comparing the 1959 and 1965 indices, thirteen communities recorded a lower index in 1965 and in 1959, the others increasing. Between 1965 and 1969, fourteen communities had a lower index for the 1969 elections when compared with the 1965 elections. But a count of the number of communities whose index decreased from election to election measures only the direction of the change, not its extent.

The direction of the index in any given community may be down for a number of reasons. The change between two points in time may be

TABLE 9.4 THE 41 COMMUNITIES, SIZE OF THE ELECTORATE
THAT VOTED FOR THE KNESSET IN 1969, AND THE
SPLIT-TICKET VOTING INDEX FOR 1955, 1959, 1965, AND 1969

COMMUNITY	VOTERS FOR KNESSET, 1969	INDEX			
		1955	1959	1965	1969
Acre	13,851	18.5	19.9	37.9	20.4
Afula	7,613	1.6	3.5	5.3	12.3
Ashdod	14,858	–	–	–	58.3
Ashkelon	16,765	–	3.4	18.8	131.3
Bat Yam	38,600	2.4	3.6	2.0	3.4
Beer Sheba	29,284	12.3	64.0	–	9.1
Beit Shean	4,539	4.3	4.2	5.1	5.5
Bnei Brak	34,488	2.7	11.2	11.0	243.9
Dimona	8,153	–	12.4	33.8	192.5
Eilat	4,826	–	4.7	23.9	33.4
Givatayim	25,388	2.8	7.8	16.2	4.6
Hadera	16,706	5.3	17.4	55.3	105.6
Haifa	118,345	1.9	2.2	1.3	2.1
Herzliya	19,251	14.6	3.0	11.7	8.9
Hod Hasharon	5,938	–	–	12.3	3.3
Holon	43,935	0.7	2.3	1.6	1.0
Jerusalem	95,331	6.4	4.3	44.1	38.3
Kfar Saba	12,465	1.6	4.4	15.3	5.6
Kiryat Ata	12,431	3.6	4.1	3.6	4.3
Kiryat Bialik	7,614	145.5	204.4	215.5	381.0
Kiryat Gat	7,542	–	6.5	39.3	13.9
Kiryat Motzkin	8,805	30.9	49.2	21.7	12.1
Kiryat Shmone	5,692	3.5	14.3	24.6	208.1
Kiryat Yam	8,866	4.1	4.8	9.2	11.6
Lydda	12,614	17.1	8.4	16.9	11.1
Nahariya	11,582	1.3	2.1	2.9	13.7
Nes Ziona	6,140	1.0	3.3	2.7	12.3
Netanya	31,141	16.0	48.3	61.9	89.6
Or Yehuda	5,125	–	11.1	49.8	31.6
Petah Tikva	43,158	3.9	17.3	25.3	60.5
Raanana	6,603	11.8	10.4	2.0	25.7
Ramat Gan	62,686	38.0	35.7	29.2	87.8
Ramat Hasharon	5,938	8.9	29.9	4.3	227.2
Ramle	13,723	1.7	15.3	13.3	13.6
Rehovoth	19,538	40.2	65.4	107.2	37.7
Rishon LeZion	22,904	60.7	33.8	77.7	221.9
Rosh Haayin	4,439	19.4	163.3	387.9	157.6
Safed	6,045	3.3	10.7	28.4	73.2
Tel Aviv	211,056	6.3	12.5	2.5	8.1
Tiberias	9,857	5.6	11.7	9.3	17.9
Tirat Hacarmel	6,440	–	9.4	13.6	6.3

small; Beit Shean recorded indices of 4.3, 4.2, 5.1, and 5.5 for the four respective elections. For one of the three time periods under consideration the index is down, but the differences are obviously negligible. At the other extreme, a very high index might persist, with the direction of the index decreasing; the index for Rosh Haayin between 1965 and 1969 dropped from 387.9 to 157.6, an impressive decline but still within a very high overall index.

The fact that the party contestants change from election to election accounts for some of the variation in the index. Consider, for example, the effects on the index of the emergence of Labor unity in the 1969 elections (see Table 9.3). In 1965 Mapai and Ahdut Haavoda ran together as the "Alignment" while Rafi and Mapam put up separate lists. By 1969, instead of having three lists running separately, the Labor party (which was formed in 1968 from Mapai, Ahdut Haavoda, and Rafi) ran in alignment with Mapam. This meant that one list appeared instead of three. This neat picture is somewhat blurred by the independent appearance of the State List, a faction of the former Rafi that refused to merge with Mapai. In 1965 the three lists, Alignment, Rafi, and Mapam, ran candidates in the national and in most local races. The 1969 Alignment ran lists in all the local communities. But the State List, which put up a list for the Knesset, participated in only twenty-four of the forty-one communities considered here. This obviously affects the behavior of the index, since the calculation includes the State List as one of the competing parties whether or not a local list appeared.

A major cause of variation between communities is the emergence or nonemergence of local parties. When a local list is successful, it affects the behavior of the index dramatically; this local list may be a base for a popular leader (some politicians who used Rafi for their personal base in 1965 set up independent, local lists in 1969), an ethnic group, or a support-your-home-town party. Some of the local parties are actually affiliated with national parties but have adopted local names or have affiliated with the national party after being established independently. In any event, the index is not sensitive to these political maneuverings, and it behaves accordingly.

On the whole, however, the index provides a good measure of the extent of split-ticket voting, which, in general, does seem to be increasing. This is more clearly comprehended when we realize that twenty-one of the forty-one communities with more than 10,000 inhabitants in 1965 had fewer than 10,000 voters. Such small sizes are likely to assure the visibility of local leaders and increase their ability to know their constituents and their problems. The fact that more than half of the communities considered here had fewer than 10,000 voters fortifies the impression that split-ticket voting seems to be increasing by community and perhaps in an absolute sense as well.

The importance of split-ticket voting seems to be growing in terms of the number of local contests whose outcomes are affected by the phenomenon. It is obvious that the impact of the split ticket is greatest at the level of local government. The monumental generalization about Israeli national politics, with all of its factional splits and mergers and ideological upheavals, is that the distribution of electoral strength from election to election barely changes (see Table 9.1). The subtle differences recorded in the total number of seats a party gains in the Knesset are less noteworthy than the pattern of continuity that election results have provided. On the local level, however, the shifting of a few thousand votes because of intraparty friction or the rise of a local personality may be enough to bring a new leadership to office. Although those votes will have little impact on the national scene, locally they may be crucial. Thus, while there is only partial evidence that the incidence of split-ticket voting is increasing in an absolute sense, it seems to be assuming a more pivotal role in the Israeli political system.

We can see this dynamic at work and gain some insight into the relationship between the alterations in the party system and the behavior of the index by studying Table 9.3. All four elections reported there were dominated by the leadership and organizational abilities of two men—Kolleck in Jerusalem and Krinitzi in Ramat Gan. In 1965 Kolleck, heading the Rafi list, won almost three times as much support for the municipal list as Ben Gurion's national list won in Jerusalem. Kolleck's success was evidently personal rather than ideological: he managed to win more votes at the expense of the rightist Gahal than from the Alignment from which Rafi had split. The same pattern continued in 1969, except that then Kolleck headed the Alignment list consisting of the 1965 Alignment, Mapam, and Rafi. When the total percentage of the vote these parties won in 1965 is compared with the

1969 Alignment, it is clear that voting behavior had not changed greatly. But the realignment of party forces had recast the face of party success by 1969. The Alignment won a large plurality, whereas in 1965 their strength was fractionalized. As before, Gahal tended to be the chief victim of Kolleck's popularity. The index was sensitive to these shifts, falling some 12 points.

If the Jerusalem case highlights the effect a popular leader of the dominant left-of-center parties has on split voting, depending on the cohesion of the dominant party, the case in Ramat Gan demonstrates how the right-of-center parties can establish a powerful base in a municipality but fail in their endeavor to translate this local success into vote winning for the Knesset. Krinitzi, who almost literally put Ramat Gan, a suburb of Tel Aviv, on the map, died in an automobile accident soon before the 1969 elections. But the Gahal list he headed continued to pull 10 percentage points more for the municipality than it did for the Knesset.[10] The tradition of split voting and popular appeal was demonstrated in Ramat Gan by an additional "local" list headed by a former deputy of Krinitzi. His success is another example of a right-of-center list benefiting from the tradition of voting for local lists headed by popular figures.

Israel politics, and for that matter the split-ticket voting index, is an artifact of the dominant Labor party—or, before the merger, of Mapai. On the national level, Labor (Mapai) has always been the dominant party. This has allowed the national party's and administration's support of local communities to be less than even-handed at times. The support the local branch gets from the national authorities, on the one hand, and the votes Labor receives from the local electorate, on the other, represent a self-perpetuating process. The more support, the more votes; the more votes, the more support. But some communities have a tradition of a competitive party structure. Most of these were at one time led by those groups that are now Gahal (Herut and the Liberal party, which was formerly the General Zionists) and the Independent Liberals (formerly the Progressive party). These center and right-of-center parties at the local level provided Mapai and Labor with the only serious political opposition in the country's history.

The relations between the center and local levels of Israeli politics are partially explained by the two variables under discussion: the dominance and stability of Labor and the tradition of competitiveness. Three main types of community become evident, when one analyzes center-local relations in these terms, that correspond closely to the behavior of the index for these communities. First, there is the community with a dominant and stable Labor branch with little or no tradition of centrist competition. Second, a tradition of centrist opposition (that is, nondominance of Labor) has sometimes arisen, with or without stability of the Labor branch. Third, there may be no competitiveness, but instability in Labor or localism. The index tends to range along this array; the first type tends to display a low index, the second a medium one, and the third a high rate.

The importance of Labor in determining the level of the index is related to the Alignment's overall success in the Knesset elections. In 1969 thirty-one of the forty-one communities gave more than 45 percent of their vote for the Knesset to the Alignment. It follows from the nature of the index that if Labor does well at the local level, the index will tend to be low. And indeed this is the case. Communities such as Haifa, Holon, Bat Yam, Kiryat Ata, and Hod Hasharon have been characterized by stable leadership in the local Labor branch and by the dominance of Labor at the polls. The emergence of popular leadership within the framework of Labor in Givatayim and Beer Sheba and the return of Rafi to the Labor fold are reflected in low indices.

The stability of a political organization cannot be measured on election day alone. Our focus here magnifies the stability immediately before the election. An atmosphere of instability on the eve of the election can easily affect the index. In Nahariya, for example, the man who had led the party and community since 1947 was opposed within the party for the nomination. In Afula the popular mayor and party leader resigned, and the index reacted accordingly. Herzliya represents the same principle working in the opposite direction: there a serious crisis erupted in 1966, after which the Interior Ministry dispersed the city council and appointed one in its place according to law. The source for this public debacle was the instability of the local Mapai branch caused by political in-fighting. The Labor candidate in the 1969 elections was a popular figure, recruited from outside of the party rank-and-file and untainted by the previous crises. Nevo's personal success coincided with Labor's traditional success in the Knesset elections in Herzliya, and the index remained relatively low. Had the elections taken place before the crises of the local branch and the city leadership were settled, the index would have skyrocketed.

In the second type of community, characterized by a competitive system in which Labor represents only one of the major parties, the index tends to be medium. For example, Petah Tikva, Safed, Jerusalem, Netanya, Hadera, Rehovot, Raanana, and Ramat Gan have all had right-of-center administrations at one time or another. The Labor party never achieved a position of dominance or continuity, and in at least one city, Ramat-Gan, never won the city hall. In many of these communities a competitive two- or three-party system has developed. This is in sharp contrast to the rest of the country, where parties other than Labor have no serious hope of winning the mayoral office and must count on coalition bargaining to maximize their electoral gains.

This competitiveness has tended to coincide with the emergence of localism—a trend toward parties unaffiliated with national organizations and stressing local interests and programs. Petah Tikva, Ashdod, Rehovot, Hadera, and Ramat Gan have witnessed the emergence of local parties in conjunction with the competitive pattern that offered an effective alternative to Labor.

The index is obviously affected by this pattern of competition. When Labor holds its own in the national election but loses votes at the local level (as in Ramat Gan; see Table 9.3), the index is bound to jump. The chances of a higher index are even greater when the party that siphons off Labor's national gains presents a home-grown list with no counterpart in the national elections. This also happens when the successful local party does much better than the national list in a particular community. The Independent Liberals in Netanya, the minorities lists in Acre and Ramle, the religious parties in Safed and Raanana, and the Free Center in Eilat do much better for their local candidates than for the Knesset.

While competition can come from local lists or small national parties, it is most usual to find Gahal representing the competition in this type of community. If Gahal also pulls well for the Knesset, the index may be low. Tel Aviv is a good example. The General Zionists (part of Gahal) had been successful there in the past. Labor's winning the mayor's office in 1959 was a major gain, for population, power, and resources are all concentrated in the country's largest city. But the General Zionist influence remains strong. In 1969 the Alignment in Tel Aviv won 44.3 and 39.5 percent of the Knesset and municipal votes, respectively, while Gahal won 30.2 and 36.4 percent, respectively.

Tel Aviv is a fascinating case study of our thesis. The Labor branch is relatively stable, but there is a strong tradition of right-of-center voting. Accordingly, Labor does fairly well but is more successful in the national than the local poll. Gahal's pattern is the reverse. Labor won the mayor's office in Tel Aviv in 1969 by a very slight margin and with heavy costs in concessions to the religious parties in forming the coalition. The necessity of choosing a mayor on the basis of a coalition and the tradition of General Zionist rule make Tel Aviv very competitive. The stability of Labor's Tel Aviv branch completes the picture and results in a relatively low index.

Tel Aviv has not produced the popular leader that Haifa had in Choushi, Jerusalem in Kolleck, or Ramat Gan in Krinitzi. If he emerges, it will have to be through a political party. Choushi and Kolleck used Labor as their base, Krinitizi the General Zionists. Popular local lists seem to be feasible only in small communities; the visibility and exposure needed for an independent list is possible only in a relatively small town. A large city such as Tel Aviv has too many interests, centers of power, and potential obstacles. The organization of a national party is necessary to harness or neutralize these factors. Localism has a rather low threshhold. Tel Aviv is much too variegated for the direct rule of a popular local mayor. It is no accident, then, that the behavior of the Tel Aviv index is similar to that of the country at large. For, indeed, Tel Aviv is the country writ small.

When localism in a small town is prevalent, the index of course reacts. Both Kiryat Bialik and Rosh Haayin demonstrate the effect of successful local lists unrepresented at the national elections. Often the local list is a reaction to the instability of the local Labor branch. This is the third type of community, with Labor instability and no competitive tradition and with a very high index. Sometimes a section of the Labor branch will break away and form a local list; sometimes a local leader will emerge and will base his appeal on the public fatigue with the impotence of the local Labor leadership. In Dimona and Kiryat Shmone local lists emerged; in Ashkelon and Rishon LeZion, Gahal benefitted. In Ashkelon the instability of Labor coincided with the emergence of a popular leader in Gahal; in Rishon LeZion a local split in Labor regarding a pollution problem led to Gahal's ascension and, with Labor's strength in the Knesset election, to a very high index. Gahal has used the combination of exploiting the failures of Labor rule on local issues and nominating a popular local candidate to its advantage. It is much less bound to the needs and weight of its party organization than is Labor. Reaching outside the party for an attractive candidate, which Labor rarely does, is often done by Gahal. The direct election of the mayor will probably change that pattern—and the prominence of the Labor party apparatus.

The popular local leader who appeared in the 1965 local elections, but much more so by 1969, tended to be new in politics. The fact that he had no experience in the party apparatus made him unattractive to established parties, such as Labor, but attractive to the voter, especially to the voter who was predisposed to split his ticket. "Stars" also appeared—army officers, successful lawyers, and managers. On the whole, these new men in Israeli politics tended to be middle- to upper-class, professionals, and Israeli-born. Many of them were from veteran families in town and were catapulted into the highest levels of local politics with no previous credentials. This description, at least in part, is accurate for such high-index communities as Hadera, Rishon LeZion, Ashkelon, Ramat Hasharon, and Ashdod.

The popular local leader's achievement as a vote-getter, even though he is not necessarily a party man, explains much of his political dilemma. It also reveals much about split-ticket voting in Israel. As often as not, a dynamic, young, and inspiring officeholder must operate in a political system that prizes order, age, and organization. If the populace is his source of inspiration, he cannot avoid the hard fact of Israeli political life that the party and his success in dealing with the government bureaucracy are his sources of power. It has been shown time and time again that a popular leader can be elected while formally at the head of a party list. But the only popular base that he can build is at the local level; it is at this level, too, that ethnic factors are most likely to be significant. While local leaders may retain their individual identities, national leaders are party men. In practice, a proven local leader is likely to be recruited into national party service in an attempt to extend his local following to the national level while "balancing" the ticket. Through this process of cooptation, the party tries to create a semblance of pluralism while, advertently or inadvertently, it weakens the leadership ranks at the local level. The populace may vote for a mayor regardless of party, but once the party calls him to national headquarters, they can no longer vote for him; they have to vote for the party. Hypothetical as these last remarks are, we are confident that the impact of the charismatic leader on split-ticket voting is greatest when he is a local officeholder. Once he loses visibility at the local level, it is by no means certain that he can transfer his appeal to his replacement. On the whole, perhaps, the national party receives more votes because of individuals now in national headquarters, but at the community level there is no assurance that the party or their successors will do as well in the next local election.

The role of Mapai (Labor) must be stressed in any explanation of split-ticket voting in Israel, since it is the largest vote-getter in the country and dominates in most of the local contests. But Mapai's importance can best be understood if it is considered in terms of other parties on the political scene. One of the factors that has assured the perpetuation of its power has been its close association with the religious parties.[11] In the national coalition, Mapai and the religious parties generally manage to divide the spoils of the local elections in an elegant and gentlemanly manner. In communities where their mandates are sufficient for forming a ruling coalition, the religious parties and Mapai generally agree between themselves regarding patronage and power. New settlements are often designated the "property" of one party or the other, and the "owner" party provides the new settlers with housing, employment, and services. When the "rival" party agrees not to compete in a community, it is little wonder that it stays solidly in the ranks of the patron party in both national and local elections. The moderate socialist Mapai and the religious parties make very strange but extremely effective bedfellows.

By controlling the municipal governments of key urban areas, the parties of the center and right (especially the Liberal party—formerly the General Zionists—and Herut) presented to Mapai the only serious opposition that it had ever known. In a Knesset debate, the then-Prime Minister Ben Gurion of Mapai referred to Tel Aviv as a "state within a state," since it was headed by a General Zionist mayor.[12] When the tide finally turned in 1959 and Mapai became the dominant party in Tel Aviv, an editorial in a Mapai publication could afford to be expansive—and revealing: "After 30 years of government by the right in Tel Aviv, it is now possible that the leaders of Tel Aviv and the leaders of the national government will finally be able to speak to and understand one another."[13]

Labor is the bridge over which the predominantly one-way traffic in power and resources from the national to the local level of Israeli government and politics travels. The data reveal no exaggerated tendency toward split-ticket voting, since there is no real division of power between the national and local levels of Israeli government and politics. Power is concentrated at the national level; local government is in a dependent, subordinate position. Local government in Israel tends to be yet another extension of the centers of power that control much of the country's political life. A tendency toward local autonomy cannot be read into the split-ticket voting data, since the incidence of such behavior is low and has not increased consistently. The impact of split-ticket voting is greatest on the politics of individual communities, but it is misleading to think of this as a muffled indicator of greater autonomy; local authorities in Israel do not have the prerequisites of autonomy. His behavior at the polls seems to indicate that the Israeli voter recognizes this fact.

New patterns of political behavior and recruitment were beginning to appear in the 1969 elections. These were largely outside of the structure of the traditional practices that have established parties and allowed them to perpetuate their strength. The parties seem to sense the change in the air. Gahal, in its attempt to compete more successfully, has adopted and promoted policies in tune with these changes. Labor, as might be expected from a party in power all these years, was slower to react. But the adaptation to the new political realities in many communities is beginning within its ranks. The decision to support the direct election of the mayor is one of the first of these adaptations. Labor has too much to lose not to adapt and too much experience at adaptation to allow us to think that the party will miss this opportunity. It is interested in maintaining and perpetuating its strength. The 1969 elections and the history of Labor indicate that changing the electoral law to provide for the direct election of mayors will be the first, but probably not the last, alteration to accommodate change.

NOTES

1. Arab councils have been ignored in these analyses. We concentrated on Jewish and mixed settlements. Examples of mixed Arab-Jewish communities are Acre and Ramle. See *Government Annual, 1966–67* (Jerusalem: Government Printing Office, 1967) (in Hebrew), p. 286.
2. Technically, the General Zionists won twenty seats and were joined after the election by two Knesset members of the sephardic list.
3. By December 1965, 72 percent of the country's urban population had local governments headed by Mapai leadership. The major turning point came in 1959, when Mapai became the dominant party in Tel Aviv, replacing the General Zionists.
4. All voting statistics are from the various *Results of Elections to the Knesset and to Local Authorities* published by the Government's Central Bureau of Statistics.
5. The Knesset elections of 1949, 1951, and 1961 were not accompanied by local elections. The election of 1950 was for local authorities only. Some communities have elected local authorities in special local elections in addition to, or instead of, the dates set for the general elections.
6. Paragraph 31(c) of the Local Authorities Act—Elections of 1965 specifies that the ballot box for the local election must be in a different room from the one used for the Knesset election.
7. For our purposes, this description of the process is probably close enough to what really happens. In reality, it is likely that things are much more complicated, with some voters splitting in one manner, some in another, and some not at all.
8. The n. used was constant for a given election year among communities and was based on Table 1. In computing the indices for 1955 and 1959 the n. used was 9—and nine lists appear in Table 1; in 1965 the n. used was 8.
9. The national indices for 1955, 1959, 1965, and 1969, respectively, are 1.8, 6.8, 4.7, and 10.1. These data, interestingly, follow the same pattern presented by Tel Aviv, the country's largest city, and provide evidence that, *on the whole,* split-ticket voting has not greatly increased over time.
10. Another powerful political leader died before the 1969 elections. Abba Choushi, the long-time labor boss of Haifa, passed away in the summer of 1968. The party organization stayed strong, and

Choushi's success in keeping Haifa Labor—and the index low—lived after him.

11. Religious parties also compete with Labor. In Beit Shean both Labor and the religious parties win nearly half the vote for both the Knesset and the local council. Competition is high, but since the split is nearly even, the index is low. In Bnai Braq, a mostly religious suburb of Tel Aviv, the religious parties' competition among themselves causes a high index. For computing this index, we have lumped the three religious parties together and this is reasonable for most communities. But in Bnai Braq, where religious party competition is intense, other "local" religious parties competed, thus inflating the index.

12. Israel, *Knesset Proceedings*, 7, 150.

13. *Hapoel Hatzair,* December 15, 1959, p. 3.

CHAPTER 10

CONCLUSIONS

VOTING IS THE single political act that captures both the spirit and the substance of democracy. With the vote, the citizen can identify with the symbols of the state and participate in determining the personnel and policies of government. The vote is an intensely individual act, and yet its potential impact on the entire society is considerable. Even in regimes where political competition is limited, the vote is used to register support for the authorities and to afford the citizen an active manifestation of his identification with the existing system. In competitive systems voting also determines the distribution of power among the candidates and their parties.

The voting act is conditioned by the influences and pressures brought to bear on the citizen and by the political arrangements that characterize the system within which the vote takes place. Electoral laws have political consequences, and hence many constitutional issues in the realm of elections—such as reapportionment, extension of suffrage, financing elections, type of ballot, use of voting machines, single-member district as opposed to proportional representation, rules of party and candidate eligibility, and formulas for distributing the left-over vote—are matters that provoke the politician's serious concern and attention. The multiplicity of electoral arrangements is clearly a monument to the ingenuity of political man and a manifestation of his striving for power. Far from being objective rules to regulate the game, electoral laws are never neutral: they favor one political rival at the expense of another.

Legal arrangements are not the only constraints on the system of political competition. Social and historical factors can be just as powerful in limiting the range of potential outcomes the development of a system might produce. These factors may not be causal in determining who shall rule for how long, but they do set parameters on the political struggle and its possible outcome. Israel provides a fascinating example of a political system whose history and social life predetermine the range of possible political outcomes and effectively eliminate the possibility of other results. It is an especially interesting case for students of politics, since the political is the variable of prime importance in these determinations.

We have seen how relationships which generally hold between indicators of political modernization and variables of social and economic development break down in the Israeli case, although they are upheld for the Israeli non-Jewish community. Modernization in Israel takes on a special meaning because of the prior establishment in time of political institutions that, in turn, determined the rate of social and economic change. Political change was not brought about by changes in the social and economic structures; on the contrary, in the Israeli case it was the political that was primary. This finding is reasonable, since Israeli history telescopes the experiences of different peoples and different heritages into a rather compact line of vision. The oriental immigrants absorbed by a predominantly European political culture adapted to the ways and behavior patterns of the established dominants. They were herded very quickly into a political experience that was foreign to their countries of origin. But adapt they did, and by doing so they gave added support to those political institutions that were already dominant at the time of their arrival.

It is not unusual to find that new immigrants adopt the styles and behavior patterns of the host community, at least in superficial ways. It is not often, however, that a host community welcomes in a short span of time an immigration larger than the size of the original community. In Israel, even though this was the case, the values and behavior patterns of the established absorbing community prevailed. The explanation for this must be in large measure political: the parties and their affiliated social and economic organizations controlled the resources for many of the needs that had to be met in the immigrants' first months in the country. Whether these were jobs, schooling, housing, medical care, or loans, the connections with a party were always helpful. It fulfilled the function of integrating the immigrant into society. The party not only won the immigrant's gratitude, and perhaps his support; it also elicited tacit acceptance of the system by coopting him into the network of benefits and debts that emanated from the party.

It would be a mistake to think that this function of integrating the immigrants into the rhythm of the country was fulfilled by a single party. In fact, it was characteristic of a number of them, especially the parties of the left and the religious parties. The parties of the center and right were less equipped, both ideologically and organizationally, for this kind of task. A circular pattern aided the leftist and religious parties to accumulate and perpetuate political power: their control of the national and semipublic institutions and their organization and party ideologies gave them natural advantages in absorbing the masses of immigrants; in exploiting these advantages, they secured the support of the new citizens, thus perpetuating their power in the next elections.

Despite the broad spectrum of Israeli parties, it is inaccurate to think of the resulting political system as pluralistic. Many of these parties attempted to organize the totality of society and encompass it within their platforms. Each party represented a rather comprehensive world view and discouraged the free flow of ideas and supporters among parties. Members' commitment was expected to be total. Since access to the political system was largely regulated by membership in a political party, credentials were carefully checked. The resulting political system was fractionalized, with each unit quite separated from the others. The proportional-representation system of elections accelerated these tendencies, for each party tended to be most wary of those adjacent to it. The boundaries established between party members and nonmembers and the lines drawn between those who accepted the ideology and those who did not were often used to distinguish between those who would be granted the parties' favors and those who would be refused them.

Another factor that worked against the development of a pluralistic political system was the implicit endorsement by almost all of the political actors of the institutional status quo. The division of power that characterized the pre-state period and extended into the first quarter of a century of independence was accepted as normal. The political roles that various groups and factions played became familiar. More significantly, perhaps, these roles were accepted and even expected by the leadership of the groups and factions, and a consensual status quo characterized the system. Few groups expected more than they had already obtained; the one stipulation was that they should not be deprived of the gains already made. The best indicator of this condition is that there has rarely been a party that campaigned in the belief that it might oust Mapai (now Labor) from its plurality position. The intriguing questions of the seven elections since independence have not been who would win or who would lose, but who would be the second biggest winner and who would be in the coalition.

The regularity of the election results has introduced a large measure of stability into the political system. The resulting pattern is clearly hierarchical, with the dominant Labor party at the pinnacle of power. If the elections make the contest between parties more visible and involve the citizenry, the truly important contest in terms of political power in Israel takes place within the Labor party itself. This contest is much less visible and takes place among the party functionairies and the party leadership. The Labor party, formed by the merger of Mapai, Ahdut Haavoda, and Rafi in 1968, has consolidated within it most of the electoral strength and almost all of the charismatic leadership of the left-of-center parties. Together with Mapam in 1969, the Labor party presented a joint list—the Alignment—to the voters. This united front for the elections resulted partially from the perceived need for unity in the face of international pressures following the 1967 war. In addition, more mundane political considerations were also important. Rafi was discouraged after its 1965 showing at the polls; at the time it hoped to offer an alternative to Mapai, but it failed in this effort. Already in 1965 Mapai had opted to align with Ahdut Haavoda, partially to stave off the threat of Rafi and partially to fill its depleted ranks of young leadership. Mapam, whose leadership problems were even more acute, calculated that aligning with Labor would assure it of more representation in the 1969 elections that it might win were it to stand alone.

The in-fighting within the party has long-range consequences on questions of both policy and personnel. But even in the general elections, the relations within the party can affect the vote. The structure of competition is influenced by the dominant party. Our analyses of split-ticket voting showed that the stability of the dominant party's local branch was the best indicator of its intensity; when coupled with the incidence of competition in the elections for the city hall, this stability generated a neat typology of the relations between national and local election results. The structure of competition as the chief explanatory variable again indicates the primacy of the political in the Israeli case.

The organization and cohesiveness of the branch center seems to be as important as any other factor in determining the division of the vote and in motivating the electors' choice of party.

The most important political fact of Israel is the domination of Mapai-Labor. The identification of the party with the epoch of independence assures that the political power at its disposal is much greater than the plurality of votes it regularly wins. The formal manifestations of this are the facts that Mapai-Labor has been the pivot of every government coalition since independence and that the crucial portfolios of Prime Minister, Defense, Foreign Affairs, and the Treasury have never left its hands. In addition, domestically sensitive ministries run continually by Mapai-Labor include Education, Agriculture, Police, and Labor. No effective opposition has risen against it; even in the urban centers, which the parties of the bourgeois center and right once held, the dominant left has succeeded in establishing its power. Duverger's description of the opposition's perception of the dominant party is very apt: "They deplore it but admit it."

The domination of Mapai-Labor and its undisputed political power create the situation in which political considerations can be so crucial in determining the political, social, and economic developments of the country. Within the constrictions of the rules of the game, the dominant party is free—and knows that it is free—to do as it likes. It is true that the rules declare some issue areas out of bounds and require exertions of time and effort in consultation and preparation. But they also assume the domination of the system by the Mapai-Labor party and therefore ultimately work in favor of its perpetuating its own power. As in most agreements, both sides gain; but in this agreement the odds are heavily in the dominant party's favor. The various proposals to change the electoral laws have unsettled the opposition—especially the smaller parties—since most of these proposals would increase the relative power of Labor. Proposals to increase the minimum needed for representation (currently set at 1 percent) are rejected by many parties; all but three who contended in 1969 won less than 4 percent.

In the summer of 1972 the Knesset approved the guidelines for switching to a mixed district-proportional electoral system, to go into effect *after* the 1973 elections. (It is obvious that even though the dominant party is committed to reform, it has been slow to act.) Even this law passed only with great difficulty: it achieved sixty-one votes, the smallest legal majority possible. Since such a change deals with a basic or "constitutional" issue, it must pass the 120-member Knesset in each of its stages by an absolute majority.

If the guidelines are translated into law, most of the Knesset will be elected on a district basis, with a smaller number elected under the old proportional system. The guidelines still have a number of formidable obstacles to overcome before they become the law of the land. Herut and the National Religious party oppose the change since, rather than making them effective opposition parties, the chances are good that Labor will achieve a majority of the Knesset seats—a feat it has yet to accomplish. The Liberal party supported the guidelines in the 1972 vote, but this support endangered the unity of Gahal, the bloc composed of Herut and the Liberals. If the Liberal votes can be denied the advocates of change, it is likely that the electoral law will not be altered. If the Liberal party remains steadfastly in support of change, even at the expense of dismembering Gahal, the law must still receive at least sixty-one votes in the various stages of law making in the Knesset. That is not an easy feat to accomplish. For, before the voting stage, the details of the law must be hammered out in committee and within and among the parties supporting the proposal. Notwithstanding the 1972 vote, there are still many obstacles on the road of electoral reform.

It is too early to tell whether electoral reform will be implemented before the 1977 elections; what is clear is that reform is likely to upset the finely honed balance within the dominant party and the relations with other parties as well. Under the existing system, the party's politicians are instrumental in determining the personnel who will be contenders for power. A system of direct elections for the Knesset or for mayor would deprive the party bosses of much of their leverage in national and local politics. It is inconceivable that the party will relinquish all of its control over the naming of candidates, but the mechanisms of that control will have to be adjusted to the new legal and political situation. Access to the system may become easier and power more diffuse, but the party will retain an active role in any event.

As to the situation between parties, Mapai-Labor has traditionally had to depend on smaller party support in order to form a coalition—especially on the National Religious party. Should Labor win a majority rather than its historic plurality, this pattern too might well change. But even if Labor can rule alone, its leadership is accustomed to working in the coalition framework, and the religious party leadership benefits from the arrangement. A period of threat to the national security, the argument runs, is no time to alter past arrangements and shrink the range of opinion in the population and the Knesset. Although there have been increasing signs of disquiet with the status quo arrangements, especially since the cease-fire of 1970, patterns which were set years ago continue to endure.

The tacit political live-and-let-live arrangements have become fundamental features of the Israeli political culture. The dominant party could do more to benefit itself through legislation, yet it hesitates. Although most of the proposals to alter the electoral arrangements would work to the advantage of Labor, it is reluctant to make use of its power to implement these changes, contenting itself instead with the arrangements of domination that have worked in its favor for so long.

Some of these arrangements are formal. Allocating broadcasting time and funds for election campaigns according to the strength of the party in the previous Knesset obviously advantages the dominant party. A practice of this kind is perfectly acceptable within the Israeli context: everyone gets his share, and power relations are likely to be continued into the next Knesset as well. Appointing staff to absorb immigration according to party strength in the Jewish Agency's institutions or dividing political tax dues among the Histadrut's parties according to their strength in the last General Assembly elections works to maintain the relative strength of parties while assuring the continued existence of all. An elaborate system of proportional tolerance has been one of the cornerstones of the Israeli political system.

The relations of proportional strength are even more remarkable because they are reaffirmed by the electorate from time to time. This reaffirmation is promoted by many of the practices mentioned. Also, the domination of the Labor party is based on a wide spectrum of appeal throughout the society; with its plurality established, the rest of the vote divides among the many other parties.

There is undoubtedly a strong tendency toward system stability in Israel. The historical evidence and the behavior of individuals and groups document this stability convincingly. It would be unwarranted, however, to project extreme stability into the future indiscriminately. Any number of developments could change Israeli politics in a fundamental way. The untimely passing of a major leader, progress along the difficult path toward peace, a major change in the electoral laws, a split in the dominant party—any of these could alter the political scene at both the elite and the electoral levels.

Nevertheless, I would argue that the basic underpinnings for dynamic stability clearly exist. Some changes will obviously occur in personnel as well as policy. But the political, social, and economic forces at work are more likely to produce an Israel ten years from now that is still readily recognizable to the present-day observer. Predictions of system stability are convenient and are often encountered as conclusions of social science research. But in the Israel I have described—centralized, hierarchical, and characterized by solid social anchors of political dominance—the probabilities that these predictions are correct continue to grow.

The social basis of support for the dominant Labor-Mapam Alignment is rooted in the control these parties maintain in the Histadrut. For the Histadrut is more than a labor union; it is an extension of the socialist-zionist power and ideology in the country. It is itself a major source of power, of course, but it is also a participant in the total power shared by the dominant establishment. As employer, industrialist, provider of services, and educator, the Histadrut fulfills functions vital to parties that see their political movement encompassing the entire social existence of the citizen. Control of the Histadrut allows the dominant party to solidify its power base by providing necessary services to both the nation and the electorate. The network of social and economic relations and obligations envelop a substantial portion of the population. The rural collective and cooperative movements—the kibbutz and the moshav—are organized within it. These groups have long symbolized many of the pioneering values developed under the socialist-Zionist banner. Reclaiming the land, the values of physical labor, mutual aid, and cooperation found their political and organizational expression in the Histadrut. If the kibbutz member was the folk hero of the epoch, the Histadrut was the provider and Mapai-Labor the mover. The network that the Histadrut represented was not only material; it was also social, cultural, and symbolic.

What I have called the Histadrut network has undoubtedly dominated the first quarter of a century of Israeli independence. The prevailing mood, the accepted ideology, the leadership, and the symbols all emanated from this network. Histadrut membership—encompassing two-thirds of the sample—may be too gross a category for many purposes, but it is powerful enough to distinguish between those who support the Labor-Mapam Alignment and those who do not. The Histadrut is the magnetic pole of Israeli politics. Those who are attracted to it—whatever the reason and regardless of the degree of attraction—are likely to support its dominant parties at the polls. This fact provides insight into the mechanism of power perpetuation operative in the society. Since so many services and activities are controlled by the Histadrut, the chances are good that a citizen will be attracted to it (leaving aside matters of ideology and workers' solidarity). Once attracted, his support for the Labor-Mapam Alignment is likely. Dependence on the Histadrut leads to support for the Alignment; Alignment strength leads to added power to the Histadrut, which in turn leads to greater dependence of the individual on the Histadrut. And so on.

The network of potential competition, the religious, is hampered in many ways. Its institutions have long been dependent on the Histadrut (sick fund, for example), just as other elements in the society are. The public image of its parties has declined as a result of recent events. Because its major party has always been the coalition partner and never the coalition pivot, the benefits that might accrue to the dominant party by virtue of being identified with the nation's strivings were always denied it. Its subordinate position has cast the National Religious party in the role of bargainer for its own interests (in the public eye), since the role of promoting the national interest has been pre-empted by Labor.

The religious network has never gained the institutional momentum that the Histadrut has achieved. Also, the religious camp itself is split over the propriety of pursuing political interests by means of parties. Identification with the religious network, then, is not necessarily translated into support for the religious parties at the polls. Accordingly, the religious network remains a potential but still largely untapped source of political strength.

The non-religious non-labor segment of the population is at the most severe disadvantage in competing for political power, since it has no recognizable social network upon which to base its efforts. In other countries the social basis for this network might be the conservative rural peasantry and the small shopkeepers. In Israel the development of this basis is hampered by the fact that the rural areas have been the major source of support for the Histadrut network and by the fact that the religious network already includes many individuals who might otherwise seek a non-socialist alternative. In other countries the bulk of this network is more an extension of past social arrangements than a conscious political undertaking. But in Israel, with its abbreviated history, only organizations that are consciously erected have the chance of competing. Carryovers from the past are ineffective, since the past is so short. While the right and center in other nations could compete effectively even though they rejected strenuous efforts at organization, the right and center in Israel were effectively closed out of competition because of their lack of organizational efforts comparable to those of the left. Gahal could compete in urban politics, since the bourgeois tradition was established there. But on a national basis its competitive abilities were strictly limited. Its inability to establish its own network of support in the social structure led it to form as a party within the Histadrut and compete with the Alignment in the Alignment's own territory. This is an indication of its separation rather than of its acumen.

In approaching the elections, the Israeli voter is influenced by these considerations. It is not surprising, considering the pervasiveness of the Histadrut network, that the parties in the Alignment should win about half the vote. Nor is it surprising, considering the domination of the Alignment parties, that its strength should be spread out over most groups in the society. The secret of success of political domination is to recruit as many groups as possible—especially those whose support can be gained at a relatively low cost. Domination involves identification between the parties of power and the relatively satisfied strata of the society. The dominant party in Israel derives most of its support from middle Israel, although its strength at other levels is also considerable. The correspondence between conservative elements in the society and the dominant party is most clearly illustrated in terms of age and sex. Women more than men, the old more than the young—in short, the conservative elements in society—support the dominant Alignment.

The competition is left with what remains. Gahal's picture is a composite reflecting its mixture of the lower-class nationalist Herut and the upper-middle class bourgeois Liberal party. The religious parties win disproportionate support from lower-income, lower-education voters. The broad middle is clearly occupied. The alternatives open to a competing party are few. Appeals can win fragments of support away from the Alignment, but in the long run this fragmentation works in the interest of the Alignment, assuring its continued dominance and pivotal position in coalition formation. The opposition can attempt to mobilize the lower classes, but they run the risk of losing their votes to the middle-class Alignment if the political promises made them are fulfilled. Moving up from a lower-class position in Israel evidently means moving to the left in voting; this indicates less of ideological import and more about identification with the dominant culture. Moving up from the middle strata, where the Alignment is strongest, means fractionalizing among the many small parties in the political system. The two main competitive parties to the dominant Alignment, Gahal and the National Religious party, will lose much of their regular clientele if egalitarian tendencies continue. The Alignment, on the other hand, seems to lose support from individuals who rise above the middle, but this support is not concentrated in any one political group that could provide effective competition. These patterns tend to indicate that the position of the Alignment as the dominant party is assured for the foreseeable future.

Analysis of the vote in terms of the four categories generated by the juncture of the Histadrut and religious variables confirms this conclusion. The Alignment benefits almost exclusively from those who are exposed to the Histadrut network and are outside the religious network. Among those who are exposed to both networks and among those who are exposed to neither, it wins half of the votes. Only among those who are not in the Histadrut network but identify themselves as being in the religious one does the Alignment do poorly. The Histadrut-non-observant bloc does well among all groups but proportionately better among the middle-aged, European-American-born with high levels of education. The non-Histadrut-observant bloc is supported more by older respondents than by others. The group exposed to both the Histadrut and religious networks tends to be Asian-African-born and has had relatively less education. Those exposed to neither network tend to be younger, Israeli-born, and with medium levels of education.

These data indicate that many of the elements in the social system associated with "modernity" tend to be either in the Histadrut non-religious bloc or are exposed to neither network. The religious network is not successful within these "modern" groups. The Alignment's future is bright because it manages to win support from most groups, because it wins increasing support from the nonexposed bloc as age decreases, and because its Histadrut non-observant members' strength rises from more than half among the young to more than two-thirds among the old. High levels of support and effectively winning the vote of the unaffiliated augur well for the Alignment's future when compared with the kind of challenge the opposition has been able to field.

Very strong forces at work in the society favor the Alignment and its Histadrut non-observant bloc. Gahal lacks network appeal, and the religious network falters when confronted with the challenge of the Histadrut network. An insight into this is provided by analyzing the vote for the religious parties. Two simultaneous processes are at work. For those who are in the religious network but outside of the Histadrut one, higher levels of support are recorded for more "modern" voters (higher education, European- or Israeli-born). Being "modern" evidently affords the citizen the strength to vote his bloc. For the religious party voters from the bloc exposed to both networks, an opposite process is at work. The higher the level of modernity, the weaker the traditional religious ties when confronted with the competing Histadrut network. The more "modern" the citizen, the less likely is the member of this dissonance-producing bloc to vote his bloc. The pull of the Histadrut is overwhelming.

The dominant party has vast advantages in the political system. It has the power to pass legislation compatible with its needs and positions. It shares in the legitimacy enjoyed by the political system as a whole. Its ancillary organizations provide for its widespread support within the population. It enjoys a broad and solid social base within the community. It is identified with an epoch of national glory, and its leadership is acknowledged as the nation's leaders. It determines the pace of political debate and thus controls the rate and direction of social and economic development.

These characteristics of overwhelming advantage are located in a political institution. While the advantages that accrue to the party seem unassailable, the entire fabric is actually very fragile. There is no struc-tural necessity that the perpetuation of power will be successfully accomplished. There is little that the opposition can do to hasten the decline of the dominant party if the party itself does not err. But relatively small mistakes on its part can seriously disturb its seemingly unassailable strength. What is important to note is that the dominant party's continued success and its possible failure are based, for the most part, on *political* decisions. In the Israeli system politics is king in the sense that the processes of tremendous force that work in favor of the dominant party can be interrupted only by political miscalculations or by tactical negligence. The dominant party may not rule forever, but it is a form that provides for long-term competitive democracy. Its loss of strength is as likely to result from its failure to come to terms with forces in the society that it could have controlled as from anything the opposition might do.

The powerful tools used by Mapai-Labor in Israel to retain its domi-nant position are the changes it introduces in its coalition-formation behavior and in its sense of timing regarding the introduction of issues into the arena of political debate. Mapai-Labor has accommodated change in public opinion by coopting the parties representative of the non-establishment opinion into the coalition. Public policy has changed accordingly. The net result is the neutralizing of an opinion position that could eventually turn into the nucleus of a forceful opposition. The religious issue has been defused to a considerable extent by having the National Religious party in the government coalition as almost constant partners. The General Zionists in 1952, the parties left of Mapai in 1955, and Gahal in 1969 were all very effectively coopted by the dominant party. Just as they became legitimate members of the government establishment, so their platforms were incorporated into the general consensus. By coopting them and their ideas, Mapai was able to transfer the legitimacy it had provided them to itself. The new notion no longer had a clear address; it was swallowed by the establish-ment and, eventually, identified with Mapai.

Keeping issues out of the public spotlight when they are likely to lead to a serious split over fundamentals is also a potent function of the dominant party. The various bureaucracies of the country have under consideration every issue that is likely to rouse public opinion. The hierarchical nature of the system and the fact that there are so many interest groups and so few free-floating issues mitigates against the spontaneous expression of public opinion. The dominant party senses which issues can be introduced into the political system and on which issues decision would best be deferred. Especially for the security and religious issues, the dominant party variously used a strategy of providing a broad umbrella to include many divergent positions or went to great lengths to defer discussion and decision on sensitive issues. Both strategies worked toward maintaining the dominance of Labor while allowing it to be responsive to shifts in public opinion.

These strategies, like others which the dominant party might employ, must be judged in terms of their effectiveness within the Israeli political culture. They are of proven effectiveness; no less important, they are also immensely appropriate in the political culture. The "national character" of the Israeli seems to be very comfortable with the hierarchical structures that have developed over the fifty years of Zionist politics in Israel. Part of this is probably the result of the uncertain economic and military position of the community for most of this period. Also, the fact that so much of the population were immigrants—strangers—led to a perceived need for such structuring in order to incorporate these immigrants quickly into the national effort. No less important were the patterns of political organization and ideological passion that characterized the dominant political structures in the formative years. The founding fathers tended to be centralizers of political power and to communicate in a dogmatic ideological style. Whether they themselves were dogmatists or not is beside the point: they radiated a confidence in themselves and their ideas. Not infrequently, it is reasonable to assume, the content of their message had fewer long-lasting results than did the style of their delivery. The society developed patterns that supported and complemented this hierarchical political style. The educational system, for example, was often criticized for not encouraging more creativity and originality in the students. The political system was an element of the same culture as the educational system. Counterparts for patterns of behavior detectable in one could be found in the other. The political system that developed was in tune with the general society.

The picture that emerges is one of an Israeli who seems quite certain about the direction his country should take and who is quite articulate, perhaps even dogmatic, about his view. On the other hand, this Israeli would be amenable to the emergence of a strong leadership "in place of all the debates and laws."

He is quite active in participating in politics—at least insofar as interest, discussion, voting, and communications consumption are concerned. At the same time, he is aware of his limited ability to influence policy, though this evidently does not lead to changes in his political or voting behavior.

The Israeli system is characterized by both very high rates of participation and by high levels of hierarchy and centralization of political power. It enjoys a great deal of legitimacy in the eyes of its members. It is this legitimacy, in fact, that allows a hierarchical, relatively closed political system to continue to generate high rates of interest and participation. One of the periodic ways of expressing this legitimacy is by voting. The vote, while unlikely to change personnel or policy because of the social, economic, and political strength of the dominant party, fulfills a crucial function for the polity.

The linkage between the mass public and the decision-making elite is expressed only imperfectly in the elections. But the vote is only one of many components of that linkage and of the political process. In the Israeli system, various mechanisms provide the linkage and take into account pressures of various groups and public opinion. Yet the role of the dominant party in influencing these groups and publics must never be overlooked. The genius of the party is in its historical adaptation to changing circumstances without losing its broad base of support. Whether this adaptation was always consistent with its stated principles is beside the point. As a study in the exercise of rule and the perpetuation of power, the case of Mapai-Labor is exemplary. We glimpsed some of the social processes at work in favor of the dominant party and some of the obstacles in the path of the opposition. Barring drastic changes in the international situation, a series of fatal political mistakes by the leadership of the dominant party, or a split in the Labor party leadership, indications point to the continued success of the dominant party when the next election day comes around for the choosing people.

APPENDIXES

FROM THE INTERVIEW SCHEDULE

OF THE TEN basic problems listed on this card, please cite the three which seem to you to be the most important ones for Israel today.

(Interviewer: Show the respondent the card with the list of problems and request that he cite the three most important ones. Mark the first problem which he cites answer 1, the second problem answer 2, and the third problem answer 3.)

		Phase (See Appendix II)		
		1	2	3
1.	1. Relations with the world powers	11	8	—
	2. Economic independence	8	13	—
	3. Peace in the area	57	58	—
	4. Labor relations	1	1	—
	5. Relations with the Arab population in Israel and the territories	1	2	—
	6. Military strength	12	11	—
	7. Image of Israel in the world	0	0	—
	8. Absorption of immigrants	5	6	—
	9. Place of religion in the state	1	1	—
	10. Relations among the ethnic groups	0	1	—
	. . . .			
	11. Other. Which? _____	0	0	—
	12. I don't know which topic is most important	2	1	—
	13. No answer	2	0	—

		Phase (See Appendix II)		
		1	2	3
2.	1. Relations with the world powers	8	6	—
	2. Economic independence	18	22	—
	3. Peace in the area	15	18	—
	4. Labor relations	5	3	—
	5. Relations with the Arab population in Israel and the territories	9	9	—
	6. Military strength	22	19	—
	7. Image of Israel in the world	2	1	—
	8. Absorption of immigrants	13	17	—
	9. Place of religion in the state	2	2	—
	10. Relations among the ethnic groups	2	1	—
	. . . .			
	11. Other. Which? _____	2	0	—
	12. I don't know which topic is most important	1	1	—
	13. The respondent cited just one important problem	0	0	—
	14. No answer	2	0	—
3.	1. Relations with the world powers	8	7	—
	2. Economic independence	18	16	—
	3. Peace in the area	9	8	—
	4. Labor relations	4	4	—
	5. Relations with the Arab population in Israel and the territories	10	8	—
	6. Military strength	13	17	—
	7. Image of Israel in the world	4	4	—
	8. Absorption of immigrants	24	27	—
	9. Place of religion in the state	2	4	—
	10. Relations among the ethnic groups	3	3	—
	. . . .			
	11. Other. Which? _____	2	0	—

	Phase (See Appendix II)		
	1	2	3
12. I don't know which topic is most important	2	2	—
13. The respondent cited just one or two important problems	0	1	—
14. No answer	2	0	—

4. Which of the above topics is the most important one in determining *your position* in terms of the political party you support:

	1	2	3
1. Relations with the world powers	3	2	—
2. Economic independence	8	8	—
3. Peace in the area	37	38	—
4. Labor relations	5	5	—
5. Relations with the Arab population in Israel and the territories	2	2	—
6. Military strength	8	6	—
7. Image of Israel in the world	2	1	—
8. Absorption of immigrants	4	5	—
9. Place of religion in the state	7	6	—
10. Relations among the ethnic groups	3	2	—

. . . .

	1	2	3
11. Other. Which? _____	1	1	—
12. No one of the above topics	10	9	—
13. I don't support any party	9	13	—
14. No answer	3	2	—

5. To what extent is it clear to you what differences exist among the various parties concerning foreign policy and security?

	1	2	3
1. Absolutely clear	19	15	—
2. Clear	31	35	—

	Phase (See Appendix II)		
	1	2	3
3. Not so clear	28	29	—
4. Not at all clear	18	18	—
. . . .			
5. No difference among them	3	2	—
6. No answer	1	1	—

6. To what extent is it clear to you what differences exist among the various political parties concerning economic topics?

	1	2	3
1. Absolutely clear	11	11	—
2. Clear	32	34	—
3. Not so clear	30	32	—
4. Not at all clear	22	20	—
. . . .			
5. No differences among them	3	2	—
6. No answer	2	1	—

7. To what extent is it clear to you what differences exist among the various political parties concerning social topics?

	1	2	3
1. Absolutely clear	12	11	—
2. Clear	32	33	—
3. Not so clear	30	32	—
4. Not at all clear	22	21	—
. . . .			
5. No differences among them	3	2	—
6. No answer	2	1	—

8. Cite the name of the main candidate, as far as you are concerned, on the list of the party for which you are going to vote for the Knesset.

			Phase (See Appendix II)		
			1	2	3
Do	1.	Golda Meir	27	32	—
Not	2.	Moshe Dayan	23	19	—
Read	3.	Yigal Alon	6	4	—
	4.	Pinchas Sapir	1	0	—
	5.	Meir Ya'ari	0	0	—
	6.	Haim Moshe Shapira	0	2	—
	7.	Menachem Begin	6	6	—
	8.	Shmuel Tamir	0	0	—
	9.	Uri Avneri	0	1	—
	10.	Moshe Sneh	0	0	—
	11.	Another candidate. Which? _____	5	4	—
	12.	Does not know the names of candidates	2	5	—
	13.	Did not yet decide for which party to vote	9	13	—
	14.	Does not plan to vote for any party	2	4	—
	15.	No answer and unclear	19	11	—

9. Do you support any party, or are you a member or an official in a party?

		1	2	3
1.	Member and salaried official	1	1	1
2.	Member and unsalaried official	6	4	3
3.	Member, holds no office	17	13	14
4.	Supporter	37	37	41
5.	Does not especially support any one party	38	43	42
6.	No answer	1	1	1

10. Which party do you support more than all the others?

			1	2	3
Do	1.	Free Center	0	1	—
Not	2.	Mapam	3	0	—
Read	3.	Independent Liberals	2	2	—
	4.	Labor Party	44	45	—
	5.	Herut	7	7	—

	Phase (See Appendix II)		
	1	2	3
6. An ethnic party	0	0	—
7. Poalei Agudat Israel	1	1	—
8. Israeli Communist Party	0	0	—
9. National Religious Party	5	4	—
10. Liberals	4	1	—
11. Agudat Israel	2	2	—
12. New Communist List	0	0	—
13. Haolam Haze	0	0	—
14. Other party. Which? _____	2	3	(Gahal)
15. Does not especially support any one party	27	24	—
16. No answer	5	9	—

11. Do you plan to vote in the Knesset elections of this next election? For what party?

Do	1. Free Center	0	1	1
Not	2. Gahal	10	8	14
Read	3. Independent Liberals	2	1	2
	4. Alignment	48	45	42
	5. Poalei Agudat Israel	1	1	1
	6. National Religious Party	3	4	6
	7. Agudat Israel	2	2	2
	8. Israel Communist Party	0	0	0
	9. New Communist List	0	1	0
	10. Haolam Haze	0	1	1
	11. An ethnic party	0	0	0
	12. Other party. Which? _____	2	1	3
	13. Did not yet decide for what party to vote	18	16	5
	14. Did not yet decide if he will vote or not	4	6	1
	15. Will not vote	4	4	5
	16. Blank ballot	—	—	0
	17. No answer	7	11	17

There are four main factors that can influence a person to vote for a particular party:

— Identification with the party (including: habit or emotional and historical ties of the person with the party)
— The party's candidate
— The party's stand on various issues
— The party's position in the government or in the opposition

	Phase		
	1	2	3

12. Among these factors, does any one stand out as the most important one in determining your vote for the Knesset?

1. One factor is much more important than the others	48	43	56
2. One factor is somewhat more important than the others	23	20	18
3. All the factors are equally important	20	24	18
4. None of the factors is important	7	10	6
5. No answer	6	3	2

13. Which is the most important factor, in your opinion?

1. Identification with the party	16	17	21
2. The party's candidate	18	21	18
3. The party's stand on various issues	37	37	39
4. The party's position in the government or in the opposition	6	7	13
5. None of the factors is important	15	10	6
6. Another factor is important. Which? ___	1	2	1
7. No answer	6	5	3

14. In the previous question, you mentioned that the subject which is most important in determining your attitude towards the party is _____. In the event that the party would change its posi-

	Phase		
	1	2	3
tion on the subject which you mentioned, would you change your vote?			
1. Yes, I would change my vote	46	40	—
2. No, I wouldn't change my vote	27	27	—

. . . .

	1	2	3
3. I wouldn't vote at all if the party would change its position	2	2	—
4. Did not cite a subject	18	21	—
5. No answer	6	9	—

15. In another answer, you mentioned that the main candidate, as far as you were concerned, was _____ . In the event that this candidate would be included in the party list, but not be given a realistic position, would you vote for the same party anyway?

	1	2	3
1. Yes, I would still vote for the same party	46	49	—
2. No, I wouldn't vote for it	19	16	—

. . . .

	1	2	3
3. I wouldn't vote at all	3	1	—
4. Did not cite a candidate	27	21	—
5. No answer	5	13	—

16. What are the chances that the party you plan to vote for will be influential and important in the next Knesset?

	1	2	3
1. Very great chance	31	26	29
2. Great chance	26	31	29
3. Mediocre chance	14	15	18
4. Small chance	5	5	5

	Phase		
	1	2	3
5. No chance at all	1	0	1
. . . .			
6. I haven't yet decided for which party to vote	13	11	5
7. I haven't yet decided if I'll vote at all	5	4	1
8. I don't plan to vote	3	3	5
9. No answer	3	3	6

17. Do you plan to vote in the coming municipal elections?

	1	2	3
1. Yes, I plan to vote	81	76	—
2. No, I don't plan to vote	10	14	—
. . . .			
3. I haven't yet decided if I'll vote	7	9	—
4. No answer	2	1	—

18. Do you plan to vote for the same party for the Knesset and the municipality?

	1	2	3
1. Yes, I'll vote for the same party for the Knesset and the municipality	49	50	66
2. No, I'll vote for different parties	18	13	20
3. I don't plan to vote for the municipality at all	8	14	1
4. I haven't yet decided which party I'll vote for in the municipality	15	13	2
5. I won't vote for the Knesset at all	2	0	5
6. I haven't yet decided which party I'll vote for in the Knesset	6	8	5
7. I haven't yet decided if I'll vote in the municipality election	—	2	0

	Phase		
	1	2	3
8. I haven't yet decided if I'll vote in the Knesset election	—	0	1
9. No answer	3	0	2

19. *(If the respondent will vote for different parties, ask):* Which party will you vote for in the municipal elections?

	1	2	3
1. Free Center	0	0	0
2. Gahal	4	2	6
3. Independent Liberals	2	1	1
4. Alignment: Labor-Mapam	13	4	6
5. Poalei Agudat Israel	0	0	0
6. National Religious Party	1	0	2
7. Agudat Israel	0	0	1
8. Israel Communist Party	0	0	0
9. New Communist List	0	0	0
10. Haolam Haze	0	0	0
11. An ethnic party	0	0	0
12. Local party	0	0	0

. . . .

	1	2	3
13. Another party. Which? _____	0	0	1
14. The respondent will vote for the same party for the Knesset and the municipality	35	50	62
15. The respondent hasn't yet decided which party he'll vote for in the municipality	30	24	8
16. The respondent doesn't plan to vote in the municipal elections at all	10	14	6
17. No answer	5	4	7

Here again are the main factors that can influence a person to vote for a particular party:

—   Identification with the party

- The party's candidate
- The party's stand on various issues
- The party's position (in the government or in the opposition).

	Phase		
	1	2	3

20. Among these factors, does any one stand out as the most important one in determining your vote for the municipality?

	1	2	3
1. One factor is much more important than the others	39	37	55
2. One factor is somewhat more important than the others	22	21	16
3. All the factors are equally important	19	21	16
4. None of the factors are important	12	14	9
5. No answer	8	5	4

21. Which is the factor, in your opinion, whose importance is greater than the others?

	1	2	3
1. Identification with the party	12	13	16
2. The party's candidate	30	30	32
3. The party's stand on various issues	24	25	29
4. The party's position	3	4	8

. . . .

	1	2	3
5. None of the factors is important	21	15	8
6. Another factor is important. Which? ___	1	2	1
7. All of the factors are important	–	1	0
8. No answer	9	7	1
9. Unknown	–	2	5

22. What party did you vote for in the Knesset
    elections in 1965?

| | | Phase | | |
		1	2	3
Do	1. Poalei Agudat Israel	0	1	1
Not	2. Haolam Haze	0	1	1
Read	3. Mapam	4	2	2
	4. Alignment: Mapai-Ahdut Haavoda	46	44	40
	5. Independent Liberals	2	3	2
	6. Gahal	12	9	12
	7. National Religious Party	3	4	5
	8. New Communist List	0	0	0
	9. Agudat Israel	2	2	2
	10. Israel Communist Party	0	0	0
	11. An ethnic party.	0	0	0
	12. Another party. Which? _____	1	0	2
	13. I didn't vote	15	19	2
	14. Rafi	4	3	–
	15. I didn't vote; I was too young	–	–	7
	16. I could not vote	–	–	5
	17. No answer	11	13	17

23. What party did you vote for in the municipal-
    ity elections in 1965?

Do	1. Poalei Agudat Israel	1	1	1
Not	2. Haolam Haze	0	0	0
Read	3. Mapam	4	1	2
	4. Alignment: Mapai-Ahdut Haavoda	38	36	38
	5. Independent Liberals	3	2	2
	6. Gahal	11	8	13
	7. National Religious Party	3	4	5
	8. New Communist List	0	0	0
	9. Agudat Israel	2	2	2
	10. Israel Communist Party	0	0	0
	11. An ethnic party	0	0	0
	12. Local party	0	0	0
	13. Another party. Which? _____	1	2	3

		Phase	
	1	2	3
14. I didn't vote	21	27	3
15. Rafi	5	4	—
16. I didn't vote; I was too young	—	—	7
17. I could not vote	—	—	6
18. No answer	11	13	18

24. If you could vote for two more parties, other than the one you mentioned, which two parties would you vote for?

(Mark answer 24 with the first *party mentioned by the respondent, and mark answer 25 with the* second *party mentioned by the respondent.)*

Do	1. Free Center	1	2	—
Not	2. Gahal	14	17	—
Read	3. Independent Liberals	9	9	—
	4. Alignment: Labor-Mapam	8	8	—
	5. Poalei Agudat Israel	2	2	—
	6. National Religious Party	3	3	—
	7. Agudat Israel	1	1	—
	8. Israel Communist Party	0	0	—
	9. New Communist List	0	0	—
	10. Haolam Haze	0	1	—
	11. An ethnic party	0	0	—
	12. Another party. Which? _____	1	1	—
	13. Did not mention another party	30	24	—
	14. Did not yet decide for which party to vote	15	12	—
	15. State List	—	1	—
	16. No answer	4	7	—

25.	1. Free Center	1	2	—
Do	2. Gahal	3	5	—
Not	3. Independent Liberals	4	7	—
Read	4. Alignment: Labor-Mapam	2	4	—

		Phase	
	1	2	3
5. Poalei Agudat Israel	1	1	—
6. National Religious Party	3	3	—
7. Agudat Israel	1	1	—
8. Israel Communist Party	0	0	—
9. New Communist List	0	0	—
10. Haolam Haze	1	1	—
11. An ethnic party	0	1	—
12. Another party. Which? _____	2	1	—
13. Did not mention another party, or mentioned only one other party	45	25	—
14. Did not yet decide for which party to vote	15	14	—
15. Will not vote at all	17	17	—
16. State list	—	2	—
17. No answer	5	16	—

26. Name two parties which are candidates for the
Knesset for which you would not vote under
any circumstances.

*(Mark the first party mentioned as answer 26
and the second party as answer 27).*

Do	1. Free Center	1	1	—
Not	2. Gahal	4	3	—
Read	3. Independent Liberals	0	0	—
	4. Alignment: Labor-Mapam	1	2	—
	5. Poalei Agudat Israel	0	1	—
	6. National Religious Party	1	2	—
	7. Agudat Israel	3	3	—
	8. Israel Communist Party	31	28	—
	9. New Communist List	40	45	—
	10. Haolam Haze	5	3	—
	11. An ethnic party	0	0	—
	12. Another party. Which? _____	1	1	—
	13. There is no such party	6	6	—
	14. No answer	7	5	—

		Phase		
		1	2	3
27.	1. Free Center	1	1	–
	2. Gahal	3	3	–
	3. Independent Liberals	0	1	–
	4. Alignment: Labor-Mapam	2	1	–
	5. Poalei Agudat Israel	1	2	–
	6. National Religious Party	2	4	–
	7. Agudat Israel	6	6	–
	8. Israel Communist Party	24	24	–
	9. New Communist List	30	26	–
	10. Haolam Haze	13	13	–
	11. An ethnic party	1	2	–
	12. Another party. Which? _____	0	2	–
	13. Did not cite any such party, or cited only one	9	6	–
	14. No answer	7	8	–

28. Do you vote as some members of your family do?

	1	2	3
1. I vote like them	30	29	–
2. I don't vote like them	57	58	–
3. I don't know how they vote	6	11	–
4. They don't all vote the same	3	2	–
5. No answer	4	1	–

29. Do you vote as those who are in charge of you do?

	1	2	3
1. I vote like them	7	7	–
2. I don't vote like them	59	67	–
3. I don't know how they vote	15	24	–
4. They don't all vote the same	3	1	–
5. No answer	16	1	–

	Phase		
	1	2	3

30. Do you vote as your friends do?

	1	2	3
1. I vote like them	10	11	—
2. I don't vote like them	64	66	—
3. I don't know how they vote	19	19	—
4. They don't all vote the same	3	3	—
5. No answer	4	1	—

All parties have main groups of supporters. Which of the following groups is the main supporter of the following parties in your opinion?

For the *Alignment:* In your opinion, which group is their main supporter?

		1	2	3
31.	1. The young	11	12	—
	2. The old	46	49	—
	. . . .			
	3. No special age group, or others. Who? ___	34	35	—
	4. No answer	9	5	—
32.	1. North Africans + Middle Easterners	7	8	—
	2. Europeans	40	46	—
	. . . .			
	3. No special ethnic group, or others. Who? ___	41	37	—
	4. No answer	13	9	—
33.	1. Workers	50	53	—
	2. Merchants, agents, businessmen	6	7	—
	3. Men of letters or the sciences	7	8	—

	Phase		
	1	2	3

. . . .

4. No special occupational group, or others. Who? _____	28	26	—
5. No answer	9	6	—

For *Herut:* In your opinion, which group is their main supporter?

34.			
1. The young	51	49	—
2. The old	9	11	—

. . . .

3. No special age group, or others. Who? ___	31	32	—
4. No answer	9	8	—

35.			
1. North Africans + Middle Easterners	39	38	—
2. Europeans	19	15	—

. . . .

3. No special ethnic group, or others. Who? _____	36	38	—
4. No answer	14	10	—

36.			
1. Workers	13	14	—
2. Merchants, agents, businessmen	32	36	—
3. Men of letters or the sciences	7	8	—

. . . .

4. No special occupational group, or others. Who? _____	38	32	—
5. No answer	12	9	—

For *Haolam Haze:* In your opinion, which group is their main supporter?

		Phase		
		1	2	3
37.	1. The young	69	69	—
	2. The old	2	3	—
	. . . .			
	3. No special ethnic group, or others. Who? _____	14	15	—
	4. No answer	15	13	—
38.	1. North Africans + Middle Easterners	19	17	—
	2. Europeans	15	21	—
	. . . .			
	3. No special ethnic group, or others. Who? _____	47	45	—
	4. No answer	20	18	—
39.	1. Workers	13	11	—
	2. Merchants, agents, businessmen	7	9	—
	3. Men of letters or the sciences	17	18	—
	. . . .			
	4. No special occupational group, or others. Who? _____	42	44	—
	5. No answer	21	18	—

APPENDIX II

THE SAMPLE

THREE SEPARATE SAMPLES were interviewed during the summer and fall of 1969, and the analysis of their responses makes up the bulk of this book. Each sample was representative of the urban adult Jewish population and was drawn from the Voters' List of the Interior Ministry. Drawing the samples and conducting the interviews was done by the Israel Institute of Applied Social Research, headed by Louis Guttman.

The first sample was interviewed in August and included 380 completed interviews. The second phase was conducted in September and October and included 1,315 completed interviews. In the third phase, conducted in October and November, 1,825 individuals were interviewed. The third phase was carried out as part of the Continuing Surveys of the Israel Institute of Applied Social Research and the Institute of Communications of the Hebrew University of Jerusalem, the latter headed by Elihu Katz.

As is clear from Appendix I, the number of questions asked regarding the elections decreased from phase to phase. The selection of questions for the succeeding phase was determined by preliminary analyses of the responses received in the preceding phase and by time and budget limitations.

The dropout rate was about 46 percent from the original samples. One of the major classes of reasons for the dropout rate related to locating the potential respondent. In phase 2, 47 percent of the dropouts were because of address unknown, address not found, unknown at given address, and not found at home after three visits. In phase 3, these reasons accounted for 41 percent of the dropout rate. Language difficulties (including illiteracy and not speaking Hebrew) accounted for 17 percent of the dropout of phase 2 and 8 percent of phase 3. Twelve percent of the dropouts refused to be interviewed in phase 2 and 18 percent in phase 3. The other reasons for not being interviewed included being in the hospital, serving in the army, being abroad, and having the interview interrupted and not completed.

The samples were drawn from Greater Tel Aviv, Jerusalem, Haifa, and Beer Sheba. These sampled areas contain 60 percent of the country's population.

The representativeness of the samples can be estimated by comparing the survey population with data from the *Statistical Abstract of Israel, 1969*. Sex, ethnic origin, education, and year of immigration are summarized in four tables.

TABLE A.1 DISTRIBUTION OF GENERAL JEWISH POPULATION
(URBAN AND RURAL) AND SURVEY POPULATIONS
(URBAN ONLY) BY SEX (AGE 25+)

SEX	PERCENTAGE IN GENERAL JEWISH POPULATION[a]	PERCENTAGE IN SURVEY POPULATIONS		
		1	2	3
Male	49	52	50	51
Female	51	47	49	48

a. *Statistical Abstract of Israel, 1969* (Jerusalem: Central Bureau of Statistics, 1969), p. 40.

TABLE A.2 DISTRIBUTION OF GENERAL JEWISH POPULATION
(URBAN AND RURAL) AND SURVEY POPULATIONS
(URBAN ONLY) BY ETHNIC ORIGIN

ETHNIC ORIGIN	PERCENTAGE IN JEWISH POPULATION AT AGE 20+[a]	PERCENTAGE IN SURVEY POPULATIONS		
		1	2	3
Born in Asian or North African countries	37	25	23	24
Born in Europe or America	46	51	49	53
Israeli born—father born in Asia or North Africa	3	5	7	5
Israeli born—father born in Europe or America	10	13	10	13
Israeli born—father born in Israel	3	5	5	5

a. *Ibid.*, pp. 42-43.

TABLE A.3 DISTRIBUTION OF GENERAL JEWISH POPULATION
(URBAN AND RURAL) AND SURVEY POPULATIONS
(URBAN ONLY) BY EDUCATION

EDUCATION	PERCENTAGE IN GENERAL JEWISH POPULATION[a]	PERCENTAGE IN SURVEY POPULATIONS		
		1	2	3
No formal education	7	4	2	3
Partial primary school including Heder	8.1	9	7 ⎫	
Completed primary school or equivalent	35	20	20 ⎬	30
Secondary school or equivalent (partial or completed)	35.2	49	49	47
University—partial, completed, B.A. or higher	14.6	17	22	19

a. *Ibid.*, p. 275.

TABLE A.4 DISTRIBUTION OF GENERAL JEWISH POPULATION
(URBAN AND RURAL) AND SURVEY POPULATIONS
(URBAN ONLY) BY PERIOD OF IMMIGRATION

YEAR OF IMMIGRATION	PERCENTAGE IN GENERAL JEWISH POPULATION[a]	PERCENTAGE IN SURVEY POPULATIONS		
		1	2	3
Israeli-born	16	24	28	23
Before 1947	19	26	27	31
1948-54	40	40	33	35
1955-59	12	6	7	5
1960-65	9	2	3	3
1966+	3	1	1	1

a. *Ibid.*, p. 44.

The underrepresentation of females is explained by marriage and the subsequent change of name and address.

The survey population born in Asia and Africa is underrepresented because of the relatively lower proportion of this group in survey areas and the higher proportion of illiteracy and insufficient knowledge of Hebrew.

Explanations for underrepresentation of lower-educated groups include a higher proportion of lower-educated among newcome population born in Asia or Africa, who are relatively less represented in surveyed urban areas, and a higher degree of illiteracy among lower educated.

Explanations of underrepresentation of newcomers include the lower proportion of newcomers in the city areas surveyed and the higher proportion of insufficient knowledge of Hebrew among newcomers.

In conclusion, it is obvious that the distribution of the samples in the three phases is very stable. Taking into account the shortcomings of available sources of comparison, the sample can be considered representative of the population.

GLOSSARY

Aguda or Agudat Israel	The extreme orthodox political party.
Ahdut Haavoda	"Unity of Labor." A left-wing party that joined Mapai and Rafi in 1968 to form the Israel Labor party.
Alignment	A labor election list. In 1969 it was composed of the Israeli Labor party and Mapam; in 1965, the Alignment list was composed of Mapai and Ahdut Haavoda.
Aliya (pl. *aliyot*)	A wave of Jewish migration to Palestine. Literally "ascending," "going up." The first *aliya* is dated from 1882 to 1903, the second from 1904 to 1914, and the third from 1919 to 1924.
Asefat Nivcharim	The "Meeting of Electors." The supreme representative organization of the Jewish community in Palestine.
Free Center	Founded in 1967, after splitting from the Herut movement.
Gahal	An acronym for the Herut-Liberal bloc. Established in 1965 as a joint list of the Herut movement and the Liberal party.
General Zionists	A right-of-center political party founded in 1954. In 1961 it aligned with the Progressive party to form the Liberal party.

Haganah	The defense force of the Jewish Community in Palestine during the British Mandate period.
Haolam Haze	"This World." A political movement founded in 1965 by Uri Avneri, publisher of the magazine of the same name.
Havaad Haleumi	"The National Committee." The executive branch of the Asefat Nivcharim.
Herut	"Freedom." A right-wing movement. In 1965 Herut, together with the Liberal party, formed the Gahal list (Herut–Liberal bloc).
Histadrut	The General Federation of Labor. The largest trade union in Israel. The Histadrut convention is directly elected on a country-wide basis, with almost all political parties represented. The election system is essentially the same as that for the Knesset.
Independent Liberal Party	Formerly the Progressive party. A centrist political party that was aligned with the Liberal party from 1961 to 1965. It then reverted to its former independence when the Liberal party joined with Herut to form Gahal.
Israel Communist Party (Maki)	Founded in 1919 on the basis of Marxist-Leninist theory and friendship with Russia, since the 1967 war it has tended to accept Zionist views.
Israel Labor Party	Founded in 1968 when Mapai, Ahdut Haavoda, and Rafi merged. It is clearly the dominant political party of the country.

Kibbutz (pl. kibbutzim)	A communal village, predominantly agricultural, governed by its members. All property is collectively owned and work is organized on a collective basis.
Knesset	Israel's 120-member, single-chamber, legislative body. Members are elected for four years by universal suffrage (voting age is 18) under proportional representation.
Knesset Israel	The autonomous organization of the Jews in Palestine in the British Mandate period.
Liberal Party	Formerly the General Zionists. A right-of-center party. In 1965 it joined with the Herut Movement to form the Gahal list. During the term of the Fifth Knesset (1961–65), the General Zionists and Progressives merged to form the Liberal party. Before the 1965 election, the former Progressives left the party and referred to themselves as the Independent Liberals.
Mafdal	*See* National Religious party.
Mapai	The dominant party in Israel until its merger in 1968 with Ahdut Haavoda and Rafi to form the Israel Labor party. It is an acronym for the Israel Workers' party, the leader of all Government coalitions since the state's establishment, and a major source of political power.
Mapam	Acronym for the United Worker's party. A left-wing socialist Zionist party. Mapam and the Israel Labor party submitted a joint list, the Alignment list, for the 1969 elections.

Minorities' lists	Lists of candidates affiliated with and sponsored by the Israel Labor party. There are two lists of minorities candidates for the Knesset.
Moshav (pl. moshavim)	An agricultural village where members work their own land and own their homes but produce is sold cooperatively.
National Religious Party (Mafdal)	Founded in 1956 by the Union of Mizrahi and its labor wing, Hapoel Hamizrahi. It has been a consistent coalition partner in the Government.
National Unity Government	The Cabinet formed just before the 1967 Six Day War, which included almost the entire spectrum of political parties represented in the Knesset. It lasted until August 1970.
New Communist List (Rakah)	A group that broke off from the Israel Communist party in 1965. Primarily Arab supported, it takes a pro-Soviet, anti-Zionist stand in foreign affairs.
Oriental Jew	*See* Sephardic Jew.
Poalei Agudat Israel	An extreme orthodox religious party with a socialist orientation.
Progressive party	A centrist political party founded in 1948. In 1961 it aligned with the General Zionists to form the Liberal party.
Rafi	A political party formed by David Ben-Gurion in 1965 as a splitoff from Mapai. In 1968 Rafi and Ahdut Haavoda joined Mapai to form the Israel Labor party. A small group of Rafi members who opposed the realignment formed the State List.

Rakah	*See* New Communist List.
Sabra	An Israeli-born Jew.
Sephardic Jew	A Jew from North Africa or the Middle East, or one descended from these, in contrast to an Ashkenazic, or European, Jew. The actual meaning relates to ritualistic usage, but the term has come to relate to place of birth in Israel.
Sephardic list	An electoral list that participated in the 1949 and 1951 elections. Its appeal was largely ethnic, but its leadership was co-opted by Mapai after the 1951 elections.
State List	A dissident group of former Rafi members, who rejected Rafi's merger with Mapai and Ahdut Haavoda in 1968 into the Labor party, and formed a new list for the 1969 elections.
Yemenite Union	An electoral list that participated in the 1949 and 1951 elections.

BIBLIOGRAPHY

BOOKS IN ENGLISH

Almond, Gabriel A., and Verba, Sidney. *The Civic Culture.* Princeton, N.J.: Princeton University Press, 1963.

Antonovsky, Aaron, and Arian, Alan. *Hopes and Fears of Israelis: Consensus in a New Society.* Jerusalem: Jerusalem Academic Press, 1972.

Arian, Alan. *Consensus in Israel.* New York: General Learning, 1971.

_____ . *Ideological Change in Israel.* Cleveland: The Press of Case Western Reserve University, 1968.

_____ , ed. *The Elections in Israel–1969.* Jerusalem Academic Press, 1972.

Benjamin, Roger W.; Arian, Alan; Blue, Richard N.; Coleman, Stephen. *Patterns of Political Development: Japan-India-Israel.* New York: McKay, 1972.

Berelson, Bernard; Lazarsfeld, Paul F.; and McPhee, William N. *Voting.* Chicago: University of Chicago Press, 1954.

Birnbaum, Ervin. *The Politics of Compromise: State and Religion in Israel.* Rutherford, N.J.: Fairleigh Dickinson University Press, 1970.

Butler, David, and Stokes, Donald. *Political Change in Britain.* London: Macmillan, 1965.

Campbell, Angus; Converse, Philip E.; Miller, Warren E.; and Stokes, Donald E. *The American Voter.* New York: Wiley, 1964.

_____ . *Elections and the Political Order.* New York: Wiley, 1966.

Campbell, Angus; Gurin, Gerald; and Miller, Warren E. *The Voter Decides.* Evanston, Ill.: Row Peterson, 1954.

Dahl, Robert A. *A Preface to Democratic Theory.* Chicago: University of Chicago Press, 1956.

Duverger, Maurice. *Political Parties.* New York: Wiley, 1963.

Easton, David. *The Political System.* New York: Knopf, 1953.

_____. *A System Analysis of Political Life.* New York: Wiley, 1965.

Eisenstadt, S. N. *Israeli Society.* London: Weidenfeld and Nicolson, 1967.

Fein, Leonard J. *Politics in Israel.* Boston: Little, Brown, 1967.

Festinger, Leon. *A Theory of Cognitive Dissonance.* Evanston, Ill.: Row Peterson, 1957.

Halpern, Ben. *The Idea of the Jewish State.* Cambridge, Mass.: Harvard University Press, 1961.

Hennessy, Bernard C. *Public Opinion.* Belmont, Calif.: Wadsworth, 1965.

Huntington, Samuel. *Political Order and Changing Societies.* New Haven: Yale University Press, 1968.

Key, V. O., Jr. *Public Opinion and American Democracy.* New York: Knopf, 1961.

Landau, Jacob N. *The Arabs in Israel.* London: Oxford University Press, 1969.

Lane, Robert E. *Political Life.* New York: Free Press, 1959.

Lindblum, Charles E. *The Policy-Making Process.* Englewood Cliffs, N.J.: Prentice-Hall, 1968.

Lippman, Walter. *The Phantom Public.* New York: Harcourt, 1925.

_____. *Public Opinion.* New York: Macmillan, 1922.

Lipset, Seymour Martin. *Political Man.* Garden City, N.Y.: Doubleday, 1963.

_____, and Rokkan, Stein. *Party Systems and Voter Alignments: Cross-National Perspectives.* New York: The Free Press, 1967.

Luttbeg, Norman, ed. *Public Opinion and Public Policy.* Homewood, Ill.: Dorsey, 1968.

Matras, Judah. *Social Change in Israel.* Chicago: Aldine, 1965.

Medding, Peter J. *Mapai in Israel: Political Organization and Government in a New Society.* Cambridge: Cambridge University Press, 1972.

Michels, Robert. *Political Parties.* New York: Collier Books, 1962.

Milbrath, Lester M. *Political Participation.* Chicago: Rand McNally, 1965.

Rae, Douglas. *The Political Consequences of Electoral Laws.* New Haven: Yale University Press, 1967.

Rose, Richard, ed. *Political Behavior in Industrial Society*. New York: Free Press, forthcoming.

Safran, Nadav. *The United States and Israel*. Cambridge, Mass.: Harvard University Press, 1963.

Schumpeter, Joseph A. *Capitalism, Socialism and Democracy*, 2nd ed. New York: Harper & Bros., 1947.

Shapiro, Yonathan. *The Dominant Party of Israel: The Formative Years of the Israeli Labor Party, 1919-1930*. Forthcoming.

Simmel, George. *The Sociology of G. Simmel*. trans. and ed. K. Wolff. New York: Free Press, 1950.

Sondquist, John A., and Morgan, James N. *The Detection of Interaction Effects*. Ann Arbor: Survey Research Center, 1964.

Weingrod, Alex. *Reluctant Pioneers*. Ithaca, N.Y.: Cornell University Press, 1966.

Wilner, Dorothy. *Nation-Building and Community in Israel*. Princeton: Princeton University Press, 1969.

ARTICLES IN ENGLISH COLLECTIONS

Barnes, Samuel H. "Social Structure and Political Behavior in Italy." In *Political Behavior in Industrial Society*, ed. Richard Rose. New York: Free Press, forthcoming.

Boim, Leon. "Financing of the 1969 Elections." In *The Elections in Israel–1969*, ed. Alan Arian. Jerusalem: Jerusalem Academic Press, 1972.

Brichte, Abraham. "The Social and Political Characteristics of Members of the Seventh Knesset." In *The Elections in Israel–1969*, ed. Alan Arian. Jerusalem: Jerusalem Academic Press, 1972.

Duverger, Maurice. "Electoral System and Political Life." In *Comparative Politics*, ed. Roy D. Macridis and Bernard E. Brown. Homewood, Ill.: Dorsey, 1961.

Gurevitch, Michael. "Television in the Election Campaign: Its Audience and Functions." In *The Elections in Israel–1969*, ed. Alan Arian. Jerusalem: Jerusalem Academic Press, 1972.

Landau, Jacob N. "The Arab Voter." In *The Elections in Israel–1969*, ed. Alan Arian. Jerusalem: Jerusalem Academic Press, 1972.

Liepelt, Klaus. "The Infra-Structure of Party Support in Germany and Austria." In *European Politics,* ed. Mattei Dogan and Richard Rose. Boston: Little, Brown, 1971.

Linz, Juan. "Cleavages and Consensus in West German Politics." In *Party System and Voter Alignments,* ed. Seymour M. Lipset and Stein Rokkan. New York: Free Press, 1967.

Lipset, Seymour M. "Political Cleavages in 'Developed' and 'Emerging' Politics." In *Mass Politics: Studies in Political Sociology,* ed. Erik Allardt and Stein Rokkan. New York: Free Press, 1970.

_____ , and Rokkan, Stein. "Cleavage Structures, Party Systems and Voter Alignment: An Introduction." In *Party Systems and Voter Alignments,* ed. Seymour M. Lipset and Stein Rokkan. New York: Free Press, 1967.

Neumann, Sigmund. "Toward a Comparative Study of Political Parties." In *Modern Political Parties,* ed. Sigmund Neumann. Chicago: University of Chicago Press, 1956.

Smith, Herbert. "Analysis of Voting." In *The Elections in Israel–1969,* ed. Alan Arian. Jerusalem: Jerusalem Academic Press, 1972.

Stock, Ernest. "Foreign Policy Issues." In *The Elections in Israel–1969,* ed. Alan Arian. Jerusalem: Jerusalem Academic Press, 1972.

Torgovnik, Efraim. "Party Factions and Election Issues." In *The Elections in Israel–1969,* ed. Alan Arian. Jerusalem: Jerusalem Academic Press, 1972.

ENGLISH ARTICLES IN PERIODICALS

Antonovsky, Aaron. "Classifications of Forms, Political Ideologies and the Man in the Street," *Public Opinion Quarterly* 30 (Spring 1966): 109–19.

Arian, Alan, and Barnes, Samuel. "The Dominant Party System: A Neglected Model of Democratic Stability." *Journal of Politics,* forthcoming.

Etzioni, Amitai. "Alternative Ways to Democracy: The Example of Israel," *Political Science Quarterly* 74 (1959): 196–214.

Goldberg, Arthur S. "Discerning a Causal Pattern Among Data on Voting Behavior," *American Political Science Review* 60 (1966): 913–22.

Gutmann, Emmanuel. "Citizens' Participation in Political Life–Israel," *International Social Science Journal* 12 (1960): 53-62.

Liepelt, Klaus. "Esquisse d'une typologie des électeurs allemands et autrichiens," *Revue Française de Sociologie* 10 (1968): 13-32.

McClosky, Herbert. "Consensus and Ideology in American Politics," *American Political Science Review* 58 (1964): 361-82.

Rose, Richard, and Mossawir, Harve. "Voting and Elections: A Functional Analysis," *Political Studies* 15 (1967): 173-201.

Särlvik, Bo. "Socioeconomic Determinants of Voting Behavior in the Swedish Electorate," *Comparative Political Studies* 11 (1969): 99-135.

Stokes, Donald. "Some Dynamic Elements of Contests for the Presidency," *American Political Science Review* 60 (March 1966): 19-28.

Zweig, Ferdinand. "The Jewish Trade Union Movement in Israel," *Jewish Journal of Sociology* 1 (1959): 23-42.

OFFICIAL PUBLICATIONS, ISRAEL

General Federation of Workers in Israel. *The Histadrut Annual,* vol. 2. Tel Aviv: Havaad Hapoel, 1966.

———. "The Histadrut Society." A Hebrew mimeographed publication of the Dues Office of the Histadrut. Tel Aviv: September 1970.

———. *Report to the Eleventh Histadrut Convention* (Hebrew), 1969.

Israel Government Annual (1966-67) (Hebrew). Jerusalem: Government Printing Office, 1967.

Local Authorities in Israel 1968/1969. Jerusalem: Central Bureau of Statistics, 1970.

Population of Jerusalem, Haifa and Tel-Aviv-Yafo. Jerusalem: Central Bureau of Statistics, 1968.

Results of Elections to the Seventh Knesset and to Local Authorities. Jerusalem: Central Bureau of Statistics.

The Settlements of Israel, Part VI. Jerusalem: Central Bureau of Statistics, 1966.

Statistical Abstract of Israel, 1969. Jerusalem: Government Printer, 1969.

Tel Aviv Municipality. *Tel-Aviv Yafo Population (1961–1965)*. Tel Aviv Municipality Research and Statistical Department, 1967.

BOOKS IN HEBREW

Attias, Moshe. *Knesset Israel*. Jerusalem: National Committee, 1944.
Cohen, Israel, and Gelber, N. M. *History of Zionism*. Jerusalem: Rubin Moss, 1962.
Nakdimon, Shlomo. *Likrat Sha'at Haefes*. Tel Aviv: Ramdor, 1968.
Waram, Shalom, ed. *The Life and Works of Giora Josephtal*. Tel Aviv: Mapai Publishing, 1963.

ARTICLES IN HEBREW PERIODICALS

Antonovsky, Aaron. "Israeli Political-Social Attitudes," *Amot* 6 (1963): 11–22.
Gorni, Joseph. "Changes in the Social and Political Structure of the Second Aliya (1904–1940)," *Zionism* 1 (1970): 204–46.
Horowitz, D., and Lissak, M. "The Yishuv as a Political Society," *Megamot* 16 (April, 1970): 108–40.

MISCELLANEOUS

Knesset Proceedings, VII.
Klaff, Chaim, and Jacobson, Chanoch. "Multi-Variate Analyses of Ninety-Four Arab Villages in Israel." Report No. 1 in the Modernization of the Traditional Arab Village Project, led by Emmanuel Yolan, Chaim Finkel, and Louis Guttman. Rehovot: The Settlement Study Center, March 1970, mimeographed.
The Zionist Administration, n.d. *The Meeting of the Zionist Executive Committee in Jerusalem*. Jerusalem; April 19–28, 1950.

INDEX

This book was set in ten-point Times Roman,
printed and bound by Science Press, Ephrata, Pennsylvania.
The book was designed by LaWanda J. McDuffie.

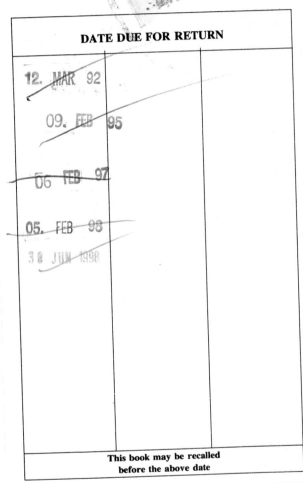

DATE DUE FOR RETURN

12. MAR 92

09. FEB 95

06 FEB 97

05. FEB 98

30 JUN 1998

This book may be recalled
before the above date

90014